Voices of Silence

LIVES OF THE
TRAPPISTS TODAY

FRANK BIANCO

ANCHOR BOOKS
DOUBLEDAY
New York London Toronto Sydney Auckland

AN ANCHOR BOOK
PUBLISHED BY DOUBLEDAY
a division of Bantam Doubleday Dell Publishing Group, Inc.
666 Fifth Avenue, New York, New York 10103

ANCHOR BOOKS, DOUBLEDAY, and the portrayal of an anchor are trademarks of
Doubleday, a division
of Bantam Doubleday Dell Publishing Group, Inc.

Voices of Silence was originally published in hardcover by
Paragon House in 1991. The Anchor Books edition is
published by arrangement with Paragon House.

"On Eagles Wings," by Michael Joncas: © New Dawun Music, P.O. Box 13248,
Portland, Oregon. All rights reserved. Used with permission.

Acknowledgment is made to Cistercian Publications for permission to quote from
Father Matthew Kelty's book, *Sermons in a Monastery*, edited by William O. Paulsell.

Library of Congress Cataloging-in-Publication Data

Bianco, Frank, 1931–
Voices of silence: lives of the Trappists today/Frank Bianco.
1st Anchor Books ed.
p.   cm.
Originally published: New York : Paragon House, 1991.
Includes bibliographical references and index.
1. Trappists—United States—History—20th century. 2. Trappists—
United States—Spiritual life. I. Title.
[BX4108.B52   1992]

255'.125—dc20   92-9639
CIP

ISBN 0-385-42430-2
Copyright © 1991 by Frank Bianco
ALL RIGHTS RESERVED
PRINTED IN THE UNITED STATES OF AMERICA
FIRST ANCHOR BOOKS EDITION: AUGUST 1992

1   3   5   7   9   10   8   6   4   2

Grief helped me appreciate my son Michael's time with us, and how it demonstrated the power of God, which is what that name means. So it is in gratitude that I dedicate this book to Michael and his love of others that made for him, and makes for us, an ongoing miracle of creation.

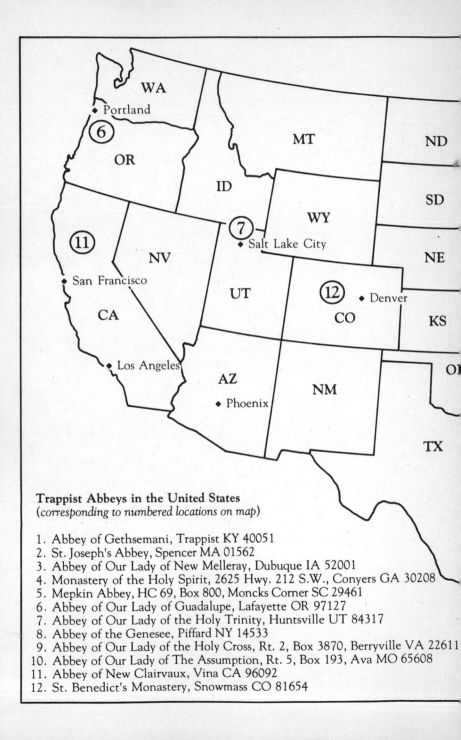

Trappist Abbeys in the United States
(*corresponding to numbered locations on map*)

1. Abbey of Gethsemani, Trappist KY 40051
2. St. Joseph's Abbey, Spencer MA 01562
3. Abbey of Our Lady of New Melleray, Dubuque IA 52001
4. Monastery of the Holy Spirit, 2625 Hwy. 212 S.W., Conyers GA 30208
5. Mepkin Abbey, HC 69, Box 800, Moncks Corner SC 29461
6. Abbey of Our Lady of Guadalupe, Lafayette OR 97127
7. Abbey of Our Lady of the Holy Trinity, Huntsville UT 84317
8. Abbey of the Genesee, Piffard NY 14533
9. Abbey of Our Lady of the Holy Cross, Rt. 2, Box 3870, Berryville VA 22611
10. Abbey of Our Lady of The Assumption, Rt. 5, Box 193, Ava MO 65608
11. Abbey of New Clairvaux, Vina CA 96092
12. St. Benedict's Monastery, Snowmass CO 81654

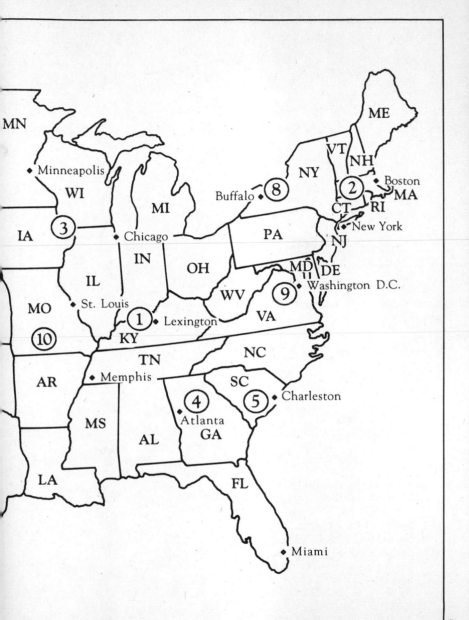

Contents

Preface   ix

Introduction   xi

Section One
KNOWN TO GOD ALONE

1. *Who Is My Neighbor?*   3
2. *Just Plain Mac*   9
3. *A Different Drumbeat*   20
4. *The Monk in Us All*   31
5. *Lord Knows, It Ain't Easy*   44
6. *All in the Family*   48

Section Two
THE LORD'S PRAYER

7. *Love Lessons*   59
8. *The Finger of God*   71
9. *Peace to All Who Enter*   73
10. *Who Knocks?*   83
11. *Pray All Ways*   94
12. *The Medium as the Message*   105

Contents

Section Three
DARKLY IN A MIRROR

13. *The Unavoidable Christ*   119
14. *What Martha Knew*   124
15. *Bums and Saints*   135
16. *Seen in an Obscure Manner*   149
17. *Called by God*   158
18. *Faces in the Mirror*   170

Section Four
A TINY WHISPERING SOUND

19. *Scaling the Mountain*   177
20. *And the Lord Was Not There*   189
21. *The Spirit in Motion*   195
22. *Finding Peace*   200
23. *Then Are They Truly Monks*   210
24. *After the Fire*   215

Bibliography   219

Preface

It is hard to believe that five years of my life have gone into this book, and even harder to realize that a single volume could hold so small a portion of all that has happened in that period of time.

It has been a time unlike any other in my life, for as I tried to take the measure of a unique way of life, I began to see the dimensions of my own, as though for the first time. God has blessed me many times, but never as he did in this instance. I know I did nothing to deserve it.

Trappist monks were the channel for that blessing. Their stories—adventures really—were a gift to me, just as their willingness to allow me to live and work with them was a precious privilege. They gave freely in trust and love, and I promised myself, even before I promised them, that I would not betray their trust.

Everything in this book is true, free of invention. Fiction would have been pale in comparison with the actual experiences of these monks. However, to honor their trust, I have changed names and locations. The monks portrayed in this book are composites and, to maintain the narrative flow, I have blended their experiences, deliberately relocating both to shield those involved.

I am sorry to see this portion of my journey ending. I could not have asked for better companions with which to share it. Perhaps though, what made our journey together so rich was not so much what they helped me to see, as how they taught me to see.

Someone once asked me what I hoped to accomplish with this work, and I initially answered, "That I may help others the way I have been helped." If only one person is helped, I added, that would be enough. Now I know my ambition has been fulfilled, because I am that one person.

More than ever before, I recognize how God is part of our lives. He/ She is present in those whom we allow into our lives, people who guide, affirm, and encourage. This book was a hard passage. Many, many people were present for me, often when I might otherwise have felt quite alone and abandoned. I leave their reward to a God whose generosity far exceeds anything I offered. Here, I acknowledge three people who were especially involved—Timothy Kelly and Francis Kline, two abbots who did the most to make a monk of me; my wife, Marie, who lovingly ensured my sanity and our solvency and who will always be, for me, the face of God I cherish most.

Introduction

I have fled you down the nights and days,
down the labyrinth ways of my mind.

"The Hound of Heaven," Francis Thompson

Francis Thompson's poem, a favorite of mine since my freshman year in college, had taken on a personal quality as I reached my late forties. I was nagged by the notion that I was on the last leg of my life and had yet to do something that could give it meaning. As my fiftieth birthday approached, I had begun careening from one thing to another, always lured by the possibility that the new path would be the answer, the direction for which I seemed to be searching.

I never acknowledged the possibility that I might simply be scared by the thought of dying. It was much easier to find fault with people and circumstances I felt certain were shackling my potential, stifling my growth. I was "choking." I needed "air, space in which to grow."

I believed I had earned the opportunity. I had been the dutiful father, husband, and loyal corporate executive. I had demonstrated further vigor with a turn as an entrepreneur and had even rounded out my profile as the ultimate sportsman, a superior competitive surf fisherman who could wrest achievement from Mother Nature's grasp. I had even prayed at the altar of psychoanalysis for five years and, freed from all my hang-ups, I had finally sought fulfillment as a free-lance journalist.

At that point, there seemed to be only one obstacle remaining between me and meaning. Though I could not have survived without my wife's patience and support (she went back to work when the struggling "artiste" didn't earn enough to pay the mortgage), I began thinking that maybe the problem was my marriage: that after twenty-eight years and five children, it was time for a change—the kind that many "sensible, mature" adults seemed to be making.

That was as far as my script had taken me when it began to undergo changes that were clearly beyond my control. The first of these took place early Friday morning, 8 June 1984. At that particular moment in time, I was busy being the dedicated professional. I had to take the quintessential photograph of Monticello, Thomas Jefferson's home, as it glistened in the slanting rays of a rising sun.

My wife, Marie, and I were both working on newspaper features and I was convinced that sunrise would provide exceptional photographs of the home, which stands on a Virginia mountaintop. Since the gates at the base of the mountain didn't open until seven o'clock, I decided to get there before dawn. I would hike to the top and begin to photograph while Marie patiently waited in our van camper for the caretaker to open up.

Our work had earned us special permission to park in one of the four spaces that were built into a shelf in front of the cottage/gift shop alongside the mansion. The mountain dropped off about twenty feet from that point to the plateau where Jefferson had once farmed an experimental garden. That is where a security guard found our camper. It had rolled away on its own from the space where Marie had parked it. It had rolled until it went over the edge of the shelf, tumbling until it came to rest in Jefferson's garden.

The fall bent the wheels, shattered all the windows, and crumpled every side. The interior had undergone an implosion that heaped it with all the equipment, cans, and clothing we had carefully squeezed into the van's storage spaces. All of it was salted with broken glass.

As a tow truck took us and the sad-looking wreck into nearby Charlottesville, Marie remarked, "This has to be the worst day of my life." We also realized it could have been her last. After she parked that morning, she had altered her usual schedule and gone to see how I was doing. She had foregone the luxury of staying inside the camper and going back to sleep as she regularly did when I went out on an early morning shot.

Michael, the youngest of our five children, was going to be disappointed, I thought. I had promised that he and a high school buddy could take the camper on a trip west after their high school graduation, which was just two weeks away. The camper would not be making many—if any—more trips.

A few minutes before noon that day, Marie and I were sitting in the office of an auto repair shop, making arrangements to fly home to Long Island. A tall, well-built man in a shirt and tie walked in. The pistol holstered on his hip caught my attention even before he asked if anyone knew where he could find the owner of the wrecked camper resting outside.

He was the sheriff, he told me when I identified myself. "You have an emergency back home," he said. "It might be best if you called there immediately."

Emergency, I scoffed to myself as I dialed. What could possibly be worse than what had already happened? The phone only rang once before twenty-one-year-old Jimmy, the middle child of our three sons and two daughters, answered. His "hello" was alarmingly solemn.

"Michael's had an accident, Dad," he said. "Is he okay?" I asked, half-hoping for confirmation. Jimmy paused for a long moment, and said, "Dad," before pausing again. He choked trying to repeat "Dad" and began to cry, but not so much that I couldn't hear him say, "We've lost him, Dad. Michael's dead."

Only part of me listened as Jimmy told me that Michael was apparently headed back to our house during the break after his first early morning class. For reasons that will never be known, his Volkswagen Beetle had swerved on a curve and collided head-on with a heavy equipment truck. He had died instantly, at approximately 8:30 A.M., about an hour after our camper had made its own final journey.

I remember putting my arms around Marie after I told her what had happened. "Please stay close to me," she said. "I really need you now." I nodded in assurance, but inside I wondered where the strength would come from. I was already drowning in my own grief.

No one can ever be said to be ready for such a blow, but I could not have been less prepared. Whereas Marie could find a measure of solace in her faith, I had no such resource. Though I had been born and raised a Catholic and had even studied for the priesthood, God had become another encumbrance in my sophisticated search for fulfillment. At best I was an agnostic.

Michael's death got me off that fence. I blamed God for our son's death and I directed all my hurt and anger at him. What right did he have to take my son? Michael was one of the most generous human beings I had ever known, happiest when he could help someone, a gifted entertainer who would do anything to bring a smile to an otherwise unhappy face. If God needed to take somebody, why hadn't it been one of the many useless bastards who seemed to live off everybody's misery?

In those pain-filled first days, I could hardly restrain my anger when well-meaning people tried to console me by explaining the "good" reasons why God might have taken Michael, or how much better off he was than the rest of us still living. I was not about to let God off the hook that easily.

I had never hurt so badly. I saw reminders of Michael everywhere. But I drew a blank every time I tried to recall him to mind. Loss is death's principle trauma and I was terrified that mine seemed to be so total. Michael's living presence had been torn away and memories that might have consoled me had disappeared. I could not believe God would be that cruel and I became even more bitter.

Things were not much better a year later. Although the loss had made me more appreciative of my wife and family, I still suffered amnesia so far as any memory of Michael was concerned. Shortly after the first anniversary of his death, Marie and I went south again to research assignments in Bardstown, Kentucky. We considered it a bonus when we learned that a Trappist abbey was only a few miles away from where we were working, and that the monks produced food products to support themselves. That sounded like a feature opportunity for Marie.

I had first learned about the Trappists when I was a Maryknoll Missionary seminarian. The monks were the elite strike force in the spiritual life—penitents who never spoke, fasted, and chanted liturgy in a way that evoked an angelic chorus.

They had swallowed a fellow seminarian who had slept on the bunk beneath mine. Tom Barrett, who was probably the most outgoing member of our class, had vanished between the moment one bell rang for "lights out" and another woke us the next morning.

"Hear about Barrett?" a classmate had whispered, his voice mixing awe and disbelief. "The Trappists. Can you believe it? Barrett, the guy they must have vaccinated with a phonograph needle. Him, silent? He'll never last."

Apparently, he hadn't. The last I heard, he had stayed a few years and then left. Another example of misplaced idealism, I thought, as Marie and I parked our car by Gethsemani's front gate at about half past five on a July morning in 1985.

The monastery was very plain looking, the kind of architecture institutions choose when utility is the only priority. White stuccoed walls met at a wooden gate that was wide enough to drive a car through. The words *pax intrantibus* (peace to all who enter) were chiseled in the arch above and formed a semicircle around a statue of the Virgin Mary standing in a niche. The three-story quadrangle behind the wall replicated classic monastic form that dated to the fifth century.

That form positioned the abbey's church on the highest point of land on the north side of the quadrangle. Inside, Gethsemani's founders had deeply struck the mortar when they laid the bricks—which they had first made from clay at the site. That pattern gave a warm texture to walls which might have otherwise appeared antiseptic beneath their stiff coat of white paint.

The tapestry of white masonry peaked in a roof whose wooden buttresses were about fifty feet above the floor. These seemed to sit atop the narrow windows that had been slit into the walls, translucent fingers of stained glass through which first and last light pierced the interior. The church was not designed to be admired. It was a place where man could speak with God, free from distractions.

There was a balcony across the rear, where guests attended the monastic liturgy. A handful of locals came faithfully, even at three in the morning, when the monks chanted their first office of the day. Retreatants and other more casual visitors used the same facility.

When Marie and I entered, about fifty white- and black-robed monks were already in their choir stalls directly below. Five minutes later, they were standing, facing forward, when a knock signaled them to begin.

I do not recall particular words or phrases from the liturgy that followed. I know I was struck by the monks' genuine reverence. They were not mouthing rituals. They were singing carefully, slowly, as one disciplined voice. They were talking to someone. I did not doubt that any more than I would doubt the presence of a catcher if I were watching a pitcher winding up.

I glanced around the church, looking for that catcher. But the tabernacle was not glowing. Nor was the crucifix over the altar moving. And the light streaming through the stained-glass windows did not alter a bit. No, everything was perfectly normal. With one exception. For the first time since he had died, memories of Michael began to flood my mind.

I could see him vividly. A happy smile wreathed his handsome face. I could actually hear him. "Dad, it's OK. It's me, Mikey." He was so real. So alive. I reached out, just to hold him, just once more. And then I began to cry because I knew I couldn't. Not ever again.

The experience absorbed me completely for however long it took the monks to finish their office and celebrate mass, a bit more than an hour. As they disappeared into the cloister, Michael and his memory seemed to go with them, leaving me heartsick, alone again with my loss.

During the summer months that followed, I received additional newspaper and magazine assignments that required me to visit two other Trappist monasteries to do research and take photographs. Each time, the experience was the same. My memory of Michael would be restored from the moment I entered any church where Trappist monks were praying. I could remember him until they had finished. Then a curtain would fall.

God seemed to be tantalizing me, holding my memories hostage. I resented being forced to go to church. But, strangely, I found myself growing envious of the monks, who, like Marie, drew obvious nourishment from a faith I had once shared. I began to feel confused. Michael's death was no less a painful mystery for which I still held God responsible. But why could I only remember my dead son in circumstances that I believed had nothing whatsoever to do with him?

My involvement with Trappists did not end when I finished the assignments. On the contrary, the subject had aroused an editor's interest in a possible book. But in order to write a proposal, I would have to spend some time actually living among the Trappists and following their routine.

I arranged to spend a week living at Holy Cross Abbey in Berryville, Virginia. I had mixed feelings about the visit. On the one hand, I was curious to get to know the monks and to learn about their way of life. On the other, I was uneasy.

I was a Catholic in name only. Given my antipathy and alienation, how could I go through the motions of worship—which I felt was necessary if I was to learn firsthand about the monks? Besides, all my previous visits had been brief and I had only been an observer. What would happen when I remained for a lengthy period of time and began to participate in the routine that had been so powerful a trigger for my emotions?

I was quite nervous when, on the first evening of my visit, I joined the monks as they sang the prayers and psalms for vespers at 5:30 P.M. When they came to the Lord's Prayer, I went no further than the first two words before my lips froze. I would not acknowledge as my Father, the agent of my son's death. I wanted no bread, needed no forgiveness, and swore against doing the will of a God who had put a knife in my heart. I stood stiffly, anger chilling any appreciation I might have had for the prayers the monks recited with obvious feeling and sincerity.

In the period after vespers, the monks go individually to the refectory for a light supper, usually fruit augmented by the leftovers from lunch, their principal meal of the day. My insides were so knotted that I could not think of food. I wanted to leave by morning and began planning to do so.

First, though, I would have to get through compline, the final choir office of the day, at 7:30 P.M. The church was dimly lit as the monks began reciting the prayers by heart. They moved slowly through Psalm four, which cites God's love for the steadfast heart, and then to Psalm number ninety. When I heard the words, my bitterness dissolved into tears. Psalm ninety is the substance of "On Eagle's Wings," the hymn that was sung at Michael's funeral mass.

The words forced me back to that moment. Marie was kneeling next to me in the front pew. All that remained of our youngest son lay uncharacteristically still in the aisle in front of us, sealed forever in a polished wooden coffin. If I put my arm out, I could have touched it.

"You who dwell in the shelter of the Lord," the hymn promised,

> *who abide in his shadow for life.*
> *Say to the Lord, my refuge, my rock in whom I trust.*
> *And He will raise you up on eagle's wings.*
> *Bear you on the breath of dawn.*
> *Make you to shine like the sun,*
> *and hold you in the palm of his hand.*

The words were a mockery. Michael's coffin, so close, so frighteningly final, was by no means the wings of eagles. I had watched his two brothers, tears streaming down their faces, help carry it into the church. It was their hands and their hearts that were visible. I saw nothing of God's palm. I didn't want to see him anywhere near that box.

As that scene flickered through my mind, reopening painful memories, I began to pray. "Please," I pleaded, "don't make me cry in front of these people. Why are you doing this to me? You took my son. Isn't that enough? Leave me alone. Please, go away. What have I done to make you want to hurt me like this?" Even if I wanted to sing with the monks, I couldn't. I had all to do to keep from sobbing aloud.

I don't remember anything until the monks stopped singing and silence brought me back to the moment at hand. All lights had been turned off, save for a single spot that illuminated a statue of the Virgin Mary in a niche above the main altar.

Turning in their stalls, the monks faced the statue and began to sing the Salve Regina, as monks have done every evening since the Middle Ages. They called on Mary, "our advocate . . . our queen . . . our life, our sweetness, and our hope. To you do we send up our sighs, mourning and weeping in this vale of tears."

I felt tears on my face as I listened, recognizing the bond I shared with that poor woman. The pain that Michaelangelo had carved into the *Pietà* was knifing into my heart. I knew how Mary must have felt when they took the broken body of her son from the cross and laid him, lifeless, in her arms. Sweet Mother of God, I said to myself without thinking, how I know.

The notes of the hymn ranged high, yet there was no audible straining as the two choirs, one soft voice, easily scaled the register, holding notes, caressing words, polishing the phrases of petition. Their tenderness had the special quality love acquires when strong men expose their vulnerability by its confession. They ended their goodnight gently, crooning its last words, "O, clement. O, loving. O, sweet Virgin Mary."

The monastery bell began slowly tolling the angelus as they finished and stood silently, heads bowed. The clanging quickened and the monks beckoned to me to join them as they filed from the stalls and walked in two lines to a point where the abbot stood with a holy-water sprinkler. Each monk came before him, bowed, and was sprinkled with the water before leaving the church. In a minute or two, the ceremony was over and I found myself standing outside in the cloister.

As the monks walked by me on their way to their rooms, I was startled to hear my name whispered. Turning around, I came face to face with my old seminary classmate, Tom Barrett, now known as Father Daniel. He was thinner than he had been when he had once emphatically dumped me with a cross-body block during a football game. But I felt the raw strength in the arm he threw around my shoulders, as he squeezed and half-carried me along into the preau, a small garden that formed the core of the monastery quadrangle.

He responded immediately to my shaken appearance and asked what was the matter. The pain pushed aside any bravado and in a rush I told him about Michael's death, the experiences I'd had in other abbeys, and what had just taken place inside the church. Tom had been standing in front of me with his arms folded, listening. When I finished, he nodded and said, "He's after you." Then, nodding again, as though saying the words had made him more certain of his conclusion, he repeated, "He's after you."

I said nothing in reply. The thought made me sick. Tom continued, explaining how he believed God never stops trying to draw us close to him. "If we resist," he said, "he finds ways to get through our barriers. I'm positive he's reaching out to you, and your experience just now is an example. I'm just as certain that your continued involvement with us is no coincidence. I think he brought you here for a very special reason."

I remained silent at first, even though I was tempted to tell Tom that if God was trying to reach me, I was not interested. While I was glad to regain access to my memories of Michael, they did not offset his loss. That thought finally overrode any desire I had to be polite and I blurted out, "Screw the sadistic son of a bitch. If he really did care about me, then why did he take my son?"

"He didn't take your son," Tom answered very calmly, "no more than he could be blamed for your death if someone shot and killed you. That tragedy would be the result of whatever reasons brought you and the gunman to the same place and time.

"We're not windup toys. We call the shots. Not God. He offers us options, opportunities—graces, as we call them—to grow into the unique individuals he created us to be. But we call the shots. Did you forget your Baltimore catechism? Remember what it gave as the reason for our creation?

" 'God made us to know him, to love him and to serve him in this world and so earn happiness in the next.' You can't love under duress. To love is to choose, and to choose, you must have free will."

Tom's logic left me nothing to say. He was right. God was no more the agent of Michael's death than I was. Michael had chosen to be driving that road at the moment when something caused his car to veer into that particular truck's path. Had the truck come one minute sooner or later . . . had the drivers stopped for coffee . . . or skipped a break . . . the accident might never have happened.

I needed to think, I told Tom, who then nodded in the direction of the church. As I began walking toward it, he called softly, and when I turned, he came over to me, hugged me tightly and said, "I'm so sorry, old buddy. Look, take it easy in there. Give God a chance. Listen. I think that's what's most important now. Just listen."

God did not kill my son, I thought as I sat in the church. Then if there is a God, I asked, where did he fit in all of this? Something told me, "love." That was God's most dominant characteristic, an all-encompassing, unqualified love—one that included every possible variety and expression.

If that was true, then God had to "feel" the love I had for Michael. It had to be part of his experience. And he had to know my pain. He knew it as intensely as he knew the loss of love that caused it. If he did, he had to feel as badly as any friend. At least that much. He had been as much a part of Michael's creation as had Marie and I. He knew the joy that had been Michael. The pain had to cut him deeply. As deeply as it did me. He had to be grieving my—our—loss, sorrowing as Christ's own mother must have sorrowed.

All this was happening in minutes, one thought after another, pulling and then sweeping me along. The God I had reviled and rejected had been waiting to mourn with me, burdened with sorrow he would share with me. I felt so ashamed. I had been so wrong, for so long. Yet God had never given up on me. The Hound of Heaven had kept following me, his arms open, no matter what I had said or done.

Then, without warning, the experience of Michael's death began to replay in my mind, but as though for the first time. I could sense it surging up inside me, a mass of agony and pain, and I wanted to get up and run. But something told me there was no need to be afraid. I heard the words, "I know. I know. As you did, as you still do, I love him too. I know."

I stayed put, weeping, as the pain poured out. But not alone. Not unconsoled. This time I wept in the arms of my God, whom I finally allowed to hold me in that monastery church.

And so, I stopped running. God had finally brought me to ground in the silence of Trappists and I knew it was there I had to listen. This book is what I heard.

Section
One

KNOWN TO GOD ALONE

He walked with God, and was seen no more because
God took him.

Gen. 5:24

1

Who Is My Neighbor?

Most people who felt as deeply as Father Bede would have shown it, but few were as tightly wound as he. As he stood before his fellow members of the Abbot's Council, coolly arguing against change in the monastery, he could have been a math teacher explaining differential equations.

Women had no business anywhere near the monastery, he said. No matter how closely their movement and presence might be restricted in the new guest house, they would still violate the spirit of monastic enclosure. A monk would have to be dead not to notice their presence. Besides, advocates of the change had admitted it was an experiment. That alone made it inadmissible. Why capriciously disturb the peace of those monks who were bothered by the mere discussion of the proposal?

Some had already spoken to him, urging that he relay their objections in the strongest terms possible. "We all know about some abbeys where this mistake has been made," Father Bede said solemnly. "I don't think it helps celibate monks at all to have ladies running around the monastery in shorts."

While Father Bede conceded that such a possibility might be remote, he was certain that any relaxation of current proscriptions opened the door to such problems. He was willing to wager that a majority of the brothers were uncomfortable with the proposal. It was irresponsible. Granted, it was all being done with the sincerest of intentions, but it was still misguided. Trappist monks were supposed to live apart, hidden from the world. They had a preeminent right to their privacy. Father Bede felt certain the Sacred Congregation of Religious would back his position if they were asked for an opinion.

Father Daniel's eyes flickered toward Dom Stephen, the abbot who sat at the head of the table. Threats, veiled or otherwise, almost always pressed the abbot's buttons. The signs were subtle but unmistakable. Normally, Dom Stephen's long, angular face was impassive, devoid of any emotion that might betray feelings or thought. But he had briefly clenched his teeth and the action caused his jaw to tense ever so slightly.

Not that Father Bede was any more comfortable in his role as opposition leader on this issue. He had in fact spoken to the abbot before the meeting and offered to abstain from the discussion, since his views were both strong and well known. But Dom Stephen had firmly rejected the offer. Father Bede may have been conservative, but the abbot knew him to be singularly selfless and thorough. There would be no surprises after Bede made his case. He would let his opponents know exactly what was facing them.

Ideally, Father Bede wanted the cloister kept free of everyone except monks. In case anyone had forgotten, he began to remind them by quoting verbatim, from memory, a portion of Article 31 of the order's Constitutions and Statutes.

"The central area where the monks live is to be reserved strictly for them," he said. "Allowing women retreatants is a first, very transparent move to open up this abbey."

Everyone knew of plans to permit retreatants to live completely within the monastic community for longer periods of time. How, he asked, was that to be resolved with the article he had just quoted? To be honest, he saw no reason why the monastery needed a retreat program of any kind. There were other monastic orders who offered formal retreat programs. People who wished could go there. Why risk diluting the monastery's solitude simply because people believed there was something special that could only be found in a Trappist monastery?

The monks earned the right to that something special, he argued. They paid the price, sacrificing family, friends, and career when they entered the monastery. They spared nothing to answer Christ's call. They had given up everything they owned, cut all ties to people they loved, and subjected themselves to isolation for life. But they accepted that deal.

They agreed to disappear from the world. They were not testing the water with a big toe and running for a towel as soon as they found it uncomfortable.

Besides, he seriously doubted whether people who experienced the life on a limited basis derived any benefit at all. Solitude had its greatest effect because it was relatively free from distraction. That gave it a necessary intensity. How could someone who still had ties to the world achieve that?

When he had finished those arguments, Father Bede moved immediately to another set of concerns he had about the retreat house. Classic Bede, Dom Stephen thought. He might vehemently oppose something, but if the majority upheld it, he would do everything he could to see that it was done as well as possible. Because even as he argued against the proposed change in policy, he knew it was a losing battle. If the retreat house needed renovating, Bede wanted to do it right.

The renovation plan called for substantial new concrete work, he said. Had the builder specifically discussed it with anyone? Where was he getting his cement? What buildings had they supplied before? What was the exact ratio of cement to sand in their mix? Had anyone charted the average drying time for their product? Had the abbey checked with friends in the county building department? The monastery was spending a sizable amount of money on the retreat house, Father Bede pointed out as he finished. It was important to check and make sure it was well spent.

Father Daniel, who sat to Father Bede's left, waited a few moments before taking his turn to speak. Though he strongly disagreed with the monastery's conservatives, he liked Bede personally. The community came first with Bede. It made opposing him difficult, but Daniel felt conscience demanded he answer his brother monk's arguments.

Pope Paul VI had been clear in his charge to the monastic orders, Daniel began. They were to find ways to share their life. Of necessity, that meant experimentation. Did anyone really think Gethsemani had moved hastily so far as change was concerned? he asked. The pope had made his suggestion in 1968, almost twenty years ago. In Daniel's opinion, the passage of time itself suggested that due consideration had been given to those monks who were not comfortable with change—any change.

Second, he asked, were critics of the proposed change going to second-guess the Holy Spirit? How did anyone know what benefits a person derived from even the most limited exposure to Trappist life? Many of the monks seated around the table had decided to join the order after the briefest possible contact—watching and listening to the monks in choir from the balcony above them. Who knew what sacrifices someone may have made to do that, or what suffering they may have undergone that predisposed them to an awareness and appreciation of the contemplative life?

Father Daniel had been speaking in a tone no different from Father Bede's, but at that point, his pace quickened. So far as the Constitutions were concerned, he suggested that those who were interested check out the article two steps removed from the one Father Bede had quoted. Unless he was mistaken, it directed monks to aid anyone who came to the monastery looking for more intensive prayer. It further specified that the monastery was not established just for the monks but for all believers.

Dom Stephen's jaw relaxed at that point. He was always relieved when someone tackled the conservatives on their own turf. Father Daniel's time at Maryknoll, and even the period he had spent separated from the monastery, had made him more sensitive and compassionate. Sharper, too. Most people would have personalized the exchange with Bede. Dan's rebuttal bearded him in his own den: the rules and regulations he was forever beating everyone over the head with.

Matthew, chapter 25, Dom Stephen thought to himself. The mandate was even clearer there. In the closing passages, Christ had left no doubt that the charity given to the lowest of the low would be credited as having been given to him.

Dom Stephen might have said that, but his policy was to listen, just as he believed it was the obligation of the council members to counsel. Listening. That was his modus operandi and, in many monks' opinion, his particular gift. He might question, in the manner of a Socratic teacher, but even that degree of projection was rare. He had candidly revealed his philosophy to a newspaper reporter who had interviewed him when he was first elected abbot.

How did it feel to be one of the world's few absolute rulers? the reporter had asked. He had heard that Trappist monks swore unstinting obedience to their abbots, that a monk needed permission to spend as little as two cents or to walk outside the gate for a casual stroll. How did it feel to have all that power, especially since it came from the very people over whom it was exercised?

It felt lonely, Dom Stephen had answered. He felt as though he had been deprived of his brothers, cut off from the informal give and take that he believed nourished his monastic existence. Many monks would think twice before telling him something, now that he was abbot. Some might even defer, to their own detriment.

"I'm not their father, and I'm not about to let grown men make me into one," he had said. If he allowed monks to manipulate him into that role, he would stifle their growth. The monastery was an uncomplicated social unit and, one hoped, free of ambition and artifice. If someone needed information he possessed, he would be happy to share it. But he believed all of his brother monks were intelligent enough to assess a situation and come up with a good decision. His job was to facilitate that process, without installing his opinion or allowing anyone to use him as a crutch.

Dom Stephen had found that his philosophy was more easily said than done. It was hardest when some monks projected onto him the unre-solved difficulties they had experienced with their natural fathers. Out-side counseling had eventually been the solution, but not before he had undergone some trying times.

Moreover, as abbot, he did have virtual dominion over his monks and when some of them dug their heels in, the temptation was strong to order them to do what he saw as best. But he knew without ever having tried, that such a policy only *seemed* to work. Ride roughshod over a group of monks and you could have a guerrilla war on your hands.

As it was, the conservatives fought him at every turn, sometimes very effectively. When the Liturgy Committee had begun using nonexclusive pronouns in the mass, the conservatives (the abbot was certain it was Bede) had written to the authorities in Rome, pointedly asking if that was permitted. Rome had dutifully and predictably answered in the negative and the abbot had to direct the committee to cease and desist.

He wondered now how they would react to the forthcoming visit of the writer from New York, Frank Bianco. After an exchange of letters, he had agreed to allow Bianco to come and experience the life while he inter-viewed monks and photographed them for a book he planned to write. At first, Dom Stephen had been cautious. There had been so much written, he had answered, and too much of it badly done, usually shot through with inaccuracy.

The writer's response to that rationale had affected the abbot. He felt something was happening in the man's life. Dom Stephen had turned down writers with clearly superior credentials. In his opinion, their involvement with the monastery would have been a journalistic exercise. The abbey did not need it.

Perhaps it was Bianco's persistence that made the abbot pause. God never brought someone to the monastery without good reason. He also believed there was wisdom in Saint Benedict's rule that no one be admitted easily.

The writer was the second person who had recently won over Dom Stephen's opposition. The first was a disbarred attorney who also refused to take no for an answer. He wanted to enter the community. The man was a divorced father of eight children, an alcoholic and over sixty years of age. The monastery's upper age limit was forty-five.

"But I'm like a little bird sitting on your windowsill," the would-be monk had told him. "Peck, peck, peck. I'm going to keep pecking on the window until you let me in." He had stayed "pecking" in the guest house for the better part of a year. Now he was a novice.

Listening. Dom Stephen believed that was the monk's job and the abbot's even more so. If God wanted someone in the monastery, he wouldn't let him or her take no for an answer. Women had been patiently tapping on the door for a long time. Men had been asking to share the monastic experience, just as Bianco was, for an even longer period. God was sending messages.

Dom Stephen watched as Father Daniel finished speaking. Bede would have to wait until everyone around the table spoke if he had something more to say on the matter. But the abbot thought Bede would pass—for the time being. He knew that Dom Stephen wanted the community's approval on the matter. That meant a discussion and vote, both of which were still some way off. There was ample time and opportunity for rebuttal.

The abbot could imagine the lengthy position papers that would soon begin appearing on the community bulletin board. Bede may have known the battle was lost but he would not give up the field without a fight.

2
Just Plain Mac

MAC STOOD back for a moment, leaning on the handle of the splitting ax. The sweat that was dripping from his face had not been drawn in vain. A small hill of split logs—perhaps an eighth of a cord—was piled in front of him. Added to the ten-foot-long row he had already split, his efforts would warm him for most of the coming winter.

The thought made him turn to look at his tiny cabin. He had used scrap material to build the rustic-looking shelter in the woods that surround Gethsemani Abbey. He fashioned the walls from one-foot-wide wooden forms once used to mold round wheels of Trappist cheese, nailing the inch-thick boards together and filling their spaces with sawdust for insulation. He had stuccoed the exterior with cement and coated that with whitewash.

The result was so airtight and weatherproof that a candle could warm the ten-by-fifteen-foot interior. It contained a folding cot, above which stretched two shelves filled with books, including a Bible, a dog-eared paperback copy of the psalms and several books by Karl Rahner.

A kerosene lantern atop an ancient library carousel provided light after sunset and a small belly stove kept the cabin cozy in the harshest of Kentucky winters. Seating was limited to a straight-backed chair with a cane seat made concave by constant use and a large rocker whose pads had grown thin in the same service.

Mac spent portions of each day in the cabin, often staying overnight, to think, read, and pray. He had been Gethsemani's abbot for five of his thirty-eight years as a Trappist, but had resigned because he felt his vocation lay in simply being a monk, subject to authority rather than exercising it.

For five years afterward, he participated in an experiment he himself had initiated in which four monks lived in a separate community in Oxford, North Carolina. The monks lived and worked in separate cabins, only coming together to chant a single choral office and celebrate mass in the morning and once again in the evening, when they again prayed the Psalms together and ate a communal supper.

Despite his aversion to abbatial office, Mac had shown a marked talent for it. He had become something of an administrative relief pitcher, called in to take over two abbeys when the resident abbots seemed unable to lead their communities. In the first instance, he had served three and a half years before the abbey stabilized and elected a new abbot from their number. The second took only two years. When asked to account for the quicker fix, Mac had quipped, "I think my curve is getting harder to hit."

In the time between his abbatial stints, he asked for and received assignments within the monastery that left him largely alone. Before the monastery began buying footwear from a commercial supplier (who charitably sold it to them at cost), Mac had been the community's cobbler. At present, he was their tailor. His skill was apparent in the neatly fitting habits he produced, despite the wide variety of sizes in Gethsemani's eighty-monk community.

He himself favored denim jeans, blue work shirts, and a pair of well-worn cowboy boots for those times when he was not in choir or at meals with his brother monks. His short-cropped hair was pure white and accentuated his tanned, deeply lined face. At sixty-nine, he looked lean, fit, and taller than he was. (I guessed his height at six feet. He was actually five-foot-ten.) He credited manual labor and daily hiking—"not the same as walking," he emphasized—for whatever physical fitness he had been able to maintain.

Not entirely so, Brother Robert, the master of novices, told me later. "The walking helps, but he's a fanatic about fasting. That's why he's as thin as that hiking stick he sometimes uses."

Rarely did anyone see him eat supper, Robert said. And frequently, his place was empty at dinner, the monastery's main meal which was eaten at noon. In addition, Robert told me about the time both of them had participated on a panel discussing meditative technique at a conference for psychological counselors.

The conference was held at a posh hotel; the meals were no less lavish. "The beef Wellington they served at one dinner was almost an occasion of sin," said Robert. "God forgive me," he added, thumping his barrel chest with a mock mea culpa, "I had seconds."

But Mac never touched a morsel. To Robert's knowledge, he did not have a bite of anything during the two-day stay. The diet showed. His lean body was a vertical curve as he stood alongside the cabin, hands on his hips. If he had strapped on a six-shooter and stuck a Stetson on his head, he'd have cornered every call from central casting for a cow town sheriff.

His background fit the appearance. He had spent most of the years before college living on his family's large ranch in western Texas. His father and mother had fully expected him, their only child, to take over the profitable enterprise when he graduated.

When he told them, after his sophomore year at Texas A & M, that he had other plans, they quickly voiced their disappointment. It turned to shock when he added that he was converting to Roman Catholicism and was fairly certain he would soon enter a Trappist monastery.

It was as though his son were dying, his father had said after a long silence. He found it difficult to believe he hadn't done anything wrong as a parent, that there wasn't something he could say or do that might change so dreadful a decision.

But although they clearly disapproved, neither parent carried their opposition beyond this initial reaction. They tearfully said goodbye on the day Mac left for Gethsemani, as they did each time they were to visit him.

Mac would not deny that his insistence on being known simply as "Mac" represented an attempt on his part to soothe his father's pain. Just as he inherited his father's physical size, he would one day take his father's name, doffing the diminutive by which he was known ("Little Mac"). When his father died, he would have assumed his mantle along with the name that had become part of the topography in that piece of Texas.

However, the principal reason for his preference was a distaste for titles. Whatever their designation, they distinguished people. Mac believed those distinctions were barriers to open relationships. When he was elected abbot, he had made it known that only the job had changed. Even fellow abbots, some of whom were given to formality, soon learned it would take a bit longer to get a reply if they insisted on using the formal "Dom." He might be known as Dom Thomas Mary MacDonald for the record, but anyone who forgot his preference would be gently but pointedly reminded of it, as I was when I visited him for the first of many interviews.

"Just Mac," he said, as he ushered me into the cabin. "As you can see, there's just no room here for extras." He urged me to use the rocker, a gift his mother had given him on the occasion of his twenty-fifth anniversary as a Trappist.

The monastery grapevine had told him of my coming. But while he trusted that venerable communications network, he was convinced that facts rarely made the passage without substantial change. He therefore asked that I tell him firsthand what it was I was trying to accomplish.

I briefly described the circumstances that had attracted me to the project and said that my overall goal was to tell readers what real-life monks do and why. Mac tilted his chair until it touched the wall behind him, folded his hands behind his head and put his boots up on the small stove. It was all very simple, he said, so much so that he wondered if there was enough to fill a book.

Monks want to give God more room in their lives, he said. The key, he continued, is self-sacrifice. It sets the stage for contemplation, which is nothing more than prayerful awareness of God's presence. A monk works at stripping himself of all that is passing, the obvious, things that satisfy the senses. The smallest sacrifice builds willpower. "Like they say, when the going gets tough, the tough get going. You need discipline. You need to learn to say no."

The obvious "things" were the easiest to sacrifice, Mac said—"things most people mean when they talk about the so-called severity of our life. You'd be surprised at how fast you get used to eating vegetables (better for you, anyway), and getting up when the rest of the world is rolling over for the other half of their night's sleep.

"When you realize you're giving away the only things you have left— the choice of what you eat, what you do for work, what you wear—you begin to know what it means to be poor. You control nothing. You don't own anything. But figure it this way. If you die, it's all gone in a flash. You never had control. You only thought you did."

The person who makes that discovery might panic, except for one thing, Mac explained. He realizes that a caring God controls. Not only is there no point in worrying, there is no need to.

"You get a taste of freedom. Ever so slowly, as your willpower gets stronger, you put more distance between yourself and things. But you get closer to God. It's like a ship that throws unnecessary baggage over the side. The lighter its load, the faster it travels and the closer it gets to port.

"If you're lucky, and God gives you the gas, it suddenly dawns on you that everything you have is on loan. That's what Christ meant when he said we were stewards and kept talking about the ones who were wise. God wasn't obligated to give you anything and he chose to give you the right to thumb your nose at him. He could have guaranteed service by making a tree. Instead he took a chance and made you, and bet that you'd be smart enough to figure it out and respond lovingly."

The basic theology behind it all was pretty straightforward, Mac continued. But "straightforward" did not mean it was easy to do. Only God could make it doable, and that grace was not guaranteed.

Obviously, he had "it," I said, or else he wouldn't have stayed in the monastery. How did he know God wanted him to stay? How did someone know God wanted him there in the first place?

Mac looked at me and hesitated. The question I had asked led to the heart of the matter, to very personal terrain that monks hold private. Most believe that area of their existence is a mystery, one that can be worn thin by too much discussion.

But I had not held back when Mac had asked me why I was writing this book. I had told him all the personal details and that relaxed him enough to return the trust.

"Merton once wrote," Mac said, " 'A monk is somebody who seeks God because he has been found by God.' You know when you've been found. Something tells you this is where you belong. That's what we mean when we say you're called to this life. God finds you.

"And the grace he gives you makes this life happy for you, like your favorite pair of shoes. The longer you wear them, the better they feel. That's not saying somebody who raises a family hasn't been called by God to do it," Mac added. "All of us are called by God to live our lives in a very certain way, doing something only we can do. If you don't hear, he keeps trying until you do.

"Remember when you were sitting in that church trying to figure out where God was in the tragedy of your son's death?" he asked. "You very correctly connected an all-loving God to your pain. That's the theological bottom line for God. He's love.

"The more we let him into our lives, the more he teaches us about love—how to love and how he loves us. Love is both the God part and the fuel for your transcendent soul.

"Once you feel you are loved, your self-esteem increases. You relax, you begin to look outside yourself. You grow in your ability to share the self-esteem that roots your peace and happiness. You really begin to love. You give without any thought of getting in return. You give the way God does, unselfishly."

I thought I was missing something. Other than asking God to come into one's life, was there something else a person had to do, something tangible, some secret of it all?

"Others."

Others?

"How do you think God works? Do you imagine he comes down in a brilliant light and says, 'Hey, Frank. I love you?' Think that's the way it happens?"

I shrugged.

"Others. It's a beautiful cycle. As God fills our heart with his love, we stop trying to manipulate others to fill that need. Instead, we reach out to them. We start giving. We give them room. We give in when we don't have to. We give them the chance to be what they are. We begin to accept them as they are. Don't you know what that does to a person? It makes them feel loved. It stimulates the growth of their self-esteem.

"We have the power to do that. Think about it. That's real power. God's power. We can take the pressure off people, and when we do that, we're no longer threatening. They can respond to us in a loving way. We and they become the channels of God's love. The biggest insight in the monastic life is realizing how we experience God in the people we contact every day."

Mac believed people made a mistake when they concluded that the monk "gives up so much" or "leaves the world." The world is simply a community of people. The monk lives in community with his brother monks. They are as much a world as any he left behind.

"Each of us brings a piece of the world into the monastery," he said. "When I walked into this place, thirty-eight years ago, I brought along my personality, my way of living and dealing with people.

"People think the monastery will be the place to straighten themselves out, but they're wrong. I've seen that reality with myself and with other monks. Whatever problem or difficulties we had before we came, were exactly the same once we were here."

I told Mac he made it sound as though there was no difference between life outside the monastery wall and life within.

"Only one. The pressure in here is to be honest, to build something real. Outside, the pressure is to compete, to win, to acquire. Like that bumper sticker I once saw that said, 'The guy who wins at the end is the one with the most toys.'

"That's what the monk is walking away from—the world's current philosophy, its overemphasis on "me first," get all you can, while you can. It's fake—fools you into thinking you've gotten someplace, even though you're just grinding out miles on a treadmill.

Was he saying that ambition was a fault? Was it wrong to try and make the most of opportunities, to make life comfortable?

"No, I'm not proposing masochism as a way of life. I'm saying you'll never find happiness in gorging yourself, grabbing everyone and everything you can in a vain effort to fill your needs."

Look at the Gospels, Mac urged. Again and again, Christ made it clear: focus on your neighbor, see what he needs, do what you can to fill those needs.

"It's a shame to see people weighing themselves down," he said. "They go along with society's prevailing philosophy like it was some psychic social security system. They get conned by all that hokum the ads promise. 'You'll be happy with this car, that hair color, this vacation.' And when tension gives you a headache, take an aspirin. By no means should you try to find out whether you're so glutted from gobbling up everything in sight, it's making you sick."

Mac waved a hand in disgust. He had been talking rapidly and, as I would learn, had become uncharacteristically emotional about the subject.

"Sorry," he said. "I just think it's such a waste. People get ground up and worn out for nothing. The closer they get to all that nonsense, the further they get from God. They waste all that good energy chasing phantoms. Their inner compass gets all screwed up.

"Real joy and peace are in the opposite direction, where God exists. Happiness, here, now, comes from adding to life, not subtracting. Turf, image, power—they're illusions, an elaborate shell game our society tempts you into thinking you can win. It's rigged and most people don't find out until it's too late. You can't take it, any of it, with you."

Mac stood up and stretched. "How about a walk?" he asked. Donning a light, hip-length denim work jacket, he led the way outside. "Seen Uncle Louie's tower?

"In the early fifties, Louie [Thomas Merton's religious name was Father Louis] had begun driving Dom James nuts with his notion of transferring to one of the hermit orders. We didn't have that as an option in our life at the time."

According to Mac, the issue was resolved by degrees. When Dom James learned that the state forestry department wanted to build a fire

tower atop a topographical high point on monastery property, he engi-
neered the appointment of Merton as its fire warden. The responsibility
legitimized long periods of time spent alone, apart from the community.

As we began walking toward the wooded area where Uncle Louie's
tower was located, I wondered aloud about the contradiction between a
hermit's existence and the human interaction that Mac had indicated as
the essence and ideal of a God-centered existence.

"Doesn't seem to square, does it?" he answered. "I think there are
periods of time when God calls you apart and you go one-on-one with
him. Maybe those are extensions of the times when you feel the need to
be alone. Everybody needs space at some point or another. I know monks
who hermit full time. We got one here who tried it for several years and is
back in the community."

Mac stopped walking and pointed at me. "I know what you're thinking.
What about that cabin I use, the one my brother monks call my 'pad'?

"The truth is, I give every monk the right to preempt me. Many of
them take me up on the offer and spend as much as a week out here on
retreat. Then I just find another branch in the woods on which to perch.

"A lot of the monks come to me for spiritual counseling. There's even a
few people who regularly come in from the outside to talk with me. The
time I spend here gives God a chance to stoke my own fire. I make more
room for him in my life. The old Romans used to say, 'Nemo dat quod non
habet'—you can't give what you haven't got."

I had to admit the cabin was hardly luxurious. It was two miles from
the monastery. There was no electricity or running water. If Mac didn't
use summer to build that wall of firewood outside, he'd freeze come
winter. I could believe him when he added, "That privy out back can be a
fearsome journey on a cold night when an old man's kidneys want attending."

But as little as it was, the cabin was something Mac owned, and I
wondered how much it took to give it away, practically on demand, when
someone simply asked to use it.

"That's when you really learn what freedom is—when nothing has a
claim on you except God. Things are easy, but I think you fight the real
battle over less obvious turf.

"For instance, everybody believes our big sacrifice is giving up sex," he
said. "But we struggle much harder when we try to surrender the very
legitimate consequences of sexuality. You see, when the mind's motion
picture theater starts tantalizing you with images of sexual fantasy, the
temptation's obvious. You can deal with that directly. But you're not as

ready or wary when the temptation comes cloaked in innocence, as it did for one monk I used to know."

This particular monk had entered the monastery at twenty, Mac said, after he made a retreat there during his freshman year at the University of Detroit. He had fallen in love with the life's beauty and peace. "He had a nice way of putting it," said Mac. "Said he didn't come to the monastery to find happiness. His life was brimming with it. He was big man on campus, the big baseball star, promising enough to pitch batting practice with his local pro team.

"He compared his life outside to a hit Broadway play, the kind that everybody raves about. Coming here was the same as going backstage after the play to spend time with the genius who put it all together." The monk had studied the flute and voice as well, Mac said. His love for music drew him to the liturgy and he quickly became the community's lead cantor.

His voice was distinguished by its ability to get everyone's attention at three in the morning when sleep gives ground grudgingly. Words that had grown familiar by years of use took on fresh meaning when he intoned them to begin the first early morning office. "O Lord, open my lips," he would sing softly. Monks would credit him as the reason that their response—"and my mouth will declare your praise"—came from their hearts even more than from their heads.

"Want to know what tormented that man?" Mac asked. "He told me it hurt just talking about it. He came from a big family, nine brothers and sisters. It was one of the things that made his life so great. He knew he'd never have kids of his own. The thought could twist him into knots. He'd fantasize about teaching a son to toss a football. He'd constantly dream about that little boy. He could describe him in detail and the dream would always end with that kid holding on to his hand, walking beside him.

"He used to fall into the blackest depression just thinking that some day the rest of us would lower him into that cemetery out there and he'd never have known what it's like to have that little kid tell him he wanted to grow up to be just like his daddy."

"Did he make it?" I asked.

Mac looked at me and grinned. Then he bent down and picked up a small stone. With a brief glance at a foot-wide tree trunk, some fifty feet distant, he drew back his arm and threw sideways. The stone passed to the left of his target.

"He'd never miss," Mac said. "That arm of his was a gift." He was looking down at the road again, idly moving the loose gravel with the toe of one shoe. "Yeah, he left. Took a leave of absence and went to live with a married sister."

The monk was exclaustrated, Mac explained. Since he had not asked to be released from the solemn vows he had made, the monastery continued to carry him on their roll. In the majority of cases, exclaustrated monks do not return. But the monk in question did.

In slightly less than a year, he returned, but to another of the order's monasteries. He was still there, Mac said, sobered after living with his sister and her three teenage sons. He had learned that the little boy in his dreams was an overidealized fantasy, a robot he had imagined would respond every time he needed companionship. His sister's sons had been real, with their own needs. When the novelty of their uncle the monk wore off, he was just another adult who liked to throw a baseball.

"Sounds like pretty normal teenagers."

"And he was like too many people who regard children and childbearing as a chance to establish their identity," said Mac. "They're takers. The creation of life is supposed to be an act of giving. Selflessness."

"That sounds a little hard, coming from a guy who never had kids."

There was no sign that my words had stung Mac. His head was bent, his gaze on the ground where his toe continued to move the gravel, as he searched for just the right stone. He found the words first.

"I may not have had any kids, but I know people," he said. "When somebody starts bitching about how bad the world is treating them, or how 'it' or 'they' won't let them do this noble thing they'd like to do, just be quiet and listen. Listen, like I listened to that monk, and see whether the smallest—just the tiniest—piece of the good they want to do winds up in their pocket."

I could see nothing wrong with the monk's dream, I told Mac. I knew many fathers, myself included, who lived to be able to make life an opportunity for their children, to share with them the good things they themselves had experienced.

"I'll tell you what was wrong," Mac said. He was looking at me now, speaking with noticeable assurance in his voice. "Everything he despaired of doing, deprived him of something. I can't recall him talking about sharing, the way you described those fathers a minute ago.

"God was good enough to let him see that. He saw how his sister and brother-in-law had to pour out to make their kids grow. I think he saw how real love comes from allowing somebody to be their own person, rather than somebody who suits what you have in mind, a nursemaid for your need."

Ultimately, the monk missed the monastery, his family, Mac continued. He realized how his fantasy had fooled him, kept him from seeing what was right in front of him. He recognized the relationships he'd spent most of his life building, the love he had enjoyed with his brother monks. He saw the things they had in common, the values they shared. He discovered that the outside world had very different priorities. Making the sign of the cross in a restaurant made everybody's head turn. And yet those same onlookers would pass people sleeping on the sidewalk without a second glance.

He returned to a monastery where the community was smaller, not because of its size, but because it had real need for a monk with his musical skills. He responded to someone else's need. And he returned to an environment where giving was the priority, where everything helped him become the person he knew God had called him to be.

"And . . ." Mac bent over. He had found the stone. He picked it up and hefted it in his palm as he sized up the trees around us. One was fairly close, decidedly wider than the first he had tried to hit.

"And," he repeated, "he learned something basic. That God calls us monks apart, to give to each other, to give away everything we have, for as long as he thinks we need to do it. We're happiest where we're supposed to be. Only God knows where that is or how long that will be, and he'll give you whatever you need just when you think you've given up all you got."

Mac wound up and threw the rock without aiming. It glanced off the side of the tree, and he turned, his smile unmistakably smug.

"Just like being a monk. Nothing to it—when you know who you are and what you're supposed to be doing."

3

A Different Drumbeat

MAC—AND Thomas Merton—were not the only Trappists who believed that God "called" everyone, and that everyone's vocation was essentially a call to contemplation. "Monks don't have any monopoly on the contemplation thing," said Brother Peter. "We just do it a little differently."

Brother Peter is one of thirty-three Trappist monks who make their living from the sale of walnuts and prunes they grow on their 640-acre ranch, better known as Our Lady of New Clairvaux Abbey. The abbey, located one hundred miles north of Sacramento, California, was founded in 1954 by forty monks from Gethsemani. It occupies the last remaining plot of what was once the lush vineyard/estate of Leland Stanford, whose donations helped establish the California university named in his honor.

Joe Osgood, a farm adviser for the University of California's Cooperative Extension, services area farms. He regards the abbey's acreage as the most fertile imaginable. Test drillings have found the same top soil at eighteen-foot depths as exists on the surface. "You throw a seed in this ground," he said, "and you better get the hell out of the way or the plant will knock you on your butt on its way up. People around here like to say the monks have an unfair advantage, but the truth is, they're real hard workers and they do everything they should to get the most from what God put here."

Brother Peter was working in his pottery shed when I interviewed him. He too asked that I forget the formality. "Pete" was just fine with him. He was slightly built, round shouldered and short, perhaps five-foot-five. His hair was noticeably thin, a condition that made his full beard and mustache somewhat wispy. Large facial features, including a hooked nose, accentuated his small head, but hazel eyes, rimmed with long lashes, softened his appearance.

Since sale of the pottery he crafted constituted income for the abbey, he had special permission to make potting his regular work. His handiwork was a well-known feature of New Clairvaux. Pete's mugs, jars, and vases found a ready market among visitors to the monastery and his pottery was also the expression of an abbey custom.

Very soon after a postulant became a novice and was thereby formally admitted to the community, he would find a ceramic mug at his place in the refectory. It would have his name and a distinctive design engraved on it, a tangible sign of the community's acceptance. (I was delighted to find one at my place not long after I arrived at New Clairvaux.)

Brother Peter's vocation had been a long time in gestation. He was the middle child of seven from a Youngstown, Ohio family, whose father and grandfather had been steelworkers. During his last years of high school, Pete's inborn talent and aptitude for things mechanical earned him a job in the mills at an earlier age than was normally allowed. That experience and his academic achievement won him a scholarship for the study of architecture at Stanford University. It was the beginning of the long journey that would take him to the Trappists.

When he was assigned a report on medieval architecture for a freshman class, Pete chose the ancient abbey of Mont Saint Michel as his subject. The choice seemed born of pure whimsy, but as he began to research it, the monks' life intrigued him.

Given his own clear-cut choice of a career, he was attracted by the ancient monks' similar singleness of purpose. He also found something decidedly romantic and appealing about the monks. Since they were always of noble lineage, they traded lives of comfort and acclaim for poverty and anonymity. Pete felt that such a decision took as much courage as faith. Too bad, he thought at the time, believing that monasteries, like dinosaurs, had disappeared.

Three years later, just months from graduation, he was living in an off-campus apartment. Life was pleasant, made more so by an existence in which he had to deny himself very little. His grades ranked him at the top of his class and had brought him to the attention of professionals in the field. One firm had tried him as an extern and then hired him part-time. There was little question as to where his talent could lead, or the doors it would open.

Part-time employment was already paying him well, more than was usually possible. His room boasted a color television set, the latest in stereo equipment, and even a well-stocked liquor cabinet. He could spend lavishly on dates and had no lack of female companions, most of whom were content with the degree of intimacy Pete offered. He reveled in playing the field and quickly ended any association that threatened his freedom.

One evening, he sought relief from the pressure of studies for final exams and was attracted by a listing for a television dramatization of Rumer Godden's book, In This House of Brede, starring the British actress Diana Rigg.

Rigg portrayed a woman in her late forties, who gave up a promising, lucrative job working for the British Parliament, and became a Benedictine nun, a female monk. Pete had heard it said that the actress was reputedly an industry sexpot and the notion of her playing a chaste, self-sacrificing nun offered an evening of ripe, farcical comedy. With a six-pack at hand, Pete settled in for the laughs.

Instead, the story moved him profoundly. It reminded him of the report he had written in freshman year. He had the same feelings, the strong attraction for a life-style about which he knew very little, and which he still believed had disappeared. Something inside him, indefinable, resonated with the idea of the monastery, as though his life and "it" were one thing.

But how? he asked himself. How could he find so vague a life so intriguing when he measured it alongside the one he was leading, one where tangible reward was only exceeded by even greater opportunity to accomplish and earn? As he kept thinking, he found himself tormented by the contradiction. Only a fool would walk away from the career that faced him. He had chosen his life's work. The lucrative job offers in the pile of letters on his desk confirmed the wisdom of that choice. A monk's life was a dead end by comparison. Nonsense, he said to himself as he forced the idea from his mind.

The whole business seemed to have disappeared from his thoughts when Pete awoke the next morning and he turned his mind quickly to his studies, the job at hand, lest the previous night's turmoil start all over again. He had lost valuable study time and he resolved to make it up by returning directly to his apartment after his last class and burying himself in his books. He would have done so if he had not gone first to his locker and noticed several library books that were long overdue. The library was on his way home, so he decided to drop them off.

The library seemed unusually empty and quiet. Only one other student was there, scribbling furiously behind a stack of books. Pete decided he could best use his time by staying in the library and taking advantage of its quiet and other abundant resources. He chose a table on the opposite side of the room from the other student, sat down, and was soon lost in his work.

He had been studying for slightly more than an hour and a half when he decided to get some fresh air. The other student had left, but the books he had been using were still stacked on the table. As Pete passed by on his way to the exit, the title of one book caught his eye: *The Silent Life*.

It was a book on monasticism written by Thomas Merton. There were other books by the same author, including his autobiography. A single large reference book was open and Pete glanced at it. The title at the head of the page read, "Religious Orders," and the very first boldface line printed beneath it was "O.C.S.O.—The Cistercians, Order of the Strict Observance (Trappists)." The second-to-last listing had been circled. It flagged the Abbey of New Clairvaux, giving its location, the number of monks in the community, and the name of its abbot.

Pete sat and began to thumb the autobiography, *The Seven Storey Mountain*. Within minutes, he had turned to the first page and begun to read. When the library closed, he copied down New Clairvaux's address and the name of its abbot and took the autobiography out on loan. Early the following morning, he finished it. There was a mailbox outside his apartment's front door. Before he collapsed into bed, he posted a letter to the abbot of New Clairvaux, asking if he could come and visit.

He graduated magna cum laude two months later and eight months after that, he received the white habit of a Trappist novice. The following are his uninterrupted thoughts about the way of life he chose.

"I like to think of our life as just another way of living. Like you do your thing and I do mine; you enjoy your life and family and I dig mine. I couldn't buy the idea that I'm more holy than you or closer to God than you. None of that. I don't have any kind of that feeling.

"I'm here because I like being here and I assume you're where you are because you like being where you are. It's as simple as that.

"Being a monk is not a job; it's a life-style that's made up of a bunch of things. This place, these guys, the work we do here. When I came here that first time, it was like falling in love. I really didn't know what this life was like, what these guys were like, but I knew in my gut that this was where I belonged.

"That wasn't a head decision. It came from the heart. I married this place, the way you married your wife. Gethsemani may be a good-looking lady, but not to me. My heart told me then like it tells me now: This is my girl and I'm going to grow old with her and probably make a beautiful love story out of our life together.

"When people ask me what life at New Clairvaux is all about, I say we're like an orchestra. Like the Philharmonic. I guess they do a lot of daily practicing, don't they? Well, I figure the rest of their life is geared to let them do that.

"Just the way that orchestra does concerts, we go to choir, seven times a day, about three and a half hours total. For the most part, our life is organized to allow us to sing in choir. Eating, sleeping, working, everything—it all revolves around choir.

"The Benedictines are monks too, but they're different. Like a different lady, you know? They sing in choir like we do, but they go out. We don't. They run colleges, give big retreats with a whole bunch of programs. If you come here for a retreat, there's no program. We make our life available to you. You do what we do.

"But that doesn't make us better. God blesses the Benedictine monk just the way he blesses me, just like he blesses people in other walks of life. Everybody gets what they need and it's got nothing to do with one being better than another, because in God's eyes, they're not.

"There's nothing special about us. I'll bet the weather bugs me just the way it bugs you. I could bitch and complain or make a grace out of it. Just like you. You talk about our silence. Well, a farmer plowing all day has more silence than we do. But he doesn't have community like we do.

"You probably pray as much as we do in your own way. But you do it alone, like the farmer is silent alone. We do those things together here. I remember when I was in high school in the late sixties, a lot of kids I knew joined communes. Some of them even did some farming and manual work just like us, but without religious components.

"Our entire daily life revolves around God. If nothing else, we hear his name mentioned every day, many, many times. And so far as I can see, that's just what I need. But notice I say, 'so far as I can see.' Because that could change.

"I know that God uses us if we let him. There's no mistaking when he comes into your life. It's as though you were driving a car. You give God the wheel and hop over to the passenger seat. We're not good passengers, though. We keep bugging God. We can't see ahead. We don't know where he's taking us and we get scared.

"So he has to assure us, in some way or other. Like he gives us a cookie to keep us happy. 'There,' he says. 'Okay? That's what I've got in store for you. Good things. So sit still and let me drive.'

"Those cookies are the opportunities God puts in front of us. We call them graces. We only get them after we walk into the darkness, trusting God to show us the way. We come out on the other side, into light, better for the trip we took, more the person God had in mind when he made us.

"That's what he was doing to me all that time while I was in college, first with the study project, then the TV show, and that setup in the library. Really something, wasn't it? If you ask me, I think God lost his cool. I think he loses patience sometimes (I know that's bad theology and some of my brothers would put me on the rack for it), but I think he does. Then it's as though he reaches down and grabs us by the back of the neck and makes us see what he's put before us.

"If we're smart enough, if we open our eyes, and our heart, we grab the grace and grow, literally, more like that plan of his. More like him.

"I haven't the slightest notion of what his plan for me might be down the line. I love it here. This is so neat. It's as right for me to be a monk as it is for other men to be bus drivers or brain surgeons or beauticians—or even architects.

"But that's now. Who knows what God's got in mind for later? I mean, there are thousands of guys in the past who entered monasteries, found peace, and felt just the way I do. Not all of them ended up in an abbey graveyard.

"When the Commies took over China, they busted into one of our monasteries over there. They tore the place apart, put the monks on trial, and then paraded them around like caged monkeys. Some of them died from the treatment. Some disappeared into the population and linked up with the Catholic Church that had gone underground.

"One of the younger monks was actually ordained a priest in the underground church. Some of our superiors arranged to bring him out in the mid-eighties and he's living here with us for the time being.

"Now, I know that sounds like a happy ending, but what about all the others? There's about a dozen of them still floating around China. Our abbot took a side trip to the mainland on one of his trips to our daughter house in Taiwan and managed to meet with them. They said they wanted to stay.

"So, who's right? Them or the monk who got out? Only God knows. Saint Paul says not to judge somebody because you might find yourself in their shoes and liable to the same judgment. (Isn't it funny the way everybody uses shoes to talk about rash judgment? Like Indians say: Don't judge a man till you walk a mile in his moccasins.)

"I've got to presume that all those Chinese monks did the same thing I do when things don't go according to plan. I pray and I listen and then I try to do what I think God wants me to do. 'What would he do if he was in my shoes,' I ask, and the answer always comes back the same.

"God always loves. That's what giving is about. To love is to give. Whenever I have to choose, I try to see which way gives me the chance to give the most. Can never go wrong like that.

"You see, that gives God control. I'm letting him call the shots. But I really don't have any choice if I want to grow. I also have to trust, because that's the grease that makes the loving move. When I do that, I'm putting myself in God's hands. I'm saying that I'll do what I think is best, even though it's loving somebody or something that doesn't seem lovable to my way of thinking. But I'm going to trust and give and whatever happens, I know it will in some way be for my good, my growth.

"There was a time when I was novice master and the novices would get all out of joint when they began to think the life was ordinary and that they had a million years ahead of them that were going to be all the same and that the guys who bugged them were going to be around as long as they were.

"That's when they begin to wonder if this life is for them. They wonder if they've got the goods to hang in there for the long haul. I mean, there's no promotions, no career, no vacations. This is it. It's this place, these people, this life. It's getting up at three in the morning when you don't feel like it. 'How will I do it?' those novices used to ask me.

"You can't, I'd tell them. And Frank, my friend, neither can you. Or me. We like to think we can. We kid ourselves. But we don't control anything at all, and when—if—we admit that, it scares the hell out of us. I'll bet that's what drove you nuts that time before your son died. Think about it for a minute. That's what mid-life crisis is all about.

"You looked at life in terms of what you had done, and you realized it wasn't half what you thought you would have done. Time was running out and you hadn't made your mark. What are we talking about? You. Your mark. Me. Mine. The illusion that we are in control. We get to thinking we're God. So we measure and want to be measured by power and possessions. We fool ourselves into thinking those give us a lock on tomorrow. That's our society's biggest scam: tomorrow and me. How happy I can make myself. Tomorrow. The tomorrow that may never come, and the me who may never make it past the next minute.

"You have to live each day as it is, for what it is, in trust. You have to trust that God loves you, and that he'll take the best shot you give him each day and make good out of it, for you and the rest of creation. I pray for that, because I believe Christ when he said that God cares for us, just like he cares for the lilies of the field or the birds that fly. If we ask for bread, he won't come across with a stone. That's the deal he and I made when I became a monk, and I don't think he welshes. That's how I try to live.

"It's one day at a time. Your vocation and your life. A gift from God. One you can accept or refuse. A chance to do your best and leave the rest in God's hands. Hey, you got any better offers?"

"IT ain't that easy," Mac said, when I later told him about my conversation with Brother Pete, whom he had met in the course of his visitations to New Clairvaux Abbey. "God has to work pretty hard sometimes before we recognize what he's trying to do and begin to cooperate. First, he has to get through to us so we listen to him. Second, he's got to help us turn off everything our society will say in opposition."

In his experience as vocation director and as abbot, Mac had frequently witnessed this struggle when a monk-to-be would first become aware of his vocation. The "call" itself was often as vague and difficult to describe as it was compelling. (In fact, Mac believed the vague calls were the strongest vocations, the ones likeliest to survive.)

"I've seen it a hundred times," he said. "A man will just feel in his gut that he belongs in the monastery. Period. That's it. Something tells him that's where God wants him. It's a real God move. Just like the call Christ issued in the gospel. 'Drop everything,' he says. 'Don't ask questions. Just come follow me.' There's no rhyme or reason to it, and the whole business doesn't seem to be related in any way to talent or temperament."

There were monks in the monastery, good monks, exemplary ones, whose life no more fit the pattern than Pete's had before he decided to become a Trappist. All they can offer is deep conviction that they belong in a monastery. "They hear God calling as clearly as you can hear me speaking to you at this moment," said Mac. "It doesn't make sense, and it's probably why people around the monk-to-be often give him a hard time. I mean, can you imagine a successful doctor or lawyer telling his family and friends that he's chucking the whole thing simply because he feels God wants him in a monastery? He gets all kinds of opposition, including a few questions about his sanity."

Virtually every Trappist vocation director I interviewed described this opposition. They believed that one of the toughest periods in a candidate's life occurs after he has decided to enter the monastery, when he is awaiting formal entry.

Sooner or later, but certainly before he departs for the monastery, some, if not all, of his friends and relatives express their doubts about the wisdom of the decision. They question the withdrawal, pointing out the alternatives. There are needs that exist in the world, they argue, needs that could benefit from the man's talents and energy. The would-be monk has to fight his way free of his own friends and their concern for his best interests. They can not understand why someone would want "to throw his life away." Such misunderstanding is commonplace.

While I was writing this book, my wife and I visited the home of a friend who asked me to describe my project to other guests he had invited. One of them was a documentary photographer who had spent several years working in Peru to preserve the work of a native photographer. She and the foundations that had funded her work believed they were securing a valuable record that might otherwise have been lost.

There was an undertone of anger in her voice as she expressed her doubt that a book about Trappists would interest anyone. My description of their life was in fact "turning her off," she said. "Who wants to know about people who have dropped out, who have shrugged off all responsibility to our society, so they could run away and indulge their insecurity?"

Thomas Merton, like other monks, generally responded by asking why monks were obliged to justify their career decisions. He doubted whether modern society could understand even if an answer were attempted.

"In a basically religious culture," he wrote, "like that of India, or of Japan, the monk is more or less taken for granted. When all society is oriented beyond the mere transient quest of business and pleasure, no one is surprised that men would devote their lives to an invisible God. In a materialistic culture which is fundamentally irreligious the monk is incomprehensible because be 'produces nothing.' His life appears to be completely useless."

Westerners (and Americans in particular) find it incomprehensible that any mature adult would willingly submit to regimentation that they perceive as designed to erase individual identity. For example, when an applicant is accepted into the Trappists, he chooses a new name, by which he will henceforward be known. He is free to choose any name, provided it is not in use by another monk in the abbey.

Like French foreign legionnaires, who also can take an assumed name when they enlist, the Trappist's former identity ceases to have any consequence. That act is as inscrutable to many people as are the motives of several Trappists who have written books but refused to take the credit of a byline.

Monks work hard at ignoring these values that dominate our society. Their cloistered life and the walls behind which they live it are an attempt to stay free of a modus operandi that can become instinctive. It is the reason why Trappist monks are generally and genuinely uncomfortable in the limelight and will politely avoid circumstances that they believe will cast it upon them. The research for this book itself had to overcome such opposition from monks who were determined to avoid publicity even though they agreed that the book might be beneficial.

When Dom Stephen put a note on Gethsemani's bulletin board advising the monks of my first visit, he described my purpose, urged their cooperation, and ended with his own opinion that my background and understanding of the order would enable me to "do a good job of it."

His endorsement did not automatically alleviate every monk's anxiety. There were many who admitted being uncomfortable in sharing the personal details of their lives with me, a complete stranger who was going to disseminate those details to the world outside.

"It amounts to a contradiction," said one monk. "Here we have publicly pronounced our desire to disappear, to expunge our public self, and then we trot out that self and put it under a spotlight on stage center. Sure, we'd like to help, but your work puts us on the spot."

In Mac's opinion, that monk was more honest than most. As he predicted, many simply regarded my efforts as an invasion of privacy and politely declined to become involved. Notably, I heard the same phrase over and over from monks if I tried to persuade them to talk with me after their initial demurral. "I'm a very private person," they would say, with a finality that sometimes bristled.

"You're touching them where they feel most vulnerable," Mac said. "Monks for the most part are very shy. People aren't born shy. That's a defense they learn when they get turned off by unloving, exploitative human beings. Instead of being nurtured and nourished by the people closest to them early in life, they get ripped off.

"So they learn to retreat and stay away, especially from a very articulate New Yorker, who sounds like he can and will dismantle all their defenses if they don't slam the door shut, and I mean slam. This place is all about solitude. You already know that's not a vacuum. It's a very active, loving presence, and it heals those people whose previous attempts to love may have gone awry.

"There's a great deal about your profession and the things you must do, that can open the scars from all those skewed—maybe I should say skewered—attempts at loving, times when trust gets betrayed. The more that happens, the more people hold others at arm's length, unwilling and often unable to let anybody get close. Try backing off a bit and respect their needs without taking offense or making them feel guilty. Don't threaten to tear them away from the only loving they have been able to achieve. Monks have suffered over the centuries when people insist they be samaritans to a bunch of spiritual hypochondriacs. Relax, Frank. Try building bridges instead of tearing down walls. Maybe you should give some thought to why you have to be the one person who succeeds where everybody else fails. There's more than enough monks around here who will talk to you very freely. That's one voice. You'll hear another in your dealings with those who decline to talk. That will come from your own heart and it's important for you to listen to it carefully if you really want to learn about our life. You have to be open to what we are, rather than what you need us to be."

4

The Monk in Us All

M<small>AC'S LAST</small> words had made me a bit uneasy. Although people may have challenged my right to report and investigate their lives before, I had never questioned that right. It was not the first time, nor would it be the last, that I realized I would learn as much about myself in the course of this project as I was going to learn about these silent monks. Something also told me Mac wasn't going to leave the matter at that.

Sure enough, there was a note from him the next morning in my monastic mailbox (i.e., by my place setting in the refectory). Why there? Because although each monk has a mailbox among those that cover half of one vestibule wall, I discovered that many of them sometimes go unchecked for days.

The practice was another example of the monks' basic reserve in dealing with "the world." They were cautious about relations with anyone "outside." "We get sucked in if we're not careful," Mac had told me. "Some people believe monks are a spiritual elite and therefore better equipped to advise and counsel. That can play to the monk's vanity and involve him in a dependent relationship that siphons away time and energy. This life works because it is intensified. We're here to concentrate on God. We artificially remove circumstances that might lessen that intensity, like using people as a crutch for shaky self-esteem. That's the same reason why we shouldn't allow them to do it either."

Mailboxes were therefore a polite concession to the customs of a world that nonetheless warranted scrutiny. Contrast the monk's regard for dinner, served at noon, as a legitimate call to solidarity. Even if he is fasting, the monk will come to dinner, reaffirming by his physical presence his commitment to the monastic family and its ongoing way of life. Therefore, if you need to get a message to a monk, you leave a note under his napkin.

"Rx for understanding why we hold the 'world' at arm's length," Mac's note began. "The books I've listed below are waiting for you in our library. Primarily medieval history. I'll get you a copy of the Rule of Saint Benedict before you leave, but use the one we have in the library for now. After you've read these, let's get together and try to fill in any blanks that remain. Have fun. Mac."

The list was short. I had already read one of them, *The Cistercians*. There was another on monastic architecture, two on medieval history, and lastly, the oft-quoted Rule of Saint Benedict. I found the small pile waiting for me in the library, alongside the in/out slips the librarian left for borrowers. The books were well worn, indicating I was one of many who had handled them. I wondered if the other readers had been grinding the same ax I was carrying to the task.

Why not? I was convinced that people in this day and age were searching for the answers monks seemed to have found. My own experience proved the point. Exposure to the Trappist way of life had unquestionably made me more aware of the need to change mine. (God will have to judge whether I have used that grace as fully as he intended.)

I believe Trappists had to make the opportunity they gave me available to other, similarly needy people. So far as I was concerned, Christ had referenced this issue clearly. Don't hide your lamp beneath a bushel, he had warned. Don't bury your talents. Mac's patient explanation notwithstanding, I could not understand why monks like Father Bede were so opposed to allowing people to come into the monastery and share their lives. But as Harry Truman once said so wisely, "The only thing you don't know is the history you haven't read." So I carried the books back to my room, sat down in the lounge chair and opened *The Middle Ages* by R. W. Southern. Inside its cover, I found several typewritten pages stapled together with a covering note on which Mac had simply written, "FYI."

It was the text of one of the conferences he had given during a retreat for guests at another monastery. It was titled, "The Monk Inside Us All." "God plants the seeds of a monk in everyone's soul at the moment of creation," Mac had told the retreatants. History proved this point, he maintained. There had been many instances before and outside the Christian experience when scores of men and women had chosen to live a monastic existence.

Mac classified each of these waves as collective blossoming of the monastic seed. Called by the Almighty, the individual undergoes what is commonly known as a religious conversion. God comes into his life directly, like a fire's warmth in mid-winter. Solitude exerts its most compelling pull, for it is there that the fire seems warmest. Everything else in life seems meaningless—cold by comparison. Monks are people who perceive the ascetic life as a way in which they can keep the newly found warmth of God in their lives.

Whenever monasticism has blossomed, regardless of the period of time or the place, the people who express it in communal form include the same elements in their basic regimen. They renounce marriage and private property. They emphasize silence, fasting, and the communion of prayer and self-supporting manual labor. The point to remember, Mac said, was that in many of its earliest manifestations, monasticism seemed to spring up spontaneously. Those people who lived as monks in each instance structured their life-style as though they were inventing it. In many instances, there was no common culture or history through which the specifics of their monastic regimen might have been transmitted.

The Essenes, a community of religious Jewish men, lived in Palestine from about the second century B.C. to the end of the first century A.D. They believed in immortality, despised luxury and pleasure, supported themselves by daily manual labor, opposed private ownership of property, and were celibate. Their routine included corporate and private prayer and periods of meditation, as well as study of the Torah.

Guatama Buddha lived virtually the same ascetic existence in India more than four hundred years before the Essenes. The Greek philosopher Pythagoras organized his followers in an ascetic way of life in the south of Italy, in 530 B.C. Though he was a "pagan," the validity of his spiritual practices led some early Christian fathers to regard him as a contemplative master.

In Mac's opinion, those manifestations proved the existence of a universal monk, an archetype that exists in every human being. Everyone experiences the call to solitude. Sometimes, Mac said, God calls softly, as on those occasions that we might simply feel a casual craving for time alone. "Why do you suppose those moments of solitude offer us such relief?" Mac asked. "Because they give us a chance to simply be ourselves, to enjoy what and where we were, to savor just being. Alone with God, we feel no need to perform, to do. The pressure is off. That good, refreshing feeling is nothing less than an experience of God's accepting love. It is the healing power of an eternal passion that is consummated in the reunion of creature and Creator. God is delighted by our act of will in which we love and place ourselves in his presence."

"That divine delight is the lover who draws each of us back and forth between twin poles, the loving opportunities of solitude and solidarity. Sometimes God recharges our batteries one-on-one, in solitude. Other times, he kindles our longing for him in the rest of creation and we wind up falling in love, or elbow-to-elbow with our fellow humans, awash in the joy of a celebration with friends or family. He pulls us to him in either circumstance, for however long he believes is necessary.

"Alone with him in solitude, we see and learn what we uniquely are, and how that is all we ever need be. Nothing more. We grow secure in the understanding love that self-knowledge represents. God nourishes us and strengthens us in solitary union with him. He affirms our value, our unique identity. Then he sends us out as apostles of his love, simultaneously exposing us to the kaleidoscopic beauty of creation. Strengthened, affirmed, secure and unthreatened, we can move beyond the limits of our self-concern and begin to see and appreciate God as he exists in everything and everyone. Solitude takes away the cataracts and we get a glimpse of the world as God sees it. As was written in the first chapter of Genesis, 'God looked at everything he had made and he found it good.' Because he loves us so, he lets us share in his vision."

That's what contemplation was all about, Mac had said. However, he qualified that conclusion: it was the ideal. Reality was a lifelong tension brought about as we moved or were pulled first toward one pole, then toward the other. God and the devil both had an interest in our choice and both bid for our decision. Obviously, a great deal depended on whose voice we chose to listen to.

"History shows us monks at all the points between the poles of solitude and solidarity," Mac said. "Whose voice did they hear in a particular circumstance?" he asked. "When was it time to go deeper into solitude, further away from distraction? When do we owe it to ourselves to retreat and recharge? When is Christ calling to us in the person of someone hungry, perhaps emotionally starved? When was our response ill advised, self-serving exploitation that only perpetuated another human being's addiction to self-destruction, a temptation that would ensnare us in fruitless co-dependency?"

Mac had penciled a note for me in the manuscript margin at this point.

"The problem," it read. "Throw open the monastery gates or build the wall higher. Which? Keep in mind that each person is at a different point on the solitude/solidarity scale at any given time. Depending on their attitude, their ability to be open to others, you can have peace or pandemonium.

"You have a perfect example in the debate that's been raging here. Some of us are convinced we should open this place up and allow visitors more latitude in sharing our life. Others feel just as certain that we should restrict access, thereby insuring more solitude. Who's right? Is compromise the answer? Dom Stephen lets you come in and refuses somebody else with the same work in mind. How does he—or we, since he makes decisions on our behalf—justify that call?

"Those may seem like a lot of thorny questions, but I didn't want you to get too comfortable with all the cushy theory I'm spoon-feeding you. Don't stay up too late reading. Three A.M. choir can put a real load on your eyelids if they don't get enough downtime. See you in church, Sonnyjim. Mac."

IT didn't take too much reading to prove Mac's thesis. People have been living like monks for a long time. Etymologists might debate that statement, since the word *monk* comes from the Greek *monos*, which means "alone." Though there was ample evidence that people had lived as monks, only rarely were they completely alone. In most cases, they lived in community part of the time.

The universal monk is a relative circumstance. As Mac had explained, we get pulled alternately by solitude or solidarity. Each individual drinks as much from either cup as is necessary, or as much as he can swallow. Man is a social animal. Even in solitude, he is not alone. God is there for the believer. Others find a force, a powerful energy to which they can relate and in which they find a nourishing peace. But not always.

Cut man off from society, separate him from sensory input, put a wall around his mind, and he may disappear over the edge of sanity. Even when he chooses solitude, man can only take so much of his God up close. Only the imprudent enter the presence of their God blithely.

"Solitude can be a jungle," Mac once cautioned, when I fantasized about plunging into the monastic life. For this reason, he said, the Trappist novice is closely monitored when he begins his initial experience with solitude. "The first discoveries in solitude are generally not reassuring," Mac explained. "You confront your essential aloneness. You learn that whatever your life may be, it is of your making. Whatever others do to you, good or ill, they do by your leave, and often at your suggestion.

"Alone with your God, you find freedom. You are freed of the need to blame, freed of whatever holds you, impotent, in your past. No longer bound by fear of failure, or the need to be what you believe pleases others, you will discover what it is to be yourself."

As I listened to Mac speaking so poetically—and mysteriously—about solitude, I had the feeling it was a place, a destination where I would find a guidebook that laid out my true self like a beautiful nature trail. I found myself tantalized by the thought that this identity, this power, lay tucked away, well oiled and waiting for me to jump start it by simply remaining silent.

The attraction grew stronger as I realized how often different organizations used periods of solitude to allow an individual an inward journey that led to positive self-discovery. That is precisely the part of the Outward Bound program that individuals remember best, a test whose passage they recall as the hallmark achievement of the experience. The U.S. Navy's SEALS and other elite military groups put their trainees through similar tests. In all cases, trainees are left alone in a wilderness area for several days. While they have been taught basic survival skills, it is obvious that they are expected to draw on inner resources, without which no amount of technique would save them.

Poets have described solitude as the ultimate spa for mental health. In Lowell's opinion, it was the "nurse of full-grown souls . . . as needful to the imagination as society is wholesome for the character." Emerson's perception of it echoed Mac's description of its essential benefit: "It is easy in the world to live after the world's opinion; it is easy in solitude to live after our own; but the great man is he who in the midst of the crowd keeps with perfect sweetness the independence of solitude."

That independence is the monk's goal: to know the person God created. Drawn by God, strengthened by him, the monk journeys to the center of his being. There he finds what only an infinite God could have made: a being free to develop his unique potential. Paradoxically, his portion of that greatness will grow to the degree that he gives it away. As Christ so often said, that individual potential is like salt, yeast, a light—useless unless it is quickened by sharing.

Solitude is hardly a social vacuum. "I was never less alone than when by myself," Edward Gibbon acknowledged, an insight that Samuel Rogers echoed when he wrote that we are "never less alone than when alone." In their study of reflective learning, two social scientists, Boyd and Fales, described this dynamic as they had observed it in adults.

Solitary introspection was "the key to learning from experience," they concluded. Initially, they noted, the individual experienced an inner discomfort as he recognized dissonance in his life. A search for solution followed, which was distinguished by unbiased evaluation of possible remedies. Boyd and Fales's research confirmed what monks have known for centuries. Solitude will challenge any self-deception and ultimately, will require its rejection.

This was why Mac had characterized solitude as a potential jungle, in which an experienced teacher/guide was essential. By extension, it is also the reason why people generally have not, and should not, commit themselves to perpetual solitude. Only those with an extraordinarily positive sense of themselves can handle the hard questions solitude will pose.

"Knowing who you are helps you appreciate *that* you are," Mac explained. "Gender, job, possessions, achievements—those only reveal *what* you are. All God sees and loves is *who*. It's our society that defines you by all the other things, all the goods that can be gone in a minute.

"The most abject beggar can do what God does—love. He can accept you as you are, that you are. That's what you learn in solitude. You understand that your mere existence in a single millisecond of time is enough to merit God's love. Think of it. Each of us was in the mind of God from the first moment of creation and to the degree that we love, we will be there for all eternity."

Solitude permits an individual to learn that he can love, that loving that makes him godlike by inviting him to appreciate everything in his life. To tolerate is to allow a difference to exist. To appreciate is to fuel growth of what is unique by affirmation. It is similar to acquiring a taste for olives, one monk explained. That acquisition broadened the person's palate.

The initial beneficiary of solitude is the person himself, as he recognizes his own uniqueness. He is called to personal integrity in which he honors that difference, just as he would affirm it in others. He must be true to his values, which are validated by God's love of all that is good. The only acceptable standard of behavior for him will be his answer to the question, How does what I do in each day of my life dispense God's love, help the people I meet to grow?

Few people have demonstrated that approach to life more pointedly than those who decided to follow Christ in the first three centuries after his death. But unlike monks before and after them, they had no need to withdraw from their society. Once they made Christ's teaching their personal credo, they became outcasts, nonpersons whose lives were forfeited from the first moment of their conversion. The world rejected them.

So far as their society was concerned, Christians were fools who failed to appreciate their lives, forswearing all pleasures and satisfactions. They fasted from food, abstained from sex, gave away all their goods, and focused their lives on what non-Christians saw as fantasy. As far as the unbeliever was concerned, life went no further than the grave. Finite existence validated the unbelievers' philosophy of life.

If this life is all there is, the natural instinct is to drink of it as deeply as possible. Unending self-indulgence becomes a necessity. Control over the quality of life masks the terror that its tenure can be abruptly ended. Power over the lives of others becomes a narcotic. Ironically, man in his struggle to acquire power does what God has never done. He tries to coerce the free will of other men. He grows at their expense, dragooning affirmation of his preference.

The first Christians rejected the impotence of that charade. They discovered real power and the immortality it conferred. They had been its object and it had changed their lives. The power of their God was love. The God who gave them life did so selflessly. Not only that, but he shared that power. He gave his creatures the power to love, to create, as well as a free will by which they could decline his invitation.

The first Christians had no use for those privileges society refused them. In point of fact, their rejection by society freed them from its cares, pressures, and anxieties. They put their lives at God's disposal. Imminent death made the world irrelevant and transparent. Freed from the constraints of ambition, pretense, and sycophancy, they could be themselves.

Since tomorrow might never come, they lived fully in the present. Temporizing represented an impossible risk. Thoughtlessness or ingratitude might never gain the grace of second-chance redemption. Acquisitiveness and possessions were equally meaningless. They invested themselves in loving as they knew Christ, their model, had done. When Saint Paul stressed the importance of earning one's daily bread, they accepted his message in its fullest meaning.

They recognized the freedom he offered in insisting that they work and thereby avoid burdening anyone with their needs, even as he himself had forgone the subsidization his work might have permitted. It was clear that their own growth as persons in God evolved from their ability to care for themselves responsibly, rather than behave as children and take from others. Besides yielding this growth, work enabled them to acquire the means of caring for the real needs of those whose circumstances made them truly dependent. Free of neurotic dependency, they worked, acquiring the self-respect that is, at its heart, God's own affirmation of the ability to add and to give.

The legitimization of Christianity changed everything. When Constantine, the last of the Roman emperors, issued the Edict of Milan in A.D. 313, he disenfranchised martyrdom as the ultimate test of faith. Not only was it relatively easy to become a Christian, it was politic. D.H. Lawrence describes a "creeping worldliness" that began to co-opt Christ's followers.

In an effort to regain the vigor that persecution once supplied, Christians began retreating from the society they then believed was jeopardizing their salvation. They searched for ways in which they could disinfect their lives and secure their souls from the ways of their world. They searched for a way of life that would help them capitalize on rather than capitulate to the endless days they faced.

The search for a martyr's life-style took the form of gradual withdrawal from the towns and villages that predominated in the Middle East during the fourth and fifth centuries. The Christian might first retreat from the flow of society by confining himself to a room within his family's house. Later, he would take up his station in a hut on the outskirts of his native village, perhaps alongside an older, more experienced hermit. Farther and farther he would remove himself. Ultimately, he would be quite alone, living in a hut, more often in one of the caves that were part of the hilly terrain that bordered the Nile Delta.

The hermits of the desert are reported to have numbered in the thousands. In fact, their ranks were large enough to constitute a problem for civil authorities left to deal with the impact and influence of this movement on the orderly conduct of society, for these authorities not only had to contend with the vacuum the hermits left in their wake, but the disruption caused by the even larger number of citizens who went to them for guidance and advice.

They became the new confessors of the Christian faith as they successfully assumed the mantle once worn by martyrs in the minds of devout Christians. They extended the ladder of asceticism to new heights in disciplining their bodies. Perhaps most importantly, they demonstrated the quintessential importance of the individual, especially as each must discover his or her unique identity within the ongoing context of a life that they now realize will be their prayer.

They restricted food and sleep, sometimes forgoing both for days. They made a priority of Saint Paul's dictum on work, spending their waking hours in their cells, weaving native materials into baskets and mats. All the while, they would pray, reciting the psalms from memory, pausing to ponder passages that might catch their mind's eye.

Their rigorous asceticism seems excessive and has often prompted critics to discount it as self-destructive masochism. They reason that the desert hermits' contempt for the human condition led to hatred for the body to which the hermits believed their souls were chained. Peter Brown offers an entirely contrary explanation in his book, *The Body and Society.* Far from hating their physical existence, the hermits regarded it as temporarily flawed as a result of Adam's Fall. Prior to that, the human body was "a finely tuned engine. In ideal conditions, it was thought capable of running on its own heat . . . capable of idling indefinitely."

Brown agrees with those scholars who conclude that the desert hermits focused their asceticism on man's skewed will. They believed its susceptibility to the allure of false goods had "crammed the body with unnecessary food, thereby generating in it the dire surplus of energy that showed itself in physical appetite, in anger, and in the sexual urge." The desert hermits "imposed severe restraints on their bodies because they were convinced that they could sweep the body into a desperate venture." They intended to restore it to the harmony and balance it had enjoyed before Adam's Original Sin.

The writings of the hermits refer to those of them who did achieve this state by long and faithful observance of their ascetic regimen. (Note: The benefits of an eremitic life never accrued from a crash program. Those who "made it" did so after long lives of unremitting self-discipline.) Saint Anthony, the most widely known of these hermits, went into nearly absolute solitude in his early twenties. When he emerged thirty years later, his contemporaries were "amazed to see that his body had maintained its former condition, neither fat for lack of exercise, nor emaciated from fasting and combat with demons, but just as it was when they had known him previous to his withdrawal."

I found many Trappists in total agreement with the desert hermit's conception of fasting and other ascetic practices. I raised the subject with Dom Stephen since, as abbot, he must personally approve any ascetic exercise, such as fasting, that an individual monk wishes to practice. It turned out he fashioned his yardstick from simple pragmatism.

"God doesn't want us to hurt our bodies, or deliberately make our lives miserable," he said. It was one of the reasons why he tended to be cautious and conservative in the matter of asceticism. Common sense ratified the desert hermit's regimen. So far as Dom Stephen was concerned, it was simply a matter of living healthfully and treating the gift of life with the respect it deserved.

That reasoning underwrote his own approach to fasting. He made it a habit to forgo something at every meal. It might be one of the vegetables, or the dessert, or perhaps milk he normally added to his coffee. He regularly abstained from all food for twenty-four hours after breakfast each Saturday. He found it had no adverse effect on his physical energy, but it did slow intellectual activity. That suited him perfectly, since he reserved Sundays for periods of solitary prayer interspersed with some form of exercise, such as jogging or hiking.

"I find it's easier to meditate when the mind is slowed a step or two," he said. "Alternating meditation with physical exercise transforms my Sundays into a therapeutic interlude that recharges me for the week ahead. Forgoing something at every meal allows me to control my appetite instead of it controlling me. It does you good to leave the table just the slightest bit hungry."

Modern science had ratified the wisdom of the desert hermit's way of life, Dom Stephen said. He cited the growing number of people in our society who had begun to meditate after it was touted as a means of reducing stress-related coronary problems. He had just received from a friend a newspaper report on findings about the link between restricted caloric intake and longevity.

He reached into his desk drawer and took out the clipping, chuckling with evident self-satisfaction as he quoted a metaphor the writer of the story had used. "Impressed with the extraordinary gains laboratory animals had shown when their gross food consumption was severely reduced," Dom Stephen read aloud, "scientists had started studying whether humans might live to the age of Methuselah if only they ate like a monk."

Those humans who have become Trappist monks are vegetarians who eat just enough fish, eggs, and dairy products to avoid protein deficiency. Research studies have found that diet to be perfectly balanced and evidently beneficial. When tested, the monks as a group had lower than normal cholesterol levels, body weights, and blood pressure readings for their ages. Trappists have regularly confounded outsiders who mistake them as considerably younger than their actual chronological age. The monks, on average, live longer lives than non-monks and remain physically active well into their seventies and eighties.

Regardless of how beneficial the ascetic practices of Trappists and their desert forebears might be, Dom Stephen said there was a principle to them all that was often overlooked. Monastic history was filled with examples of what the abbot labeled "copycat spirituality," the result of shallow thinking that completely ignored divine intention.

"God never uses a cookie cutter to create," he said. "Different people pray differently." A particular prayer form might be good for one and not as effective for another. Dom Stephen believed it was his job to be sensitive and open to the differences and thereby help each monk capitalize on the opportunities a monastery provided for human growth. Each life was a different prayer, a unique way of loving. Anyone who studied the lives of the desert hermits would recognize how that fact was precisely what made their life-style so "red hot new."

Aside from a biography of Saint Anthony, the most telling insight into the mind of the desert hermit can be found in the short anecdotal accounts that have been published in the collected form. A wry humor abounds, but even more abundant is the simple wisdom the hermits gleaned from their lives and shared with each other, as they did everything else. Most notably, their monasticism is distinguished by pluralism.

"That's what made it work so well," said Dom Stephen. "They gave the Holy Spirit all the room he needs to do his job." There was one anecdote that illustrated his point, he added. It concerned a hermit who went to his abbot one day and told him he felt it was misguided for the monks to busy themselves working when they could be devoting themselves exclusively to prayer. They worked for "bread that perisheth," he said. Then he should do as he believed best, his abbot replied, and allowed him to stay in his cell reading while his brother monks continued working. Hours later, the prayerful monk grew hungry, poked his head from his hut, and asked the abbot why he had not been called for dinner.

Because his brothers took him at his word and presumed his prayers provided all the nourishment he needed, his abbot answered. In Dom Stephen's opinion, the hermit's apology indicates he got the point.

The hermits operated from a basic respect for each other that was God-affirming, Dom Stephen explained. "If a hermit felt called to sit on a pillar like Simon the Stylite, that's what he did. A large number of them had no rule, no vows, nothing except their response to a call as they perceived it, not as someone interpreted it.

"I'm convinced monasticism has always gotten in trouble when it tried to organize individuals as though they were robots. Every life is unique. God orientation makes it a prayer. A certain percentage of that prayer, that God-oriented life, should be made with others. And a certain portion of it must express the distinct, solitary personhood that God meant it to be. It doesn't take a genius to see that logic, but it takes a gift to make it grow. Thank God for all the spiritual fathers and mothers who knew enough to recognize they don't know it all and were grateful to God for allowing them to be present to him in those they served."

5

Lord Knows,
It Ain't Easy

S<small>WEET</small> L<small>ORD</small>, don't turn away from me, Mac prayed as he massaged his hands one with the other, trying to loosen the grip of arthritis. Age gave the lie to the gospel of fitness, he thought. People were kidding themselves when they worked out, convinced they could stave off aging. It was like restoring an old car. The metal was fatigued. Its life was running out. You could bang out the dents, fill in the holes, and cover it with new paint. A masquerade. Underneath the shiny paint, death had already been seeded. Any attempt to burden the car with normal service was liable to overstress the tired metal and the car would break down.

On good days, Mac could belie his age. The woodpile outside his cabin proved that. It was the work of a man with springtime in his muscles. But Mac knew fall lay in ambush behind the next moment, likely the next morning. On too many of them, he had awakened stiff, his back nearly in spasm, his hands fixed by arthritis into what he sometimes feared would be permanent claws.

He was between a rock and a hard place. Aspirin would help. But his stomach could only take a mild dose before it kicked back. And while the infirmarian had offered to get him buffered aspirin, Mac's arthritis had gone beyond the point where medication's renewing grace could help. Run the old car too hard and it very well could break down, therapy notwithstanding. Today would have been tough on a Mercedes, Mac thought as he recalled his agenda, and *I feel like a worn-out Model T.*

The monastery's regular cook had himself been laid up with a hernia operation, and the prior had asked Mac to fill in. Filling in had begun at a quarter past two, when Mac awoke, dressed, and walked through the damp, chill morning air to the monastery, where he prepared the community's coffee. There was enough time left after the chore to pour himself a steel tankard of the hot liquid, but not many more minutes than it took to toss down a few mouthfuls. Not nearly as much as Mac needed to let his stiff fingers absorb the heat that seeped so comfortingly through the walls of the cup. *Sweet Jesus,* he prayed, *stay with me.*

The abbey church was cold. Winter was a bullying enemy in Kentucky. It would sally against constitutions softened by summer, subject them to its numbing threats and then withdraw, allowing the false hope of Indian summer to return like a mirage. The abbey's elephantine heating system was little help in the battle. It could be prodded to life, but only with great effort. Once alive, it could not be switched off except at great expense. So the plumber, Brother Martin, and the abbot waited until they were both certain that winter had taken up permanent residence. Only then would the monastery and the church get the heat that would relieve its masonry from a tomblike existence.

The cold knifed into Mac's sandaled feet as he stood in his choir stall, waiting for vigils, the first choir office of the day, to begin. Holding his hands against the bare skin of his forearms inside the sleeves of his cowl gave them only a brief period of protection from the chill. More than an hour and a quarter passed before Mac got the chance to hold them beneath the hot water of a lavatory tap and try to get them limber enough for his next chore. When he returned to the darkened church for a half hour's meditation, he felt the first tremors in his back, a minor version of the pain in his hands. *Sweet Lord, not just yet,* he prayed. *Help me hold up my end. No pun intended, Lord,* he added quickly.

He had been appointed to the abbey's Liturgy Committee and his responsibilities included preparing the readings for the various choir hours. These had to be typed into the monastery's word processors so that they could be duplicated and handed to the readers. The hot water had loosened his fingers and made Mac fantasize about a hot tub into which he could invest his back for the same dividend.

He finished the computer work in time for lauds at a quarter to six. Community mass followed, after which Mac returned to the kitchen, where he worked several hours preparing dinner—for eighty. Since he was also serving at that meal, he had to wait until the community finished eating before he could eat his own meal. If he ate hurriedly, taking no more than ten minutes, he would have enough time for a thirty-minute nap before he was due at the barn. He was stiff when his alarm woke him and he muttered aloud as he grabbed the back of the rocker to pull himself upright. Sweet Lord, just a little longer, he asked. Sweet Lord, I'm not asking for me. Just so I do what I have to.

He met Brother Gabriel, one of the novices, at the barn. Together they were supposed to clean the stalls of accrued manure and see that it was spread on the garden plot. Gabriel was in the predictably stormy passage of novitiate. Loneliness had gripped his entire being as intensely as arthritis owned Mac's bones. It was the Cistercian way, the deceptively simple movement into solitude, free from distractions, but also devoid of all the props and comforts those distractions normally provided. Only the self remained.

As though by plan, all the monks who had so warmly and enthusiastically received Gabriel when he first came to Gethsemani now seemed caught up in their own affairs. Even God seemed to have forgotten him. The sweet satisfactions that had once filled all his prayer had gradually diminished until now prayer was cold, dry, empty. The life was an unending routine that promised an eternity of time in which to repeat every unsatisfying moment.

Mac had been there and as abbot had helped other monks make the passage. Everyone who stayed came to that point—more than once. That first time was the toughest because it was unexpected. They had answered God's call and after an initial period that was spiritually sweeter than they ever imagined, they found themselves in a vacuum. The spiritual consolation ended and they found themselves alone and empty-handed. There were no friends, no long weekends, no change of scenery, nothing.

It was disorienting and frightening, primarily because it looked as though it might go on forever. It was like talking into a void. No matter how hard they tried, nothing changed. In fact, trying harder just intensified the nothingness, since it drained them of energy.

They had to learn to accept. They had to realize that God was there but in a way different from any they had ever experienced. They had to say yes to the God who was present to them in circumstances different from any they had faced in their lives.

The crisis was always evident to the older monks. They kept their distance, knowing that any attempt to comfort their younger brother deprived him of the chance he needed to learn to live with himself, to develop the resources he would need to live with God on God's terms. He had to realize that God accepted him as he was. There was nothing he needed to do (or could do) that would alter that acceptance, except to say yes to it all.

Until he did, the monk's turmoil made him fidgety, nervous. Lack of sleep showed in dark rings under his eyes, and his face grew haggard as appetite disappeared and he ate haphazardly. His old superficial identity was falling away as he used games and ploys to try to change his circumstances and found none of them worked. God was not playing games, nor were any of the monks around him disposed to do so.

He had to *be*. That's all, just be. Yesterday didn't matter. Tomorrow might never come. He had to learn to live in the present. Mac remembered working in the kitchen when he was a novice. He'd driven himself frantic, poring over cookbooks, measuring exotic spices, doing all the things he was sure would transform the monks' menu. Consequently, about the same number of people liked and disliked the food as had before.

He was not in a contest, the novice master had told him when he complained of the lack of appreciation for his efforts. Mac had offered the monks a deal. Some accepted it and complimented him and some declined and continued complaining. "Let it go," the novice master said. "You're not here to impress God and you couldn't do that anyhow."

Mac tried to remember that as he and Brother Gabriel began to shovel the manure into the back of a pickup truck. He measured his motion, rationing his effort. He could not do what he once did very easily. Sweet Lord, he said to himself, but how much less can I do before I'm not doing anything at all? He got his answer when he tried to load ever so much more manure on the next shovelful. The sharp pain in his back brought him erect and he stood there bending backward gingerly in a futile effort to ease the gathering spasm.

Brother Gabriel stopped and leaned on his shovel, lost in thought that filled his face with pain of a different sort. Mac glanced at the young brother, waiting for him to look up, mustering the courage to ask his help in getting to the infirmary.

"I never imagined it would hurt so bad," Gabriel said, his head still bent as he stabbed his shovel into the steaming manure. Mac waited silently for a moment. Then as he began to hobble away, leaning heavily on the shovel, replied, "Me neither. Sweet merciful Savior, me neither."

6

All in the Family

ALTHOUGH ABBOTS have the advantage of being elected to their job, a simple majority is all it takes. Some would never accept close election, wanting no part of a house in which their supporters were barely neutralized by their detractors. They can be elected for an indefinite term or for six years. After more than fifteen years, Dom Stephen was still riding the crest of an original, overwhelmingly favorable vote that put him in office indefinitely.

It was only after I had visited several other abbeys that I realized there was a real basis for the affection and respect he commanded. In every other monastery, the reaction to the abbot was mixed. The best situations were those in which some monks strongly disagreed with the abbot on one or several issues but bowed to the majority after they had expressed their views. Dom Stephen was one of those who had that. The worst were those in which the abbot faced opposition on every issue and the monks who opposed him often spoke about it being time for a change.

Dom Stephen's monks did not want to lose him. They worried that he worked too hard, especially with his added responsibilities as father immediate to Gethsemani's daughter houses. He visited each one every other year and could not have been more generous with his time. He never discouraged any monk from one of the daughter houses who sought his continuing counsel.

When it came time for Gethsemani's own visitation by Dom Jacques of Notre Dame de Melleray, the mother house, several of the abbey's monks urged the French abbot to insist that Dom Stephen cut down on his work load. "I'm all for him taking a leave of absence," said one. "We'll only lose him for six months that way. If he keeps going full tilt, the pressure has to damage him and we'll lose him for good."

The concern was a tangible element at Gethsemani and made it the loving place that everyone who had ever been there remembered. "It's the spirits of all those monks who prayed their lives here," said Mac. "It's in the walls and the fields. You find it in the old abbeys, like our mother house, Melleray. When an abbey makes it past the first one hundred years, you know God has a special place for it in his heart."

I theorized that whatever Gethsemani had could be traced in its lineage. When I mentioned that to Dom Stephen, he immediately offered to write the following letter of introduction. "In the near future," he wrote to Dom Jacques,

"You will receive a letter from Frank Bianco, who is writing a book about our order. As part of his research, he has spent time living with our community here at Gethsemani, as I believe he would like to do at Notre Dame de Melleray.

"We have found him to be well informed and particularly sensitive to our life, and have therefore felt confident in sharing it and our experiences with him.

"I hope your circumstances will allow you to grant his request to visit with you and your brothers. Please consider any hospitality shown to him as though it were extended to one of us."

The carbon he sent me had a line written across the top: "Good luck. I just hope they don't lock you out because of me. You're in our prayers."

THE French farmland stretches to the horizon, a purposeful patchwork quilt. In the unrelenting flatness, the fifteen-foot-high white cross stretching skyward at the crossroads commands attention. Contrast emphasizes its presence. Its man-made form is unmoved by breezes that ripple the rows of ripe, golden grain in the field to the left. It remains rigid when wind rustles the leaves of gnarled apple trees platooned on the right.

But the cross is too familiar to the farmers who live and work in this part of the world, as disregarded a detail as Notre Dame de Melleray, the twelfth-century monastery a quarter of a mile distant. Astride roaring tractors, beret-topped Bretons shuttle past both. With scythes over their shoulders, they stride by. They no more see those sights than they hear their sounds.

Yet monastery bells beckon insistently every quarter hour from four o'clock in the morning, when they first summon the monks to prayer, until eight o'clock in the evening, when they signal bedtime. Though their sound is audible for miles around, it earns no more notice than the squadrons of sparrows that wheel noisily overhead most of the day.

Neither disrespect nor irreverence prompts such behavior. The monks are estimable neighbors, sensitive to the needs of the people who live and work around them. Local folk rent the abbey's fields at eminently fair prices and participate in its stately liturgy. The monks own as much place in their affection as they did in the hearts of their forefathers who prized "les moines qui ne parle jamais" (the monks who never speak). No, the behavior simply reflects the tendency to take for granted the constants of daily existence, however grand or unusual they may be.

The cross, though, is more unusual than grand. It is set in a masonry base roughly fashioned to resemble the prow of a boat, artistry undistinguished except for the plain metal plaque pinned to the left side. "On this spot," it reads in French, "on October 26, 1848, the monks of Melleray stood and embraced forty-four of their brothers who left for America. There, in Kentucky, they founded that nation's first Trappist monastery that still stands today."

Notre Dame de Melleray swarmed with monks in the middle of the nineteenth century. More than two hundred crammed its ancient buildings, many of which had been built before Columbus set foot on America's soil. But today, attics into which monks spilled in search of sleeping space are the realm of spiders that spin elaborate lace on the partitions. Only spiders toil amid the crates of unused tins in the cannery and the empty floors of the three-story granary. Webs mark their monopoly in the winery where casks the size of small cottages stand in empty rows like a deserted village.

I was prowling Melleray's dusty attic early one morning, looking for a vantage point that might give me a good photograph of the surrounding countryside in the early morning light. The attic was a large space, with perhaps fifteen feet between its uppermost roof beam and the flooring. Small dormers had been let into the slanted slate roof about every ten feet.

The attic seemed to be used only for storage. There were boxes filled with new sandals of the type I had seen the monks wearing. Others contained hymnals and work clothing. Spare metal bedframes leaned against the wall in one section.

A wall separated the main attic from the portion over one of the wings that had been added in a later period of the abbey's history. The door leading to this section was ajar and I walked through. To the left was a small room, approximately the size of a monk's cell. The door to it was closed. I could see the rays of first light streaming through the dormer windows opposite the room and I walked toward them.

There were thick ropes hanging from the overhead cross beams in my path. If one of them hadn't been knotted, I would not have given them more than passing notice. The knots were evenly spaced in the fashion of a gymnasium climbing rope. Another of the ropes was slung through a pulley fastened to the beam. One end hung loose, about waist height. The other was fastened to a five-gallon metal pail half-filled with sand. I studied a pipe that ran from one beam to another. Someone had done enough chin-ups to leave two shoulder-width handprints on it.

It was enough to make me remember when I was a skinny high-school freshman and had responded to the inspiration of a Charles Atlas magazine ad by making barbells from pipe and cement-filled cans. As I considered the incongruity of such a fantasy being fulfilled in that ancient attic, I became aware of someone standing behind me.

I turned and saw a slightly built monk, perhaps in his late thirties, standing there, a proud smile on his face. Though I had been at the monastery four days, I had not seen him in choir or at meals. My curiosity must have shown, because the monk held his hand out, palm downward, and rubbed the thumb and other fingers as though sprinkling something. He next touched his forehead with the tips of his index and middle fingers.

They were Trappist signs, the medium by which all members of the order had communicated when a rule of silence had been common, continual practice (not a "vow" as is commonly believed). Since few abbeys still observed the practice, I had only glanced through a book of Cistercian sign language. I shrugged, at a loss for the monk's meaning.

He smiled again, leaned a bit forward, tapped his chest and whispered, "Air-meet." *Ermite*; French for *hermit*. Now he turned and pointed toward the small room, the door of which was slightly open. "Air-mee-taj," he whispered again. *Ermitage*. That was his *hermitage*.

I pointed to the ropes and then to him. Oui? I mouthed. He nodded. Then he pulled the loose habit sleeve up on his right arm and flexed it in a universally recognizable configuration. Charles Atlas would have been proud of the baseball-size bicep that popped into view. I made a thumbs-up sign to indicate how impressed I was. He cocked his head quizzically. I made an OK sign, whispered, "magnifique," and made the thumbs-up sign again. His smile betrayed slight embarrassment, his nod, understanding.

He pointed to my camera, then to the window, his face now posing the question. I nodded. Follow me, he motioned. He walked to one of the dormers, pointed again and nodded vigorously. If the abbey were ever put up for sale, the view from that window would sell the place.

It was his personal view and with a wave of his arm, he invited me to capitalize on it. "Merci," I whispered. "Ne rien, mon frere"—(Don't mention it, my brother), he replied and, with another wave, walked back to his hermitage. Just before closing the door, he turned toward me, made a thumbs-up sign, and grinned. Then he pulled the door shut and I was left alone once more in the dusty silence.

NOTRE Dame de Melleray was a never-ending sensory feast. I relished the simple breakfast I ate after vigils ended at about half past four. Coffee lovers' heaven. Two ten-gallon pots waited on the cast-iron kitchen stove, one filled with hot milk, the other with strong French coffee. A ladleful of each, laced with a tablespoon of sugar, filled my saucepan-size aluminum cup. At the end of one refectory table, on a cutting board, cheese and crisp French baguettes were put out.

Sitting in the silent, dimly lit refectory, munching on a fist-sized chunk of bread, sipping that sweetened, scalding coffee, would have been special by itself. But to do so with the sounds of vigils still echoing in my mind was special in a way the word can't convey. Melleray's monks were few—sometimes only twelve for an office—yet their chant had heart. I can not imagine anything that simple sounding so beautiful; it was especially so when they would break into harmony in mellifluous French. The sound would resonate in that vaulted stone nave as though the church were a musical instrument and the monks had been the craftsmen who had made it and were now the only ones who knew best how it should be played.

Often, as I sang with them in that eleventh-century church, I would wonder how it must have sounded when the community was at its high point, with two hundred monks. When Melleray was built in 1142, not even the most optimistic abbot could imagine such a surfeit of spiritual riches. I venture that the most imaginative of them could not have envisioned the abbey as it is today.

Twelve of the abbey's monks work five hours daily, six days a week, in a state-of-the-art, fully computerized typesetting operation. The abbey, which had depended upon agriculture for income since its foundation, changed to the typesetting operation in 1986. A sixteenth-century barn was renovated and air-conditioned to provide a suitable environment for the work. There the monks, whose predecessors once composed with quill pens and parchment, use modern technology for the same purpose.

Melleray's monks shepherd original manuscripts through all those steps of the publication process short of actual printing. Their reliability and relatively low pricing has brought them a surfeit of work from publishers of textbooks and travel guides. Their labor, like that once done by two hundred, earns all that is needed to keep the abbey solvent.

But in 1848, the monks of Melleray reckoned their flourishing circumstances as a mandate for multiplication. They decided it was time to found another monastery, to consider filling one of the requests for a new foundation that always follow the grace of abundant vocations.

American Catholicism was itself in the throes of expansion. In 1808, Baltimore's Bishop Carroll had responded to the increase of American Catholics with the creation of new dioceses in Boston, New York, and Philadelphia. A sizable migration of Maryland Catholics begun in the late 1780s to the area around Bardstown earned that tiny Kentucky metropolis the distinction of becoming the fourth new episcopacy.

The new bishop, Joseph Flaget, had forwarded a request to the superiors of the Trappist order for consideration if and when a new foundation was planned. There were no Trappist monasteries in America, and so the bishop scored an ecclesiastical coup when the monks agreed to settle in his infant diocese.

While the new foundation would increase the bishop's place in the pages of history, it would further obliterate any trace of the founders. Each of those monks of Melleray, men who worked at disappearing, had already relinquished family, friends, and even the names by which they had been known when they entered the monastery.

They could receive visitors no more than twice a year. Letters were similarly restricted. Continual silence within the monastery reduced the interpersonal communication by which individual history and identity are perpetuated. Monks could and did work alongside each other for decades without learning a single detail of the lives each might have lived before entering the monastery.

Now the monks would put an ocean between themselves and even that limited existence. They brought with them all they needed to live in complete independence and isolation. Each carried two blankets and a straw mattress. The community baggage included plowshares, parchment hymnals, and bake ovens—everything necessary to fashion and fabricate the circumstances into which monks could retreat from the world without a trace. Once they arrived at their destination, they would draw their silent life around them. They would have no need to knock on a neighbor's door to borrow, nor to travel to town to buy.

Even en route, the Trappists lost no time in hiding their existence. An account of the trip, written by their superior, Father Eutropius, describes how the monks constructed a temporary monastery in the steerage of the *Brunswick*, the eight-hundred-ton sailing ship that took them to America. There, behind a wooden partition, they observed their regular schedule of work, prayer, and study, sustained by fresh loaves of bread and soup from their traveling kitchen.

In the latter days of the voyage, they shared that meager menu, the fruits of their austerity, with fellow passengers. Ironically, these others were also pilgrims, bound for a utopian commune in Texas. Only the monks' generosity prevented the passengers from fighting when the last of their scanty provisions petered out.

It was raining when the monks, riding in open wagons, arrived at the site of their new home in America. Many were fairly young. Father Eutropius, who later became the group's abbot, mentions that the youngest was only seventeen at the time. Their first years were as difficult as any endured by the nation's pioneers. Arable land had to be cleared, crops planted, and a proper monastery constructed.

But whereas the pioneers would *adapt* when possible to ease their hardships, the monks *endured*. They wore the same woolen habits while they worked beneath Kentucky's brutally hot summer sun, even though they might have sought dispensations which would have allowed them to change. Neighboring religious voiced their concern at this physically overwhelming condition. "At least allow your monks to eat more," they urged Father Eutropius.

There was to be no such compromise. Thirty-eight monks would survive (one died en route; four left the order; Father Eutropius resigned from the abbacy because of ill health and returned to France). They eventually built a monastery with two million bricks "burned" at the site, a steam sawmill, and a flour mill, which they also allowed local farmers to use. Their lives ended as do the lives of all Trappist monks to this day, marked by a simple ritual.

When a Trappist monk dies, his body is carefully washed and clothed in the better of his two habits, its hood up around his head. He is placed in a plain wooden coffin kept for that purpose, and brought by his brothers in procession to the abbey's church. A single lighted candle is placed at the foot of his coffin and for the next twenty-four hours, the community will sit by his head two by two, in shifts, praying the psalter.

After a funeral mass, the dead monk is carried to the cemetery, located on the north side of the abbey church. There, at the grave site, the body is removed from the coffin and slowly lowered into the arms of the infirmarian, who waits in the open grave. He settles his dead brother. He cushions the head with a pillow, crosses the arms over the chest, and closes the hood of the white cowl over the face before climbing out.

The abbot is the first to take a shovelful of earth and drop it into the grave. Then, any of the monk's blood relatives who are present do likewise. Two of the least senior monks complete the task. Finally, a white cross made of iron or wood is placed at the east end of the grave. It bears nothing more that the monk's religious name and the date of his death.

When Gethsemani's founders died, they were buried in a plot of ground that eventually wound up outside the growing monastery proper. The remains were subsequently moved to the new cemetery alongside the abbey church. There, for the sake of practicality, they were reinterred in a common grave marked by a large metal cross that stands at one end of the graveyard. In a way, that unplanned pragmatism may have aligned the monks more closely with the purpose they had chosen for their lives, as well as with the brothers they left behind in France.

A wrought iron fence rings the graveyard at Melleray, alongside the abbey church. But it contains noticeably fewer graves than its American daughter house. Despite the monastery's considerable history, I counted only one hundred crosses. A plaque in the infirmary seemed closer to the mark, even though it only listed 250 monks who had died.

"Where are your missing monks?" I asked the abbot, Dom Jacques.

He cocked his head, uncertain that he understood. Though I had thought he spoke English very well, I found he did not. Faced with a visitation to Gethsemani, his first, he was anxious to improve his grasp of

English. Toward this end, he frequently referred to a pocket-size French/ English dictionary, intent on building his vocabulary.

I explained the discrepancy I had found between the memorial list and the cemetery.

"Oh, yes," he said, smiling. "Yes, I see. Missing. No, all our monks are there. No one is missing." It would not do, he explained, to have the cemetery growing endlessly. If a monk died, they would open up the oldest grave, gather any bones that remained, put them in a cardboard box, and position the box beneath the head of the monk who was to be buried.

"So the dead monk becomes his brother's pillow," I suggested.

"Pillow?" Dom Jacques asked, reaching for his dictionary. "Pillow, pillow," he repeated, holding the unknown word in mind as he searched for its French translation. "Ah, yes. *Oreiller*—pillow. That's right," he said, grinning at the growth of his vocabulary. "Pillow. When I die, my brother who never knew me, will be my . . . ," he glanced back at the dictionary, "pillow, and eventually, we will both be the . . . pillow . . . for a monk neither of us ever knew."

But although monastery archives fixed the resting place of all the monks who had been buried, he added, only the name of the last-buried monk would be listed on the cross that marked their graves. Given the goal of the monk's existence, he said, even that degree of record was superfluous.

"After all, it's only necessary that we be known and remembered by God."

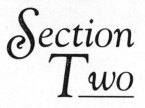

Section Two

THE LORD'S PRAYER

". . . and one of them, a lawyer, put a question to him to try him: "Master, which commandment is greatest?" Jesus said to him, "Thou shalt love the Lord, thy God, with thy whole heart and thy whole soul and thy whole mind. This is the greatest of the commandments and the first. And the second, its like, is this, Thou shalt love thy neighbor as thyself."

MATT. 22: 35–40

7

Love Lessons

NOT A happy camper, Dom Stephen thought as he watched Brother
Gabriel walking toward him in the cloister. Not when smiling requires
such obvious effort. On instinct he reached out, took Gabriel by the arm
and led him out into the preau.

Brother Gabriel shrugged when Dom Stephen asked how things were
going. The black mood could still get pretty oppressive, he said. Coming
to Gethsemani didn't seem to dent it much. If anything, it was sometimes
worse. Whenever he felt as though he were shaking free of it, he found
himself facing a bleak, blank nothingness. "When's God going to give me
a break?" he asked. "When is all this self-analysis going to start paying
off?"

"He already did," Dom Stephen said. "He brought you here. Maybe all
that's needed is that you learn to listen differently. Not better. Differently."

Gabriel looked away in an effort to conceal his impatience. From where
he stood, coming to the monastery had not made life any easier at all.
The abbot was not making any sense. "I'm sorry, Stephen," he said. "But
I've turned my life inside out since this thing first hit me and I don't see
that the problem has gotten any better. I'm getting nowhere fast."

"No, no. Not true," said Dom Stephen, "You're learning. You're finding
out that taking aspirin for a pain ignores the real problem. We all do that.
We fool ourselves. We pretend we've dealt with the problem because we

did something about it. It's really a cover-up. When our attempt to live like Christ blows up in our faces, it takes courage to sift through the debris. Sooner or later, we have to confront ourselves. We have to account for the part we played. That may not suit the scenario or the role we're used to playing."

"I know what part I played. The schmuck. I was naive, just like always. I gave everything I had to a relationship and people on the other end held back. I'm too damn trusting."

"Gave? Held back? Didn't you get your money's worth? Somebody sold you shoddy merchandise? What are we talking about?"

Brother Gabriel was getting annoyed—a totally new feeling. He had felt powerless until then, overwhelmed by rejection. Now he felt cheated and he could also understand the abbot's meaning, even though Stephen was probably being facetious. Right. Stephen was right. He had been duped. The other party had not been open. The phony had welshed on the deal. "Right," he said. "I got screwed."

Dom Stephen glanced at his wristwatch. The council meeting was scheduled to begin in ten minutes. "Sounds like you've discovered a whole new dimension to your problem," he said, looking up. "All I know is the only times I've heard love and business mentioned in the same breath, somebody had been patronizing a prostitute."

The abbot paused. He had been trying to listen, allowing Brother Gabriel's words to trigger his comments. He did not want to influence Gabriel, even though the young novice's turmoil was alarming. He might be on the verge of leaving. The temptation to reassure him was strong. He could mature into a good monk—he was bright, talented, and he was young. God knows how hard-up we are for young blood, Dom Stephen thought. Every year we all get older, the median age gets higher, and the old monks wonder if we're really on our way to becoming dinosaurs, and not just spiritually either.

Dom Stephen knew his position could make intervention in Gabriel's anguish easy and he also knew that would be wrong. Novices had to work this through by themselves, with more than a little help from the Holy Spirit, of course. The abbot would try to stay out of the way. He would act as a consultant to the process, available whenever he was asked, an objective resource.

Brother Gabriel was traveling through a tough stretch of the monastic terrain. Old experience could mislead him. He could wind up going around in circles. God was trying to show him a new way, the road that led to a life in which friendship was not a transaction and prostitutes were not perceived as lovers. Gabriel was confusing bartering with giving. That was not surprising, given the way present-day society operated. I'll be nice to you if you'll be nice to me. It was civility masquerading as love.

Dom Stephen's task was to help Gabriel discover that for himself. It was not something the abbot could accomplish when starting time for the council meeting was minutes away. "Look, I've got to run," he said. "But I'd really like to bat this around with you some more. Can we make time in our schedules sometime soon? What say? Maybe we can go for a walk tomorrow or the day after, when we won't feel pressured by schedules. OK?"

Brother Gabriel nodded. He wanted time to think over the abbot's comments. "Sure thing," he said. "And thanks for taking the time to say hello. I'm sure I'm not the only monk with problems. I really do appreciate the concern."

The smile on Brother Gabriel's face was not as joyous as Dom Stephen might have liked, but it was far more genuine than the one that had led to the exchange. He was glad he had stopped. He smiled, reached out, and squeezed Brother Gabriel's shoulder. "Let's make sure we do that walk before too many days go by," he said.

Brother Gabriel waved in acknowledgment. He wasn't sure he felt better, but the abbot's comments had given him something new to consider. Maybe he had overlooked something in that past relationship. It didn't seem so. He'd been dumped. There was nothing he could have done about it.

Unless there was something about the people he chose, the choices he made. That theory didn't seem to hold up much better. He had never had trouble making friends, or keeping them.

Before joining the monastery, he had been the most easygoing, accessible of people, everyone's best friend. It had been a long time since he wondered about his ability to win acceptance. He was worried about that now. What made him think the monks would not accept him like everyone else? When the time came for them to vote him in, they'd do it. Why not? He could fit in anyplace. Hadn't he always done so?

He could not have been more different from the construction workers with whom he spent two summers during college. He loved music, sailing, romance languages, Eastern religions. Yet he quickly felt, and was treated, as if he had worn a hard hat all his life. Their ways were a new suit of clothes. With a few adjustments, their life fit. He liked how they sounded. Not just their earthy jargon, but their direct, physical philosophy. They thrived on life's tougher portions. They just bit in and chewed.

He consciously adopted their mannerisms and patterns of speech. He soft-pedaled those parts of himself that might distinguish his life from theirs. He listened and nodded, and learned to like his coffee hot, black, and heavy on the sugar.

Brother Micah, the other novice, reminded him of the construction workers. He even looked and walked like Marty, the foreman who had taken Gabriel under his wing during his first weeks on the job. Micah was big like Marty. He had the self-assurance that size bestows. Gabriel was willing to bet that little, if anything, had ever threatened either man.

Circumstance drew Gabriel and Micah together. Both were novices and custom restricted them from social contact with other community members, since the instinct to share is highly developed among older monks. While it might be born of generosity and concern, it might also be an attempt by a wavering ego to shore itself up—self-affirmation by cloning.

Aspiring monks might understandably be susceptible to the pressure represented by such advice. Gabriel's anxiety was not unusual at his stage in the monastic life. Acceptance is the unprofessed monk's priority. He knows that his fate will one day be put to a vote by permanent, professed members of the monastic community. History has shown that monks develop as individuals to the degree that they first get to know and accept themselves. That happens best if they are left alone.

The abbot and novice master are the sole sources of information and counsel for Gethsemani novices. Both men scrupulously avoid imposing their personalities or preferences. They believe God has called the monk-candidate to the monastery so he can hear that unique voice that was his from the moment of his creation. To adapt any other's voice, another's way, would be an imitation instead of the original that God intended.

Gethsemani novices go to choir and meals with the community. But they live in a separate part of the monastery, study there, and generally work together. These were the circumstances that allowed Gabriel to get to know Micah. He liked working with him. It was like having another pair of hands that made the most distasteful jobs easier. Mistakes became anonymous, regarded only as the reason for a good laugh. If Micah had a black moment, he never took it out on those around him.

Yet, Gabriel politely demurred when he felt that Micah was attempting to move their relationship up a notch. After he refused his brother novice's suggestion that they share one of the hikes both were known to take each week, Micah pressed him for an explanation. They got along well together. Why the turnoff? he asked.

"Please don't be offended," Gabriel said. "I'm not very friendly to myself right now and I really don't have a lot to share. Under any other circumstances, I'd be the one doing the inviting. But I can't just now. I need to regain control of my life. I've got to sort things out and I just know I've got to do it alone. I'm even having a tough time talking to the abbot about it. Be a friend and give me some room. OK?"

If the incident left Micah confused, describing it to Dom Stephen brought him no closer to understanding. "What does a guy do," he asked, "when a brother who obviously likes you as a friend, and looks like he can use a shoulder to cry on, turns you off when you offer him yours?"

Dom Stephen thought a moment before speaking. There was something to be studied in someone who became unsettled because somebody else declined his advice. "He makes certain he wasn't selling something," he answered, "rather than giving it away."

AT the council meeting later that same day, Dom Stephen told the members that I was returning for another visit. I had spoken with him by phone and he had agreed to my spending additional time within the community. There had not been any violent reactions from my last visit, he said, and he did not anticipate any if I were to come again.

Father Bede thought differently. Things only *seemed* to go smoothly during my last visit, he said, because of the forbearance of many monks. Like him, they had taken pains to avoid contact with the writer. They consoled themselves with the thought that there would be no other intrusions. He considered the situation highly irregular and monks who believed so might not keep their own counsel a second time. It was unfair to force them into a corner where they had to compromise principle or appear inhospitable.

Brother Robert, the novice master, did not believe the matter would ever become the problem Bede envisioned. Even if monks chose to express their disapproval, it might be beneficial to the work the writer was trying to accomplish. He reminded everyone of their own related experience. There was a very distinct honeymoon period for all newcomers to the monastery. New monks were a somewhat refreshing presence, especially to monks who still needed the stimulation outsiders provided. But that novelty wore off almost at the same time as the older monks began to reveal an all-too-real, flawed humanity.

Disenchantment resulted on the new monk's part and very often precipitated the first crisis in the monastic vocation. Up close, his new brothers were not the saints they had appeared to be when seen from the tribune, the visitors' gallery. The process could take as long as four or five months but, as everyone on the council now agreed, given the pressure generated by the writer's probing questions, several weeks might be more than enough.

As far as adverse reaction was concerned, he added, perhaps it was important that the writer get a taste of the rougher side of community life. He had said he wanted to experience the life firsthand, and friction was part of it.

"He's not a kid," Robert said. "If somebody gives him a hard time, I think he'll be up to handling it—and maybe even learning a little about himself at the same time."

If there was nothing else in the way of new business, the abbot said, the council could adjourn. He looked around the room as most members began gathering their papers. All looked up and several even frowned when they heard Father Bede ask for the floor. If he started, the advantage gained in efficiently dealing with a long agenda would be lost. Guaranteed, he would filibuster for another three quarters of an hour at the least.

As Father Bede stood up and began speaking, Brother Saul realized he himself was only watching. He had stopped listening the moment his brother monk had begun. Now, as Saul tuned out even further, his vision glazed, like an unfocused camera. People have a hard time changing, he thought to himself. It's what makes them predictable. It's what made Father Bede boring. Maybe that's why new monks were so interesting. Robert was right. You didn't know them. They were a new ingredient in the monastic mix. But, man, you prayed to God that they stayed that way. You prayed that he would give them the courage and strength to be as different as he made them to be. A lot of times, it even happened, although you'd never know it looking, or worse yet, listening, to Bede.

Brother Saul blinked and told himself to be charitable. That same inner voice urged him to give God some credit. Maybe Father Bede might surprise you, it said, if you give him the chance. He looked over at Bede and his ears caught the droning phrases. Not in this lifetime, he thought, as he heard Bede saying something about the new guest house. He steeled himself not to look away again.

Father Bede felt obliged to point out that the contractor was not clearing off the building site quickly enough as he put the finishing touches on the guest house. Such neglect exemplified the man's disorganization, in Bede's opinion. A real professional would never let leftover materials accumulate.

"It's unsafe," he said. "Uneconomic . . ." He glanced at Dom Stephen, who was watching him impassively, as were all the others at the meeting, except Saul. When Saul sensed Bede's eyes canvassing the members to make certain of their attention, he shifted his own gaze toward the window, through which he appeared to be staring absentmindedly. Bede continued.

"It's . . . un . . . worthy of the work."

Saul looked back. He was not quick enough to restrain the smile that betrayed his surprise. The fainter, sheepish smile on Bede's face revealed the price he was paying for his admission. He just wanted to go on record, he continued. "The building was . . . well . . . passably well done." He was not about to deny ". . . credit where credit was due." The man had done better than Bede had expected. His voice slowed. "It just showed . . ." Everyone was watching. Bede began to sit down before he was finished, eager to escape the spotlight his words had focused on him. "I just thought it demonstrated," he said hurriedly, and then hesitated, his body midway between standing and sitting. "I just thought . . . it's a good example of the power of grace."

"A real conversion," said the abbot, standing and thereby signaling the end of the meeting. As the others began moving their chairs away from the table, he added, breaking into a smile, "Maybe he's got a mason named Joshua working for him."

The remark made Bede's face stiffen and may have hastened everyone's departure, including Saul, who bit his lip to keep from smiling. *Joshua* was the title of a book that had just been read in the refectory during dinner. The mystery that had cloaked its selection had blossomed into full-blown (and predictably heated) debate as the book was read.

Joshua was the name of the novel's hero. The plot revealed him to be Christ, reappearing as a humble stonecutter in the twentieth century in a small American town. This time, however, his disappointment was not with the Pharisees and Sadducees but with Christian religions and leaders whose failure to love was evident in their treatment of him and each other. They moved to silence his exposure of their hypocrisy, while Jewish believers welcomed and supported him for his affirmation of the love and acceptance he found in their midst.

A friend of Father Daniel had sent the book to him as a gift. He had loaned it to Saul, who was one of the three members of the abbey's Media

Committee. After reading it, Saul had agreed that the book contained a message that some of their brothers should hear. But he doubted whether he could win the votes of his fellow committee members, who took pains to avoid any choice that might be branded as propaganda.

Daniel suggested they give the book to Dom Stephen. They waited patiently until he returned it with a small note of thanks that included the comment, "A little on the light side, but a provocative thesis." Saul made a point of seeing him the next day, ostensibly to discuss abbey business. He waited until he was on his way out of the abbot's office before he "casually" mentioned the book.

Did Dom Stephen have any objection to *Joshua* as a selection for reading in the refectory? The abbot thought the question was unusual, since he always deferred to the Media Committee's judgment. The thought made him hesitate and search Saul's face before replying. He regarded the man he had appointed as the abbey's business manager to be one of its more effective politicians—someone who never asked idle questions. "No," he said. "I wouldn't vote it down if I were on the committee."

Blue Highways was the next book scheduled for reading. But when Brother Ignatius went to the refectory ten minutes before dinnertime, the book had vanished. It should have been right atop the lectern where he had left it that morning. He was frantic when Saul appeared. Less than five minutes remained until the community would be filing in for their meal. Saul handed him *Joshua*. The abbot had read it, he said, when Ignatius looked at him suspiciously. "Called it thought-provoking," Saul added. "He assured me he would have voted to approve its selection if he was on the committee when the book was considered."

Only three days of reading passed before Father Bede was in the abbot's office. Would he be good enough to verify his alleged approval? Bede asked. Did he know that the book offended a great many of the brethren? Not the least of their objections was its consistently negative characterization of Catholic clergy, up to and including a fictitious pope. They were scandalized by the disrespect shown the hierarchy, Father Bede said. He believed that the book gratuitously vilified people who were appropriately obedient to God's vicar on earth. It never credited them for their great courage in standing up to a self-indulgent, weak-willed laity intent on a hedonistic life-style.

Dom Stephen consciously restrained himself as he continued to listen. Here we go with pervasive hedonism, he thought. Father Bede confirmed his fears as he swept into the all-too-familiar lecture. It all boiled down to a matter of rules and law, Bede said. "They were made to be obeyed," he said. He could not understand how liberals managed to delude themselves. All they ever did was relax existing rules, lower standards, and excuse human frailty. Christ did not run from his cross. Why couldn't people—monks especially—learn to shoulder theirs?

No question about it, Dom Stephen thought, as he had many times before, the sons of insecure fathers make good drill sergeants. They learn the rules but they scourge themselves more viciously than they do anyone over whom they exercise authority. Father Bede was as tough on himself as he was on everybody else. He drove people crazy with criticism. But his own work was flawless. He would go without sleep and use all his spare time, if necessary, to ensure that outcome. Sadly though, it was never enough.

Only Dom Stephen knew that. That part of the abbot's job was a never-ending revelation. In the course of his abbacy, he learned the pain that every monk carried deep within him. It was the other side of the story that few people ever knew existed. He knew where and how a personality had been abused and neglected. It was always the same: somewhere along the way, God's love had been short-circuited. Someone had failed a commitment, betrayed a trust, exploited innocence.

Bede was one of the most deeply wounded. He exemplified those people whose capacity to love had been crippled by their earliest experiences. When they tried to love in their turn, their misguided attempts had only resulted in more hurt for themselves and those to whom they reached out. It was a miracle if their ability to love was any more than tentative thereafter. If, as in Bede's case, misfortune shadowed their early attempts, love became forever suspect. Half-digested theology often twisted the experience in their memory. They blamed themselves for the failure and any hurt it had generated. That fed guilt, which they carried into the monastery, where it flourished and became their raison d'être.

In Bede's mind, God's compassion was a remedial program necessitated by sins. Penance was an obsession that distorted his view of life and made proscription a reflex. More than once, Dom Stephen had tried to make Bede see how he confined God to a single dimension, made him a judge who only sentenced wrongdoers, a warden who supervised their detention. Christ's love rarely got through to Bede. "God forgave you, Bede," the abbot said. "Stop making your guilt an identity. We're human. We're all capable of the worst imaginable evil, but also of the most heroic good. Get with the program, Bede. Make the good—and God—a part of your life."

Cautiously, Bede would try, as did everyone from time to time. Dom Stephen called it "the God thing," the relentless loving by one's peers. "If they can accept me," each monk reasoned, "then I can live here without pretense."

As the monk grappled with old history and tried to free himself from its confinement, the community's compassion was critical. Its expression was often heroic. They had to support and love someone who may have consistently made such effort difficult. They had to love enough to sustain God's presence for everyone concerned and provide a new and badly needed learning experience for their brother. Father Bede was one of those who did not make the loving easy.

As Bede stood in front of Dom Stephen's desk, holding his arms rigidly by his sides, the abbot remembered the monk who asked him, "How do you doctor a wounded porcupine?" He wished he could laugh. He wished he could make Bede see the humor in the *Joshua* mischief. He knew that would never work. Someone had stretched a rule. That would never be funny for Bede.

It was the abbot's responsibility to see that all views on a particular issue were represented in a fair hearing, Bede said. *Joshua* was one-sided. Would the abbot assure equal time to him and the constituency he represented, perhaps with a book that embodied their views?

Dom Stephen resisted the temptation to ask if Bede felt as democratic about all dissenters (for instance, those who wanted to ordain women). Or how about providing a forum for the nuns who had recently come out in favor of contraception for the poor? He knew the answer. Bede allowed the same voice to his opponents as did a judge who asked convicted prisoners if they had anything to say before he passed sentence.

The choice of any book was the Media Committee's purview, Dom Stephen finally replied. It was unfortunate if their authority had been circumvented, and he would personally look into the matter to see how that had been done. If he found the community's well-being and peace had been jeopardized, he would of course take such steps as were necessary to prevent a reoccurrence.

"Lighten up," the abbot had said as Bede turned to leave. "It's only a book. Have a little faith in your brothers' ability to put things in proper perspective."

"I don't believe," Bede said, "that one should compromise in matters of principle. History shows all too well that where the dust of errors is allowed to gather, mountainous heresy results."

"I wonder," said the abbot, "how much of that dust ever amounted to more than a convenient molehill."

The following week, the monastery's Conventual Chapter, comprised of all solemnly professed monks, convened. They were scheduled to vote after discussing the proposition, Will Gethsemani Abbey allow women to use the new guest house? Father Bede was the principal speaker against the proposal. In unemotional tones, he recapitulated every argument he had made in daily memoranda posted on the community bulletin board during the previous month. Anyone sincerely interested in finding the truth could do as he had done, he said. They need search no further than the monastery's library. Policies, traditions—the accumulated wisdom and unmistakable intent of established authority—were there in black and white. Women were not permitted inside a cloistered male community. Although the guest house had been built outside the monastic quadrangle per se, it was still an integral part of the abbey. A questionable precedent was being set.

Many monks wondered about Brother Leo's contribution to this opposition. During the previous months, the inroads of Parkinson's disease had confined him to a wheelchair. He seemed to have changed. Although he still was given to outbursts of temper and his conservatism was thought to be as immutable as before, he no longer was as implacably cold to certain monks as he had once been. Dependency had deprived him of that luxury. You looked at people differently when they had to help you get to the john or take care of those times when you didn't make it.

He nevertheless proceeded to surprise everyone with the vehemence of his presentation. It was vintage Leo. At one point, he gestured so vigorously, a few monks fully expected him to leap from his chair and begin stalking about as he once used to do. He dramatically marshaled his voice as he wound up his speech. He was not one for words, he said slowly, but Gethsemani was at a crossroads. Declining vocations already threatened its existence. Many of the older, seasoned monks had confided in him. He paused, allowing that revelation to gather its force. He bowed before the wisdom of these monks. He could not betray their number or names, but their identity alone would overwhelm any opposing point of view. He paused again. There were some who were convinced they heard him say next, "This may come as a surprise to some of you." If he didn't, his arch delivery said it for him.

"I came here to get away from women," he said. "Much as I love this place, it could be the Holy Spirit is calling me elsewhere. Might be he's calling a lot of us. Maybe he's saying the same things to us that he told the desert fathers. The faith is in danger. It's our turn to stand up and be counted."

No one knew how many of the twenty monks who voted against the proposal did so at the Spirit's urging. Fifty yes votes insured that women would be allowed to use the retreat house one week out of every month. That policy would be tentative, subject to review in a year's time. Brother Saul thought the abbot had handled the issue in his usually adroit fashion. He had seen to it that there was no consideration of opening the retreat house to couples, the natural next step. Berryville Abbey was already doing this, and their new guest house was booked solid year-round.

The vote had put the matter of the guest house to rest. The abbey had been relatively peaceful until the *Joshua* incident. Dom Stephen thought the abbey had been too quiet. He had braced for an explosion when Bede surprised him and everyone else with his endorsement of the guest house builder. He was overdue for an outburst, and that kind of concession was out of character.

Thoughts about the guest house reminded the abbot to call Sister Joan, the chaplain at Bellarmine College in Louisville. She had spoken to him about bringing a group of coeds from the college's Newman Club for the inaugural retreat. He might as well get the ball rolling.

The new policy was probably going to go over beautifully. Sometimes it seemed as though Bede and Leo operated on automatic pilot when they protested. There was an unreasoning tyrant somewhere in their heads. God help us if that despot ever gets complete control of them, the abbot thought. And Lord, while you're at it, Dom Stephen added, glancing heavenward, make sure those two don't gang up on the writer. He's got a tough enough job as it is, trying to figure us out.

8

The Finger of God

AT ANY other time, the idea of making a retreat at a Trappist monastery would have been an interesting exercise in feminism. However, for eighteen-year-old Betty Ryan, the notice from the Newman Club on her college dormitory's bulletin board was a message for which she had been waiting. She believed she could change things. All you had to do was believe. You had to have faith. She was convinced there was something she could do, something she had to do, something that would help her father.

It had all begun under circumstances that make the word, "simply," a euphemism for deadly. Dick Ryan noticed his shirts were getting too tight around the neck. He had not gained weight. Then why? He asked that question of his company's doctor when he went for his annual checkup a few weeks later. A biopsy provided the answer. At age forty-five, after years spent in splendid health, Dick was in danger of dying. He had lymphoma—cancer.

Don't panic, the doctor told him. They faced a tough battle, one that some people had lost, but time was on their side. They had caught the disease in its early stages and that increased the odds of successful treatment. It had added decades of life for some people. Dick had every reason to believe he would be among them.

While the doctor's optimism eased the blow, it still fell hard on Dick. Two years before, he had set out on his own after years of working for others as a construction carpenter. The quality of his work had quickly been publicized by word of mouth. Success coincided with need. When bills came due for his daughter Betty's college education, the money was there.

As far as due bills were concerned, the cancer went to the head of the line. Treatment for the disease was expensive in terms of both money and time. Dick learned he would probably not be able to work during the initial treatment period. Although his business could continue with a reduction of effort on his part, profit would be proportionately cut by the need to hire labor to replace him.

Betty wanted to take a leave of absence from college when she learned the news. It was more important that she continue her studies, Dick assured her. That wasn't fair, she complained. She was old enough to help carry the burden rather than add to it like a helpless infant.

Dick had hugged her and then with one arm still around her shoulders, thanked her for being so characteristically caring. "They say love's the best medicine," he said, "and you and your mother can fill that prescription better than anyone I know. I'll be able to concentrate on beating this thing, if I know you're doing what you have to do. OK?"

Betty glanced up at her father as he squeezed her shoulder. He had already begun chemotherapy and wore a baseball cap to cover the resulting loss of hair. She had tried not to stare. The sight of him without his black curls unsettled her. As she listened to him say she would always be his little girl, one of the two women in his life, she lost her composure and began to cry.

"Daddy, I'm so scared," she sobbed. "I don't want to lose you."

Dick Ryan put both arms around his daughter and somehow managed to avoid breaking down himself. He was as frightened as she. They had to be brave, he finally said. He was not giving up and he didn't expect her to either. God was still on their side. Nothing like this ever happened without some good coming of it. He had believed that all his life and he was not going to change now.

"You pray for me, kitten," he said, as he wiped the tears from her face. "Pray that God shows us what we need to see. Let's stay as close to him as we can so we won't miss anything he has to tell us. OK?"

OK, Betty said to herself as she stared at the bulletin board notice. The women from her college's Newman Club would be one of the first groups permitted to make a week-long retreat at Gethsemani. Count me in, she told Sister Joan later that day. Christ had found strength and answers at Gethsemani. There was no question in Betty's mind that she would find hers there as well.

9

Peace to All Who Enter

"JUDGMENT DAY," Brother Saul muttered aloud as he shook his head groggily. "This is what Judgment Day will feel like for everybody who's going to hell." The alarm clock had roused him from a dead sleep and he stretched several times, struggling to break free from it.

Sleep had been fitful, as though he had a fever. His pillow was wet and he could feel perspiration running on his shoulders and neck. He had moved his bed in front of the open window, but the night breeze had been warm—a mirage that only reminded him of the unrelenting heat.

He finally pulled himself up, stumbled to the sink in the corner of the room, and began splashing cold water on his face. On impulse, he put his head under the tap. That helped. As he toweled his short-cropped white hair dry, he glanced at the clock. Ten of three—early enough to grab coffee before vigils began at 3:15.

Standing, he raised his arms and slipped the full-length white habit over his head. He could feel himself begin to sweat anew by the time he added the black hooded scapular and cinched it in place with a wide leather belt. God bless sandals, he thought, as he slipped his bare feet into a pair of well-worn Birkenstocks. Was it true, he wondered, that hell was really an endless summer in Kentucky?

He walked to the window and looked down into the preau. In the darkness, he could barely distinguish the fountain in its center, from which water flowed regardless of time or season. What little sleep he had managed had been coaxed by its relaxing sound.

Saul's room was on the third and uppermost floor of the monastery. His "cell" was almost exactly the same as those in Melleray Abbey, Gethsemani's mother house. Whatever personal statement a Trappist on either side of the Atlantic might wish to make, most of it would be on such canvas as a twelve-by-fifteen-foot room provides.

The door was centered in one wall with a single window directly opposite in another. Normally, Saul arranged his single bed headfirst against the wall in between these. A digital alarm clock and a copy of the psalter in French, open facedown, covered the top of a small five-board wooden bench, alongside the bed. The sink, with a shelf and mirror above it, was wedged into the corner that flanked the bed.

A small desk and a wooden clothes closet occupied each of the room's other two corners. One side of the closet was shelved, the other open for hanging garments. The wooden desk was embellished only with a bookrack stretched above and across its back. Books were crammed in the rack. Others were stacked on the desk's edge, hemming a spiral notebook. It was open, a ballpoint pen lying across the last words Saul had written before going to bed. He walked to the desk and paused to read them.

"Why can't I just put Father Bede out of my mind? There's seventy other monks in this place and somehow he manages to get under my skin every day. We've been together in this place for forty years and I still haven't had one really friendly conversation with him.

"We communicate. Right. All you have to do to get a word out of Bede is work at something, anything, he thinks comes under his authority. Then he's overflowing with words, everyone of them barbed. Even his "hello" has an edge. Makes me feel like I'm coming into grammar school two minutes late and there's the assistant principal, Mr. Preeby, waiting by the door.

"That little scheme Dan and I worked with *Joshua* has him steamed. I'll bet he's been hammering the abbot about it. He'll get around to squaring the account with us somehow. Nobody ever gets one up on that guy, especially if he can find a rule to justify his reprisal.

"I keep hoping he's going to change, but I think he's passed the point where he might have mellowed. If anything, he's getting worse. He's more inflexible now in his sixties than he was forty years ago in novitiate. I really think he needs help. Whatever he's been chewing on all these years is poisoning him.

"He's so damn critical. I've never heard him say a good word about anything. It's not like he slips and says something hurtful that he doesn't mean. I think he means whatever he says. I know he does. I'll bet he feels it's all a matter of fraternal correction, like we still have the chapter of faults. If we're all so bad, if everything is so unsatisfactory, why the hell has he stayed? Why have they let him stay?

"Talk about somebody in need of healing or acceptance. I wonder what his story is. I guess Stephen knows. Maybe he's trying as hard as he can, but it's not in a way I can see. Wouldn't it be funny if he's over in his room right now, writing in a journal like this, about how tough I am to live with?

"Maybe he's laying in bed right now, asking God, 'Why the hell did you make that creep Saul for?' Maybe he and I are each other's cross. The happy ending will be if somehow we don't let the problem become bigger than us. Somehow, I hope to God that our faith will keep us clinging by our fingernails, and in spite of whatever hell we put each other through, we won't quit. The joke will be that we'll die and they'll bury us side by side in that graveyard.

"Maybe all that matters is that we love God enough to say, 'I love others for your sake.' Not just friends, or people with swell attributes and virtues. They're easy. I'm attracted to them. But it's that pain in my ass, Bede, that I've got to keep trying to love. You love him, God, I know that. You made the jerk. You're crazy about him. And you know what? Sometimes I think you got terrible taste."

Saul shook his head and looked up. Bede—or actually, his impression of Bede—owned a chunk of his energy and he disliked that admission. Saul looked around his room. This would probably drive Bede nuts if he ever saw it, he thought. Running shoes and work boots lay on the floor in front of the open closet. A pair of sweatpants and a sweatshirt hung from the arms of the chair where he had tossed them after his run the previous afternoon. His light cotton bathrobe hung from one of the closet's two doors.

He was sure Bede's room was letter-perfect neat. So what, he thought. He probably suffers from constipation. If you live life, you don't worry about leaving the cover off the box while you enjoy what's inside. Anyway, it made no sense to stuff yesterday's soiled, sweaty clothes into the unaired closet interior. You waited till they were dry—and indisputably dirty. That was time enough to return them to the monastery's common laundry. It was the same reason why you didn't put away shoes you wore every day.

"The hell," Saul said aloud. "I don't have to justify anything. This is my space. If there's books laying around, maybe this is a parole for them. Bede would put them back in those shelves so fast, you'd think they were convicts looking for a chance to hop the prison wall."

Actually, the clutter did crowd the room and make it seem smaller. It also betrayed an ego under siege. Saul had only recently begun to acknowledge that possibility. Mess it might be, but it was his mess. It was his. As he walked to the door, the scene reminded him that egocentricity was the toughest of weeds, regenerating often by runners. He resolved to do something about it. It was pretty bad when you became possessive about a pigsty. He would straighten everything in the very near future. Soon, he thought. Sometime soon, he said to himself, as he purged the indictment from his conscience by flicking off the light, plunging the room into neatness.

Quietly, he made his way down the two flights of stairs to the first-floor refectory. The refectory was still dark, but as he walked toward the lighted kitchen at one end, he could see Brother Boniface shuffling about. The pilot light on both coffee urns glowed red and he blessed the old brother's diligence. In his opinion, anyone who got up earlier than everybody else and saw to it that coffee was hot and waiting was at least halfway to paradise.

Gethsemani's refectory kitchen, like those in most Trappist monasteries, is a serving pantry where the monks can pick up the adjuncts for their meals. It is off-limits at other times of the day. Eating between meals is frowned upon.

Food prepared for dinner, the principal meal which is eaten at midday, is brought by servers directly to the monks sitting at the refectory tables. However, they assemble the components of breakfast and supper themselves and eat those meals privately. They can do so whenever they choose, during the hours set aside for that purpose.

Saul appreciated having a cup of coffee before vigils, an indulgence many abbeys permitted. He found that the hot liquid loosened his vocal chords. Generally, he returned to the refectory after the office, for breakfast. Two pieces of toast with margarine seemed sufficient. He had been eating the homemade granola, but found that choice had added up to extra poundage, something he had been intent on avoiding.

He walked to the table where clean dishes had been stacked for use and took one of the quart-size stainless steel mugs from the wire crate on the table's bottom shelf. These were the beverage containers the monks could use as individual serving pitchers. Saul preferred this mug as his principal drinking cup, since it could hold all the coffee he invariably drank with his meals.

He stepped to the coffee urn and filled one of the mugs approximately halfway, easily a pint. As he did so, he passed Brother Boniface, who caught his eye and winked a recommendation, nodding toward two large trays of corn bread that the cooks had baked the night before.

At eighty-five, Boniface was the abbey's oldest monk. His path to Gethsemani had been circuitous. He was fifteen when he lied about his age and volunteered for the army during World War I. While in France, he had befriended a French Trappist monk who had been drafted into that nation's army. The monk-soldier so impressed Boniface that he chose to remain in France after his discharge and journeyed to his friend's abbey, Bellefontaine.

Traumatized by combat, the young American found peace and meaning in monastic life. He remained at the abbey for six months, at which time he asked to enter the order. The abbot, however, urged Boniface to seek admission to an American monastery, believing that a familiar culture would improve his chances for a successful vocation.

Boniface entered Our Lady of the Valley Abbey, then located in Rhode Island, a daughter house of Bellefontaine. He could—and would, for any interested party—recall the circumstances that led to his inclusion among the group of monks who were sent to found a daughter house in Argentina. Most considered their selection a benediction. In Boniface's case, however, it amounted to banishment.

Although his seniority had made him a popular favorite at the abbey, he never lost a certain contentiousness. Ultimately, it was the trait that led to a confrontation with the abbot, Dom Edmund. As guest-house cook, a privileged post, Boniface had more contact than usual with guests. But he was not about to exploit those relationships in the interest of fund-raising, as he said Dom Edmund once suggested.

Contact with the outside must have confused his loyalties, Dom Edmund told him one day when the two chanced to meet by the abbot's office. Should he consider taking away the guest house assignment? he asked. A monk passing by clearly heard the overly loud reply. "If I understand your meaning, Reverend Father," Boniface said, "then you should absolutely take my job away. And if you need any suggestion as to what you might do with it after that, I'd be delighted to offer one."

It was not long thereafter that Boniface's name was added to the list of monks bound for South America. When the option to return was offered to the American monks some years later, Boniface accepted, but transferred to Gethsemani instead of returning to Spencer.

Saul's own combat service in France during World War II had given him common ground with the old monk. Saul was an esteemed comrade in arms, a fact that enhanced Boniface's dealings with him as cellarer.

For his part, Saul found the older monk's forthright personality refreshing. After all, some people were deaf to all but the most direct of brotherly counsels. And Boniface never hesitated to express his opinion. Dom Stephen had been one of the most recent beneficiaries of his observations.

"That new guest, the writer, has the makings of a monk," Boniface had told the abbot less than a day after I had arrived. "Always smiling, works hard, and never misses choir, which is more than you can say for some who call themselves monks. You're not going to let him slip through your fingers, now, are you?"

When Dom Stephen told him that such designs might needs be altered by the fact of my marriage, he blithely replied, "Well, maybe his wife might be considering the convent. Which of us, after all, is up to knowing the infinite mind of the Almighty? I'd think on it, Reverend Father. I'd surely do that, if I were you."

Saul felt that the old monk's sense of humor was the least of his virtues. At his age, he could have been taking it easy, if he wanted. Instead, he took a regular turn at work, kept his mind active with prodigious reading (which led to some interesting pronouncements on the community bulletin board), and never missed choir.

As an assistant refectorian, it was Brother Boniface's responsibility to prepare the coffee every morning, refill the water pitchers and various seasoning dispensers at each table, and clean up after meals. Saul believed that Boniface knew how to live the life, and his example edified far more monks than it sometimes scandalized, his ad hoc—and ad hominem—commentary notwithstanding.

He stopped Saul, who was walking outside, and, grinning mischievously, traced a sign of the cross over his coffee. The world was still and quiet, under a canopy of glistening stars. Saul sipped the hot coffee and felt its warmth chasing the cobwebs in his mind. No matter how tired he might feel, he never regretted getting up when most of the civilized world was turning over for the other half of its night's sleep.

The hours before dawn had a note of happy anticipation about them. Something new was about to happen. Something new and fresh. Saul believed his monastic vocation was born during the nights he spent on the open deck of the troopship that ferried him to Europe. Even then, as foreboding as the journey might have seemed, Saul could find beauty and peace in the night sky. If one lived to see another dawn, one found a clean slate waiting. Most times, what got written depended entirely on how one dealt with the day.

There, on the gently rolling deck, Saul got the same sense of God that he found when his father had taken him camping as a little boy. The night had a pristine purity, especially when seasoned by campfire. Nature seemed eager to share with those who could make the necessary sacrifices camping required. Sitting quietly with his father, he would simply soak up all the good feeling and free association made him wonder about the God who fashioned things that were at one moment both profound and simple.

Only later did he relate this to monastic practice. The desert hermits customarily rose with the first hours of the new day to chant their first office. Christ had repeatedly given priority to watchfulness. The fragility of life demanded that God's presence never be far from one's thoughts or actions. Let God's call, whenever it might come, not find one sleeping.

The spirit might have been willing, but in Saul's experience, even given his personal predilection for choir and early morning, the flesh was sometimes wanting. He remembered the first time he overslept his alarm. The luxury did not last a quarter hour, until the exact moment when the monastery bells tolled the beginning of vigils. A giant's hand could not have shaken Saul more forcibly than the sound of those bells as it traveled unobstructed across the open courtyard to his room on the top floor.

Saul drained the cup, wondering which of the psalms were scheduled for the morning. After forty years in the monastery, he knew them by heart. Many times, he could go through an entire office, realizing only at the close that his mind had wandered. Often, distraction would betray him and he would find himself singing out of turn.

He agreed with Mac that what really mattered was the faithfulness to the practice. It was important that the monk come to pray with his brothers. The psalms were never to be found wanting. Whether or not you got anything out of them depended on what you brought to them. Come as their friend and they warmed your soul. Come as a stranger and they let you drift in your own alienation. Father Matthew was right: they talked to the human experience.

The monk's choir was undoubtedly the single greatest influence on new vocations. For the largest majority of people, experience of the Trappist life was limited to what they could see and hear during the chanting of the Divine Office, as the practice is known. In most cases, it was all that was needed to change their lives forever. Saul was one such case.

In 1946, he had been a sophomore studying engineering at New York University's Bronx campus. He typified the legion of returning veterans for whom the GI Bill was a ticket to opportunities they might never have experienced. He had lived in a small Ohio town before being drafted at twenty and the experiences of army life and overseas combat had cast him on his own resources. Values, implanted early in his life, had flowered and formed him as an individual. After his discharge, the glitter and glamor of Manhattan were entirely manageable. Just another new place, filled with people whose own newness neither unsettled nor elicited response from Saul. He could live alone. He needed very little, if any, approval from others. Unlike students away from home for the first time, Saul was quite content to stay by himself. He preferred it, in fact. Until he met Kathleen Sullivan.

He first saw her at a mixer that Saint Vincent's Hospital School of Nursing regularly hosted for its student nurses. In a hall full of bright, pretty—and eager—young women, Kathleen was the oasis. The men hovered around her as she held them all in thrall, smiling, drawing out the shyest of them.

It took the better part of the evening for Saul to break into that circle and win a single dance. He was hardly surprised to discover that Kathleen's social calendar was booked solid into the weeks ahead. Unless, she said, Saul wanted to accompany her on Wednesday night when she went to Miraculous Medal novena at a nearby Catholic church.

For several weeks, Saul juggled his tight weekday schedule to squeeze the time for the round-trip subway ride to Saint Vincent's, the novena, and a too-brief time with Kathleen, whose own schedule was closely circumscribed. When she was assigned to a month-long tour of night duty, he was grateful to regain the precious time. However, within two weeks, he found himself willing to give it up to another lady whom he realized had come into his life. The third Wednesday found Saul attending the novena at a church not far from the New York University campus in the Bronx.

He liked the simple prayers and hymns and the ritual they comprised. They nourished a part of him that had first emerged during those long, thoughtful nights on the troop transport, and later during lonely tours of sentry duty. Neither jeopardy nor fear could shake the strength and peace he found in those moments. Now he began to rediscover the riches of a faith he had known but only practiced by rote since early childhood.

On Christmas break, Saul made his way to Gethsemani for a retreat. After the first day, there was no doubt in his mind that he was meant to live as a monk. He would have stayed if the assistant guest master, a young monk with a Texas drawl, Father Thomas Mary MacDonald, had not urged him to go home and think it over. Better to decide in an atmosphere free from the strong influence the abbey invariably exerted, Mac had advised.

Mac did not share those opinions with Dom James, Gethsemani's abbot at the time, whose policy was to accept everyone who knocked at the gate. It was as though someone were giving a prize to the abbot who recruited the most vocations. Gethsemani could do without some of the people Dom James was letting in. Mac had listened to some of them explain their notions of the life. If it were up to him, he would have sent them packing. That might have spared the community the unfortunate scenes that were taking place with disturbing regularity.

They usually occurred when the monks were at meals or in church. As the pressure of solitude bore in, the more neurotic of them would collapse. They would suddenly begin babbling aloud, ranting about visions or some other hallucinations that had taken hold in their troubled minds. It happened so often, the monastery's infirmarians had a procedure in place. They would quietly go to the monk's side, help him to his feet, and lead him away. Before the day was out, the man would be under treatment in the psychiatric ward of a Catholic hospital in Louisville.

Gethsemani was bursting its seams and that didn't help matters. There were over two hundred monks in the abbey, twice the number it had been designed to house. The majority, like Saul, were returning veterans. They hailed from every branch of service, from generals to buck privates. All had experienced the fragility of the human condition. They had seen nations collapse, watched best friends bleed and die.

They were a principal component of a worldwide movement toward prayer and peace, the natural reaction to the overwhelming violence and destructiveness of war. The monastery was never more of a countercultural statement. *Pax Intrantibus* was chiseled in the granite arch over Gethsemani's main gate: "Peace to all who enter." By giving their lives to the monastery, the veterans would pray for peace by making it their life's work.

Saul became part of that phenomenon on a bitterly cold day in late

January 1947. He sold his few belongings, visited his only sister to say goodbye, and used a one-way Greyhound ticket to get to Louisville. He had hitched a ride to the monastery. He never doubted that he would remain there till the day he died, and except when he thought about Bede maybe occupying the adjacent grave, he could not have been happier about the prospect.

10

Who Knocks?

SEEN FROM the visitors' balcony above it, Gethsemani's church before the start of vigils resembles the opening act of a staged play. The curtain rises on the darkened church. Movements prove to be monks arriving soundlessly, noticeable only because their white habits refract the tiniest light in the dark. They glide to their stalls (monks rarely hurry) and disappear in the shadows. Since the seats are folded up, one kneels on the wooden floor, while another may stand, his elbows resting on the top of the stall. Others quietly lower the hinged seats and settle themselves, heads lowered, hands folded in their laps.

Brother Gabriel was one of the first to arrive one morning in July, when I was making my second visit to the abbey. He later told me he liked to "warm up" with private prayers before vigils. He would invariably kneel, tuck his body into the stall, and lean his forehead against the partition. He concentrated on the Jesus prayer, silently repeating it over and over, letting the mantra-like rhythm carry him in its gentle current. "Lord Jesus Christ, Son of God, have mercy on me."

Gabriel hungered for those precious milliseconds when his mind would be swallowed by the silence. Sometimes, not often, he would feel as though he had awakened, that time had somehow gone by and he had been somewhere else. He couldn't remember when he had last been there. Weeks? Months? He had come to realize that wanting it to happen might prevent it from ever happening again. God drew you close on his terms.

That was the most difficult part of the spiritual life to understand. Your job was to open yourself to God, but in ways that seemed to contradict everything you had ever learned. In a sense, all your instincts were wrong. You loved God by letting him love you. God was in the silence. Yet, the moment you began working to create silence, you drove it away.

The finger of God had touched all creation. He still was touching it. His creations were there for you to appreciate. Every time you did, you opened yourself to God and became the channel of his nourishing love. That made sense to Gabriel, except . . . nothing and no one stood still. You listened to the music of your heart and found yourself dancing with life.

People like Brother Micah pulled you from the sidelines. That smile, the ever-constant cheerfulness, made you forget yourself, at least temporarily. They called to that person inside everyone, the one who succeeded, contributed, the friend that everyone valued.

The invitation was familiar to Gabriel. He thought he had gotten it from Linda. There were no unshared feelings, no differences of opinion. She saw life as he did, dreamt some of the same dreams. It all began to happen; they spoke of plans and futures. Then what did I do wrong? Gabriel used to ask himself.

They had been dating steadily for six months when Gabriel mentioned his intention to go away on retreat, alone. He had been doing so since his sophomore year in college. Linda was disappointed. Shouldn't a couple as serious as they had become search for opportunities to deepen their relationship? she asked. Wasn't separation divisive? It seemed to her that the strongest relationship was one never splintered by consuming hobbies or solitary passions that siphoned off precious energy.

By all means, go, she urged, but Gabriel didn't. It was a small sacrifice, given what their relationship had meant. The past tense had been appropriate, Gabriel realized much later. Things were never the same after he missed the retreat. Accounting had become part of the relationship. There were questions of whose turn had come for a contribution and how much each had done. Gabriel could recall suspicion creeping into the equation. Was someone holding back? It was as though a secret addiction had been uncovered and each watched the other for relapse or regression.

The strain made reduced contact tolerable, eventually preferable; there was always a legitimate reason. Special presentations, grant proposals, special courses—things good friends wished for each other. Before long, Linda had to consider a career move to another city. The move seemed to make more sense to both of them than other career opportunities had in the past. Gabriel helped her pack and tried to ease her first weeks of loneliness with phone calls. He even flew out to see her one weekend. Slowly the relationship dwindled until it no longer existed.

His relationship with Linda had been a major event in Gabriel's life, a purposeful attempt on his part to "get married." Marriage was one of the predominant goals he had formed when he left a religious teaching order. Or maybe, he sometimes thought, the order had left him. He originally had intended to be a social worker like his father, but had modified that ambition (he believed) after a recruiter for the teaching order spoke to him during his senior year in college.

He stayed slightly more than two years, never coming close to realizing the adventure the recruiter had promised. He found instead an order that was as rigid in applying outdated teaching methodology as it was in insisting its members conform to a single, "time-tested" spiritual regimen. He said as much to his superior one day, whose suggestion that he reconsider his vocation neither surprised nor disappointed him. He knew he loved teaching and wanted to continue. And if religious life hadn't worked out, perhaps marriage was the answer to his need for community.

He had been teaching music for three years in a Salt Lake City high school when he met Linda. He was ready for a serious relationship, one into which he could blend his interest in music, travel, and his extracurricular work as director of the student band and chorus. When the relationship soured, Gabriel invested even more energy into those interests. There was no one to object to them, or to the weekends he frequently spent at the Trappist abbey in Huntsville, Utah. He would laugh when Father Simeon, the guest master, warned him that unless he changed his ways, he was going to wind up a Trappist someday.

"Careful, Gabriel," he said. "God's a relentless lover."

He would later admit that the monk's words were on his mind when he made plans to use his sabbatical for a six-month trip to Asia. Part of the time would be spent visiting Buddhist monasteries.

The first monastery intrigued him. The second allowed him to stay for two months. There he befriended a twenty-five-year old monk who had committed himself to remaining in the life until he was thirty.

Gabriel quickly learned of the reverence and respect the people of Asia have for their monks. He was impressed with their approach to prayer, especially meditation. For several years, he had been practicing centering prayer, as Huntsville's Father Simeon had taught him. Constant distraction had nearly led him to abandon the practice.

The young Buddhist's ability to concentrate was awesome. He told Gabriel how he had spent a month of eight-hour periods focusing only on his breathing. He referred Gabriel to the works of an Indian Jesuit, Anthony de Mello, who he said had adapted Buddhist technique in a way that was entirely consonant with Roman Catholic theology.

He also helped Gabriel put distraction into perspective. There was a story he had read in which a disciple asked one of the desert hermits for help in reducing distraction. The master suggested that his disciple hold his cloak open so that he might catch the wind. Impossible, the novice replied. It was just as impossible to try to do away with distraction, the master answered.

The two months passed quickly. Too much so, Gabriel thought. He was sad to leave a place in which he had found so much peace, especially since he had come to the monastery untroubled and happy. He found that his exposure to the Utah Trappists and now the Buddhists had gone beyond mere taste for the monastic life. It was now an appetite.

On his return to America, he spoke with Father Simeon about his experience and conclusions. It was time to test them, said the monk. He encouraged Gabriel to go to an abbey where his love of music would have the best chance of developing: Saint Benedict's Abbey, a small community of eighteen monks, located in the Rocky Mountain community of Snowmass, Colorado.

Gabriel wrote to Saint Benedict's abbot and asked if he could test his vocation by staying with the community for six months. The initial reply was no. But three days later, a second letter arrived from Dom Alexander, the abbot. It contained an unqualified yes.

Saint Benedict's, better known as Snowmass, had decided to test a new program. In it, men could come and live within the community for a six-month period. There was to be no presumption from either party for any commitment beyond that time. Gabriel entered, one of eight men. At the end of a year, all but he had left.

Going in, Gabriel, at thirty-three, had presumed that celibacy would prove difficult for him. He enjoyed his relationships with women. Except for the time he had spent in the teaching order, he had never gone without a sexually intimate relationship. He believed that the sacrifice would be offset by the gain of something that he craved even more: solitude, and the intimacy with God that he knew it could foster.

His hopes seemed threatened at first by Father Thomas, a young monk who had been given charge of the new program. Like Gabriel, Thomas had been in a teaching order, where he had been ordained. He had been a

Trappist for nine years. He too was deeply interested in music. In fact, it was love of music that had initially cast them at odds.

Father Thomas was highly introverted, a man much more at peace when by himself. He liked nothing better than to take his flute, hike to the top of one of Snowmass's surrounding mountains, and play a duet with the winds. But in the opinion of Dom Alexander, he was in danger of overbalancing in the direction of solitude. He needed to develop his capacity to be with people, to relate to them.

It was for that reason that Dom Alexander placed Thomas in charge of the new program. It was a trial. The job required him to listen, to counsel, to become involved. Instead, Thomas kept his charges at a distance. He reverted to the role of a doctrinaire teacher, a martinet. He believed it was unprofessional to become involved with one's pupils. Familiarity interfered with the discipline that learning required. Young monks-to-be had a great deal to learn, he told himself. At least he thought so until he met Gabriel.

Music might have brought the two men together sooner. The liturgy nourished both. Thomas sensed the depth of Gabriel's knowledge and, although he never admitted this feeling to himself, he feared it. Gabriel's presence was a challenge that could weaken Thomas's control and his plans for the other novice monks, whom he believed would only respond to a strong hand. They seemed to be encrusted with the slovenly habits of a laity that had been reared on oversimplified melodies and hymns. The sound of music that was potentially beautiful, when sung badly, brutal-ized Thomas's psyche like a salted broadsword. One was supposed to sing what was on the page, stretching when necessary, rather than relaxing with what one's untutored peers found comfortable.

Gabriel had only been at the monastery two months when Thomas used precisely that characterization one day. He was preparing the class for Holy Week. They were having difficulty singing a particular psalm tone that most remembered singing differently in their parishes. One student went so far as to say so and wondered aloud whether Thomas was insisting on an optional, rather than an absolute, rendition of the phrase in question.

He was not only wrong, said Thomas, visibly annoyed, he was out of line. His job was to listen and to do as he was instructed. That was the way of monks and, Thomas added, especially those whose musical educa-tion had been so badly neglected. There was too much to learn to allow for idle debate. Besides, debate was something that took place between equals, which he and his pupils were not.

The student was right and Gabriel knew it. He waited until the class had ended and the others had gone before saying so to Thomas. Annoyance escalated to anger, as Thomas's worst fear took shape in front of him. What made Gabriel think that he, a rank newcomer, could correct a monk who had been placed in a superior position over him? Did he know what obedience meant? If, among other things, his ignorance extended to that basic fact of monastic life, then Thomas would be happy to open his eyes. "There is one way to progress in a monastery," he said. "Keep your ears open and your mouth shut and do as best you can to do as you're told. Right?"

"Wrong," Gabriel countered, his face growing red with emotion. The way of the monastery was the way of Christ. His presence in each and every person required a respect that ruled out blind obedience. Furthermore, one did not teach by embarrassing one's pupils. The surest way to turn a student off was by demanding compliance with something the student knew was wrong. "Finally," said Gabriel, "I am your equal, not only in music, but in the eyes of God who brought us here to be brothers to one another. I will not allow you to treat me otherwise."

The rejoinder stunned Thomas, who had never been questioned. He smiled weakly and turned to walk away. Gabriel called out. One moment, he demanded. The matter was not over, he said, as Thomas turned toward him. Did Thomas understand what he, Gabriel, had just said? And did he, in light of what had been said, have anything to say in reply?

Head down, in a low voice, Thomas apologized. He repeated the apology in front of the class the next day. It was the beginning of a friendship between him and Gabriel that slowly gathered strength. Music was the initial link. They delightedly mined the richer veins that had been buried by the avalanche of changes after Vatican II. The nuggets they drew forth and their own expertise formed a core around which the other monks clustered—precious metal that everyone could own. The abbot happily consented when they asked permission to attend the music festival in nearby Aspen and to take classes that were offered in the institutes.

Though Thomas was in his late forties, he gave high priority to physical fitness and was delighted when he found that Gabriel shared that interest. Both monks enjoyed hiking and they took frequent, day-long excursions to the peaks of the surrounding mountains. During the next winter, when the monastery became perpetually white with snow, they strapped on cross-country skis and spent hours traversing the abbey's extensive acreage.

Trust developed between the two monks. They talked freely about their past, about incidents and people they felt had both sanctified and scarred them. They found it easy to admit to each other difficulties they encountered in the spiritual life. Their discussions brought new insights as they brainstormed about particular problems. For Gabriel, part of each day's happiness was going to choir and looking across to where his friend Thomas was standing.

Thomas buttressed the weakest point in Gabriel's monastic life. Snowmass was too "open" for Gabriel. Guests and visitors seemed ever-present. When the office was over, Dom Alexander encouraged the monks to join him as he went to the church vestibule to meet with guests, to talk with them, and to be available for those who needed advice or counseling. That situation troubled Gabriel. He felt that the monastery had relieved him of the need to "figure people out." He didn't have to say the right thing, or even remain silent when he disapproved of something that was said. He was right on target, Dom Alexander told him, and that philosophy was no less appropriate with the guests. "Just be yourself," Dom Alexander had assured him.

Gabriel found that difficult with the guests. They had certain expectations, which put him on stage. He felt he had to listen politely and offer advice. He had to play the monk. It was intrusive, distracting. He could not ignore their presence right behind the monks in choir, or their participation during mass when everyone stood in a large circle around the altar. It was like praying under a microscope.

Don't worry, Thomas had said. He felt as Gabriel did and frequently argued his opinion in the chapter of professed monks. It's only a phase, he told Gabriel. Someday, the pendulum would swing back. It always did when it was at such an extreme. Keep to yourself, he advised. Exercise your right to privacy and immerse yourself more deeply in the solitude. God has brought us together to be of comfort to each other, he said.

And then he was gone. One morning, Gabriel looked up and Thomas's stall was empty. There was no note on the community bulletin board. No explanation. When Gabriel approached the abbot, seeking information, he learned what he had already suspected had taken place. Although he had been consoling Gabriel, Thomas himself had felt pressured by the abbey's fluid relationships with outsiders. In one of his last talks with the abbot, he admitted he could not tolerate the circumstances any longer. People were pressing in, he said. He felt suffocated and needed time to get away and reconsider his vocation. He would be in touch with the monastery and anticipated writing to those monks whom he felt had a right to know specific details about his decision.

Gabriel waited, but after several weeks, he realized Thomas was not going to send him a note. He also began to see how Thomas and Snowmass were fatally intertwined in his own mind. Everywhere he turned, he saw ghosts of his absent friend. Places, rituals, and routine had become the grist of a common experience. All were now emotionally empty, only reminders of a vanished relationship.

Including Gabriel, there were only two other monks who refused to meet with the guests each day, so he was plunged into an unaccustomed solitude. Thomas's presence had once softened isolation's edges. Gabriel tried to separate his loss from the process of becoming a monk, but found it increasingly impossible. He wanted relief from all the memories that prodded him into mourning the loss of another love. The monastery was not working. He wanted to leave.

Wait, Dom Alexander advised. He cautioned Gabriel not to permit his relationship with a single individual or circumstance to define his total relationship with God. Such confusion often trapped people in grief and anger.

"You don't have to let go as much as recognize that it's gone," the abbot said. "God brought you and Thomas together the way he gave you your talent for music and he inspires you to express yourself in that form. We find it so hard to accept the fact that it's all temporary. But things change. We change. Our growth, the identity God gave each of us, is the product of inexorable change. Whenever we become attached to anything, we try to stand in the way of change. We can't. We're setting ourselves up for a fall.

"Ownership is the self-delusion of frightened, insecure people. God gives us roses, sunsets, youth. He invites us to drink deeply, allow experience to expand our being . . ."

"Isn't that the real trap?" Gabriel interrupted. "Isn't God just setting us up for that fall you mentioned? He points us down a path that leads straight into an ambush."

"No, no," Dom Alexander said. "He shows more faith and trust in us than we show in ourselves. He's telling us, 'Come on, you can do it, let go, there's more.' He wants us to up anchor and explore. We keep insisting the world is flat and we'll fall off the edge if we sail beyond our horizons. We're frightened children who insist that the world we know is all the world there is."

There was just one thing wrong, Gabriel thought. He still hurt. Once again he had reached out, trusted, loved, and all he had to show for it was pain. It served him right. He still had not learned the lesson from his experiences with Linda and the teaching order. He was still making room in his life for others. And when they decided they didn't like the arrangement, they left, and Gabriel had empty space to fill.

"I don't think I belong in this monastery," Gabriel said.

Perhaps not, Dom Alexander said. Why not try a larger abbey before giving up the idea entirely? he suggested. Things might be very different. People often feel there's a great difference between a small and a large abbey, although opinions vary as to what that difference might be. "You might find what you're looking for," Dom Alexander said. "A new place would also be free of painful reminders."

After some thought, Gabriel agreed. With one year of novitiate to his credit, and Dom Alexander's blessing, Gabriel wrote to Gethsemani and asked if he could transfer, with the possibility of making the move permanent. The answer came within a month: yes.

By the time I visited Gethsemani, Brother Gabriel had been there seven months. Five more and he would make his first temporary vows. He was glad he had taken Dom Alexander's advice. Gethsemani provided him with space. He found that in a large community, it was possible to get lost. A monk need only do what he is assigned and be present at the community functions of choir and meals.

Actually, Gabriel's desire to maintain a low profile honored conventional wisdom. Nervous bridegrooms are nothing compared to a monastic community that is being asked to approve a new monk and to allow him to become part of their life. Often a substantial number of the professed monks who are entitled to vote on the matter will suddenly grow wary. They can and have asked for more time, which effectively shelves their prospective brother monk.

A desire to cauterize his personal history had alienated Gabriel from his brother monks. They in turn responded simply to what they perceived as his legitimate desire to be alone. He was taking care of business, they felt, and the novice who does not look for opportunities to relieve the intensity of solitude has the makings of a good monk.

Gabriel later told me he wished he could have been as certain about the purity of his motives. He initially classified my presence in the community as no different from the policy he had opposed at Snowmass Abbey. When I asked him what had happened to change his mind, he said he was not quite sure. He still was not comfortable with the idea of laypeople coming in and living temporarily as monks, but he found out one afternoon that he was very uncomfortable with monks who were deliberately going to try and make such people feel unwelcome.

He had been helping to tend Brother Leo in the infirmary one afternoon when Father Bede stopped for a visit. In obedience to the Rule of Saint Benedict, Gabriel refrained from joining in the conversation and continued doing his chores. Although Leo and Father Bede spoke to each other as though he were not in the room, he knew that at least some of their remarks were for his benefit.

Leo believed the abbot had at the least circumvented the Rule by not consulting with the community's professed monks before allowing a journalist to live among them. That was an intrusion. He heard about the constant picture taking. That had to be distracting. All the interviews were not much better. It never works anyway, Leo had insisted. It was impossible to understand the life unless you lived it. Reporters could only see it from their own narrow perspective. Every time a monastery allowed them to visit, they blew things out of proportion. Most of the time, they talked to the wrong people anyway.

"If I get the chance, I'll set him straight," Leo said. "Maybe if I distract him, he'll lay off the rest of the community. What the hell, it'll give me something to do, where I can be useful to the community, spare them a lot of that endless interviewing, and keep the distortions down to boot.

"Trouble is, the press treats us like we're a bunch of monkeys in a zoo. I'll tell you one thing—that foxy abbot of ours got taken on this thing. He thought he'd put one over. Knew damn well, he did, that this thing would never have gotten past a community vote."

Father Bede had listened attentively to the old monk, reassuring him as soon as he had finished. Others felt the same way, himself included. He was personally sure, however, that Dom Stephen did not mean to be insensitive. Father Bede just hoped the Holy Spirit would find a way to insulate the writer from those monks who never learned to keep their mouths shut. They were the ones who would tell stories just to make themselves look and feel good. He was particularly concerned about the younger monks, all of whom reflected current society's lack of respect for tradition and established convention. They could be a problem. Their naivete also made them easy prey for a crafty reporter.

"Maybe it's just as well that we find out which ones give in to the temptation," Leo said. "It wouldn't hurt to let them know that this is the kind of thing that shows just how much they value being members of this family. People have a way of remembering things like that when they're trying to decide who they're going to welcome as a brother."

Gabriel told me Leo's last remarks came back to him one morning just before vigils began. I had been assigned the stall next to Father Michael, the vocation director. Prospective candidates used it during the week-long visit they made for their first taste of the life.

When someone was using the visitor's stall, the vocation director would usually arrange the various hymnals when he did his own. The task was not overly complex, but it required familiarity with the ordo, the daily schedule. A non-monk might find it confusing. I had heard of unwanted visitors being left to grope through the unfamiliar texts and was happy to see that Father Michael and Brother William, who flanked me, made certain my hymnals were always set.

On this particular morning, neither monk was there and both had obviously presumed someone else would substitute for them. I busied myself, but as the minutes ticked away, I gave up trying to make sense out of the ordo. When the abbot knocked on his stall as a signal to begin, I was resigned to spend forty-five minutes in silence. The community had only finished one verse of the opening hymn when Brother Gabriel left his place two rows behind me and walked to my stall. Quickly and quietly, but hardly unnoticed, he began arranging my hymnals. In a few moments, they were all ready, their place ribbons set so I could easily follow along. Gabriel had not so much as glanced at me during the entire time and just before he moved to return to his place, I tugged at his sleeve. When he turned, I flashed him an OK sign. The smile with which he responded gave his face a lift plastic surgery could not have matched. Wherever his old girlfriend may be, I'm telling her here and now she made a big mistake letting that guy slip through her fingers.

11

Pray All Ways

Dom Louis, New Clairvaux's abbot, was deeply disappointed and his expression showed it. How could someone in the religious life be blind to the unique privilege of priesthood? He had wanted to be a priest for as long as he could remember. The thought of being a priest, of sharing the high point of Christ's own life, overwhelmed him. How could a monk, of all people, forgo that richness of experience, as Brother Peter was now doing?

He had asked Peter that question many times during the past year and the answer was always the same. Pete wanted nothing to distinguish him from the rest of the monks. He believed priesthood would set him apart and his sense of solidarity could not suffer that.

Pete knew how Dom Louis felt and found it hard to articulate his stand without hurting his brother's feelings. But he had found it increasingly hard to ignore the strength of his own convictions in the matter.

Besides, he had found ample support for his position. When Mac had been father immediate, he told Pete that he felt the same way: that if he had it all to do over, he would not have gone on to the priesthood.

Ironically, it was monks who originally gave priority to the priesthood. During the Middle Ages, nobles had supported monasteries on a quid pro quo basis. Praying was the monks' job. That was all they did, all day long, better than anyone. That kind of prayer was a one-way ticket to eternal salvation, an immediate priority in medieval society. Nobles were more than willing to pay the fare, but they wanted first-class accommodations. If the mass was the ultimate prayer, they argued, why say it so infrequently, as was the practice? Their benefactions and tithes bolstered their argument and more than covered the cost of changing the practice. Priests began offering the sacrifice of the mass at least once a day, even with a small—or nonexistent—congregation. And priesthood grew to preeminent status in the process.

During the reevaluation of liturgy initiated by Vatican II, many felt the private mass was a contradiction. A congregation was as intrinsic to the concept of mass as was a priest. In monasteries, where monk-priests had celebrated mass with only a server, or alone if none was available, concelebration came into vogue. One principal celebrant actually consecrated the bread and wine while other priests, generally standing nearby, recited the appropriate prayers with him.

In Pete's opinion, concelebration particularly emphasized the elitism he meant to avoid. It gave a special place to the priest and ranked the congregation in another, lower category of worship. He could not do that, he told Dom Louis. He had never been more conscious of his brother monks than he was now. If the mass was to be a communal activity, like choir, then he wanted to feel he was one with them, not separated in any way.

Community had taken on new meaning for Pete in the last two years. Events had allowed him to see it as the single seamless garment so often used as a metaphor for the mystical body of Christ. Ironically, that concept had come alive two years before, as though for the first time. Just when he had been ready to leave the monastery, he saw how his brothers had become his life.

New Clairvaux Abbey was then at its lowest point in years, so far as able-bodied personnel were concerned. Vocations seemed to have dried up and there was more work to be done than hands to do it. As harvesttime approached, everyone took on additional tasks. For a monk like Pete, one of the monastery's more capable men, that amounted to service on the House Council and the positions of vocation director, irrigation technician, and potter. Even though he had been excused from the minor hours of choir, there just was not enough time in the day to do all the jobs he had been assigned.

He had been making his rounds of the monastery's network of irrigation ditches late one afternoon. Certain canal gates had to be opened to flood growing areas; others had to be closed. There were only two gates left, spaced a half mile apart, when the front tire of the bike he was riding went flat. Without the means to repair it, he would have to walk the remaining distance, rolling the now-useless vehicle, and then cover the two miles back to the monastery on foot.

He was at the extreme end of the property, close to the small bridge that spanned a bordering river. He can remember the sound of his work boots on the bridge's wooden planking and he can remember closing and latching the monastery gate behind him. A passing truck had even stopped to offer him a lift as he walked down the road toward town. He refused, but the driver's question had started him thinking.

Where was he going? He shivered in the cooler temperature of the waning afternoon and looked about. He knew why he was going, but not where. Circumstances in the monastery had become difficult, but life there was still precious. Whatever—whoever?—it is that I want from life, Pete thought, I know it's not out here. He shivered again.

God led me to the monastery, he said to himself, and allowed me to find more of the things that have made my life joyous—people who give priority to things I love. I left a world that never even came close to appreciating those things. My body may be tired and cold, but I know in my heart that it's warmer on the other side of that gate than it is out here. If I've hit a plateau, maybe it's time to sit still and look around instead of working so hard trying to find ways to go farther up the mountain.

He turned and began walking back, pausing only long enough to let himself through the gate and to pick up the bicycle from the spot where he had thrown it. He was still searching for an answer several months later when the community made its annual retreat. Gethsemani's former abbot, Dom Thomas Mary MacDonald ("Mac") was the retreat master.

In his closing talk, Mac had suggested that after he left, the community share experiences about the retreat: that if he had touched them in any way in their life, they should say it aloud, allow their brothers to receive the benefit of it, and share it gratefully with the Lord.

Pete was one of the first to share at a special meeting of the community the week after Mac left. It had been an especially difficult time for him, he confessed—one in which he had felt hurt and likely had been the agent of hurt for others. He was aware of praying those last months, of asking for the grace of healing. He believed God had chosen to give him that grace in the retreat.

Throughout the retreat, Pete told his brothers, he had felt a growing sense of unity with them. It was their presence, their commitment, their common objective, that distinguished the monastery from its surrounding vicinity. "I just want to tell all of you," he said, "that I am very grateful to God that he has called me to this community, because I feel that I really belong here, to each of you, and that you belong to me. I'm humbly grateful for what I know God has done to me through each of you. I'm honored that you all accept me as your brother."

That had been a turning point in his monastic life and Pete had tried to explain it to Dom Louis. The dynamic of his existence lay in losing himself by serving and relating to his brothers. He had grown wary of anything that smacked of promotion or status. That did not mean he wouldn't accept responsibility. He would, but only on condition that his term in any superior office be specifically limited.

Dom Louis had been touched by Pete's explanation. He was troubled as well. This action, coming from so highly respected and revered a monk, would send a signal to many in the community. He did not know how many would be able to see and appreciate it as a brother's individual statement, valid and necessary for him. He feared for those who, lemminglike, might precipitously imitate him, and so be sidetracked from finding their own individuality.

The abbot wanted his new monks to be trained theologians and he had seen to their education. He went to great lengths to assemble the monastery's teaching faculty. He would bring them in for six-month periods, during which the monks who were studying concentrated on that single subject in which the visiting professor was a ranking expert. Dom Louis saw to it that men and women, Catholic and non-Catholic alike, ranking experts in their fields, formed the minds of his monks. Who knew what might be thrown at them some day during a stint as guest masters? He wanted them to be on solid theological ground if they ever advised people. They should know what Catholicism, and other religions as well, were about.

Once Dom Stephen, the abbey's father immediate, had directly asked Louis if he wasn't obliquely ushering all his monks toward priesthood. The decision is entirely theirs, he had replied. He had no intention of pressuring anyone to do something they felt the Holy Spirit wasn't ratifying. But he was willing to wager that everyone who took that step would find the priesthood as rich a source of spiritual strength as he did.

Not one day went by when he failed to celebrate mass. Even when he traveled, he carried the necessary equipment to do so. He might arrive at a destination (motels on occasion) too tired to brush his teeth, but as appealing as the bed might seem, mass came first. His teeth might fall out for lack of attention, but Dom Louis would never fail to honor his priesthood.

Pete was a good monk, a holy one. Many of the monks had chosen him as their spiritual director. The abbot himself was among them. If anything ever happened to Dom Louis, he had no doubt the community would probably want to choose Pete as their new abbot. Not now, though. Abbots had to be clerics, priests.

That policy was being maintained by the Holy See. The order's abbots, meeting in a general chapter, had, on several separate occasions, voted to change the policy and allow brothers to become abbots. But their recommendation had been turned aside each time it was sent to Rome for ratification.

As a general policy, the overwhelming majority of Trappist abbeys did not consider priesthood to be part of the monastic vocation. In fact, if a prospect gave priesthood as part of his overall ambition, he was told to go elsewhere to fulfill it. An abbot could and still did ask monks he thought were capable to undertake the studies and accept ordination. But usually this was the result of practicality, in that the abbey's need for priestly services was being satisfied.

Dom Louis was frankly concerned that it might not be possible to guarantee those services in the future. Two of the three other monks who were studying for the priesthood had begun talking about doing as Pete had done. They had spoken to Pete and he had shared his thoughts. Monks did not have to be priests, he had said. They were laymen, not clerics. One of the first Christian monks, Saint Anthony, was never ordained. Monasticism remained a lay movement even when it spread to the Western church and was institutionalized by Saint Benedict. In fact, the Saint had warned against admitting them to the community. Treat them just like everyone else, he advised, and take care that they don't stir things up.

There had been moments when Dom Louis felt similarly wary of historians who used stories like that to discount the priesthood and by extension the theological studies that led to it. It was as anti-intellectual as it was anticlerical. It was his responsibility to lead his monks. They needed to study, to know. He was appalled by specious definitions that would have treated theology and priesthood as simply fuel for a fascist bonfire.

Intellectually, Dom Louis accepted the idea that there were as many prayer modalities as there were people. Pete was taking a major step in a direction very few had taken. But he had done so after careful consideration. Dom Louis might not appreciate what he was doing, but he did not have the authority as abbot to dictate when a matter of personal spirituality was at issue. If the monk believed he saw the will of God in a particular practice, the abbot was obliged to help him as best he could. He might not understand or appreciate Pete's choice of prayer, but he was only the abbot. His job was to help the monk pray, not to mandate one way of praying.

"WAS he talking about priesthood or prayer?" Mac asked, when I told him what Pete had shared with me. "Let me tell you how it has changed for me and maybe that will tell you something about one monk's prayer at least.

"Saint Bernard talks about coming to the monastery to see God. But when we get here, that's not what God lays on us. What he lays on us is self-knowledge. Then the second phase is a compassionate viewing of our brother. Only then do we reach that image of God that brought us here.

"That's not what you expect—what I expected—when I entered the monastery. What drew me in at the beginning was love for the Christ I discovered in the Gospels. In the thirty-odd years I've been here, that has changed an awful lot.

"I remember getting a sense of that union, that communion. Whereas at first it was a desire to be face-to-face with God, with Christ, at some point I began to see how I could make that desire an everyday part of my life, just by being free and open, by simply being present and available for God.

"It was a surrendering for me, about fifteen years ago, in which I had to allow God to be, in whatever and however circumstance he chose. So then, my prayer became a two-part harmony, in which desire and design were one. First, there was my wanting to be in that love relationship with God, and then the other [part]: my wanting to surrender and let him be through me, to act through me. I got a sense of my being a channel for that presence. That gave me a sense of value and worth.

"Now I've begun to see how God keeps moving past my expectations. I have a sense of finding him in places and people that I didn't expect to. The ecumenical movement, the changes we've undergone in the monastery, they've all stretched the traditions, the different religions, allowing us to experience different faces of God, to find him in wider and wider circles.

"A while back, a group of laypeople started a commune, a monastic experiment, on a chunk of land nearby. They tried to live like us, except there were husbands and wives [with] kids, and they held down regular jobs. They shared what they had, including regular periods of prayer, the psalms, meditation.

"Well, in spite of its good intentions, it didn't work out. Maybe the problem was they were learning the words to old songs instead of listening to see what tune God was playing. Anyhow, one of the last couples was this man and woman with two kids. They had been Catholic, but they'd sort of stopped.

"But they hadn't stopped with their God life. They'd go off on a nature hike and that appreciation of God was their meditation. That's how I got to know them. They came in here and I used to take hikes around here with them. We'd talk and laugh. But they didn't come for counseling with me. We just shared that experience. It took me out of my monk head—no, it stretched it.

"What I had to look at was this phenomenon of people who left "the church" but who hadn't gone slack. They had a relationship with God but not with the institutional church. So far as they were concerned, they and it were at two different points in time. Maybe the church as such had even become an obstacle. No hard feelings on their part. It was like they moved away from this neighborhood where the church had been one of their neighbors.

"Tragically, the lady developed a brain tumor. They went through all that terrible business with chemotherapy and radiation. She had this beautiful red hair and she lost it all. She couldn't eat and toward the end, the cancer got into her bones. She couldn't even walk.

"Somehow the illness brought her back to this neighborhood of Catholicism, back to her old neighbor, the church. She'd go in the hospital for treatment and her husband would take her in the car, come back out here, and carry her into our church for mass and the psalms. He was so tender and loving—as big a man as she was little. Mutt and Jeff. To see him carrying her in his arms, little tiny thing, helpless, hurting, it was like this heartbreaking pietà, because you knew she was dying and a part of him was dying too. Actually, she didn't last all that long. Maybe six—no, seven months. She died a few days before Christmas.

"That was another face of God for me to see. That relationship I formed with that beautiful couple brought me into contact with people who had been raised in my tradition and who didn't find it helpful. I got to see these people who had checked out of the institutional church, not because they wanted to live a sensual, sinful life. Not because they were angry or ticked off at something [the church] had done or didn't let them do. No hard feelings. And they didn't stop growing spiritually. They heard a different tune and sang it for a while.

"Knowing them helped expand my repertoire. I got a chance to see that God's not just here, but he's over there in the Pentacostals, in Buddhists, in that couple whom I might have judged as having washed their hands of him. It made me grow more compassionate.

"I think there's another example of what I'm trying to say, in the feeling some monks have about priesthood. I thought Pete would eventually make the move he told you about. That was a tough call for him. A lot of people feel he's being disloyal. I think those critics miss the point. The guys who back off from the priesthood aren't knocking it. It's perfectly OK with them if you want to do that. But they want to move toward God in a different way. That's all.

"I sometimes get lumped together with them since I don't concelebrate. To me the priesthood is a service for which I have been called and to which I have been anointed. The service is a ministry of word and sacrament that I bring into play when there is a need for it. If I'm presiding, I'm the priest. Then, I put it out there as best I can. When there is no need, I don't have to put it out there.

"I went on a trip once with another priest and we were in this city on Sunday. He had to find a place where he could be the celebrant at a mass or concelebrate with another priest. Me, I just wanted to attend mass with the other people, to celebrate as one of them. I didn't feel the need and it didn't make sense to me to get all dressed up in the vestments and stand around as window dressing.

"Don't get me wrong. I have a deep feeling for the mass and the liturgy. It's what got me into the church in the first place. And it got me through one of the toughest periods I've had so far in the monastery.

"This life may look tranquil, but it's anything but that. They talk about the desert as part of the spiritual journey. Some call it acedia—a time, maybe a place in a sense, when everything dries up. This place, and this life, lose their meaning. You get hit with anxiety of the most terrifying kind. "You've wasted your life," a voice inside you screams. You've thrown it away. All your sacrifices, everything you've endured has been as so much water poured into a hole in the sand.

"That's when monks start to look forward to visitors, to going outside. They begin to think of all the ways they could contribute if they were out in the world. They become desperate about doing something before their life is completely gone.

"When it hit me, I thought I'd lost it. The faith. God. Everything. I

stopped believing. I didn't go around broadcasting the matter, but I tried
to fight it. To do something about it. Wrong move. I realized it was
novitiate all over again. I had to accept God being present to me in a
different way.

"So I just hung on. I nourished my dry soul with the beauty that is in
the ritual, with the sound of the music. I listened to the very practical
wisdom that overflows in the psalms. I even took to reading the "kill 'em,
crush 'em" psalms, the ones that are categorized as those of disorientation. If there was a God, then those words fit my feelings. He had
abandoned me. He'd run out.

"I also quickly acknowledged the illogic of that complaint. If there was
a God, he'd given me life, something I'd done nothing to earn. When a
man and a woman make love and a child is born, they make something of
their love. They not only share it with each other, they share in the
creation of another being. We're born of love. God's love.

"Anyway, at the time, I could think all that through, but it was a cold
and tasteless portion. But I made up my mind that I was going to be a
brother to my brothers. Many of them had shown me love. Now it was my
turn. It's easy to love in the sunshine. But the test of love comes in the
rain, when it's dark and cold and your heart feels empty. So I resolved to
go to choir, to go to mass, even to celebrate it when it was my turn. I was
going to be there with and for my brothers, the people with whom I had
once shared God's love.

"They knew. Somehow they knew what was happening to me. And
they went out of their way to respond to my emptiness. It was as though
they were going to fill this huge void that was inside me. They knew I was
at the point when guys leave, and it was like they were saying, 'Don't go;
we really like having you here.'

"Dom James was the abbot at the time, and a more sensitive guy
couldn't have been found. I know some guys hate his guts. There's one old
laybrother here who claims he's got affidavits from every monk who ever
got a tough time from James and left. He says they're all in the hands of an
attorney who is under standing orders to make them public the moment
any favorable biography of the old abbot gets published.

"Well, James may have been tough on some guys, and I know he was
tough on himself, but he gave me all the room I needed. No pressure. No
prodding. He didn't excuse me from any obligation while I was here. But
if I wanted to get away, he offered to bankroll a trip, wherever, howsoever
long I wanted. No strings.

"I stayed. That's when I met that couple that had dropped out of the faith. Dom James let me go out to see them, develop the friendship. I said her funeral mass and blessed her remains before they lowered them into the ground. The sight of her husband and two kids standing by that grave, tears rolling down their faces, broke my heart. They had such a special [kind of] loving.

"I knew there couldn't be an end to that kind of love. I didn't know that in my head. I knew it in my heart. I felt it there. And that's where and when I got my God back.

"It was a prayer. That entire experience was a prayer. Because through it all, I never stopped thinking about God. Just like any atheist. God's more a part of the atheist's thoughts than he is for many so-called believers. Saint Augustine defines prayer as a turning of the mind and heart to God. Well, my heart may have been empty, but it wasn't closed.

"I realize now that my resolving to stay and *be* for my brothers was an act of God, an act of loving. The attachment I formed with that family was no less. Christ said, 'Where two gather in my name, there I'll be.' That's what a church is—the institutionalization of prayer, a structure formed by people loving, by a loving people.

"You can see that now in our society. More and more people are getting interested in the spiritual life. Two of our monks, Basil Pennington and Thomas Keating, have become meditation gurus. They teach the centering-prayer variety. If they held a workshop on the top of Mount McKinley, it would be full. Their books and tapes are best-sellers.

"God's calling those people, Keating, Pennington, those they attract, all of them. He's letting them hear different music. It may be that such interest will bring about a change in the monastery. Something more fluid. A way people can move in and out as they need [to].

"I don't know if monasticism as we now have it will be able to respond to that. There's too many older monks who have paid their dues, made commitments to God as they understood him. I may disagree with their notion of what this life is and should be, but I can't indict them for bad faith. And I can't deny them what they need to sing their particular song. So maybe a new monasticism will have to come into being. Another song.

"Maybe it won't even take place in the church as we know it. For the last couple of years, the Catholic church has been in a desert. People have looked to it for relevance and too often they've gotten rhetoric, a broken record. That's the problem with institutions like ours. They confuse unity with uniformity. Prayer isn't a confrontation. It's confluence in the name of Christ.

"Think of that for a minute. And remember Saint Augustine's definition. Know what? If you do anything lovingly, anything in which you're giving, you've got the makings of a prayer. You've got your mind and your heart involved, and there's no question that you have a connection with the Almighty. No matter where you are, no matter what you're doing, you can pray. That's pretty potent. It's a powerful force, prayer is. God help anyone, or anything, that tries to stand in its way."

Give us this day at New Clairvaux Abbey a loaf of Brother Adam's bread.

Lest the machine covet a dollop of Snowmass Abbey's cookie dough.

They also pray who fix the machines that spray New Clairvaux orchards.

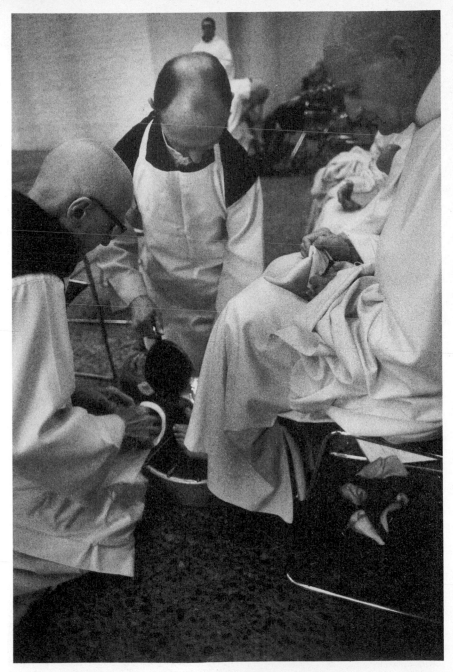

As did Christ, so do we at Gethsemani Abbey on Holy Thursday.

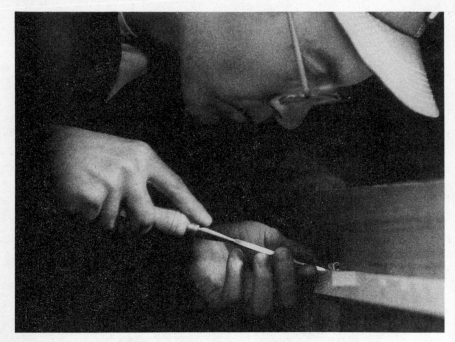

Time and patience enough for a Gethsemani monk's craftsmanship.

Praying by morning's first light at New Clairvaux Abbey.

Prayers to season New Clairvaux's annual picnic in Lassen National Forest.

Rocky Mountain High watching a Snowmass monk in prespike mode.

"*Lord, when did we see our Gethsemani brother hungry?*"

Monk's bread begins its journey from the production line at Genesee Abbey.

12

The Medium as the Message

PERFECTIONISTS ALWAYS look as though they have just stepped out of a recruiting poster. Everything is pressed, buttoned and tucked, precisely as it should be. At three o'clock in the morning, when many bodies and bones rebel at any movement, Father Bede was a picture-perfect monk as he walked to his place in choir. When he bowed from the waist before entering the row of stalls, his movement was the prayer of a young tree bending before the wind.

I waited eagerly for the moment when he would intone the opening prayer of vigils. Everyone had been silent since the ending of Compline at eight o'clock the previous evening. At a signal knock by the abbot, all would stand and turn to face the front of the church. A pause no longer than an inhalation followed. Then Father Bede's voice, a passable tenor, beautified by practice and control, would lead us back to spoken communion. "Oh Lord, open my lips," he would sing. Another pause and then everyone would continue, "and my mouth shall declare your praise." Hours before dawn, in an otherwise silent world, a new day would begin at the Abbey of Gethsemani.

Vigils, lasting approximately three-quarters of an hour, is the longest of the choir offices. It is one of the three "major" choral offices, the others being lauds, at approximately six o'clock in the morning and vespers, which takes place in the evening at 5:30. These latter two take the better part of a half hour.

In addition, most monasteries also schedule several smaller periods of choral office. These are the "little hours," spaced throughout the day, beginning after lauds: tierce (8:00 A.M.), sext (12:00 M.), none (2:00 P.M.), and compline (7:30 P.M.). The psalms sung during the little hours are unvarying. Church law requires that every hour include at least one of each from these categories: psalms, hymns, prayers, and scriptural readings.

Indeterminate adjectives are appropriate to describing monastic prayer life. Not every monastic schedule includes all the offices mentioned, although all do include vigils, lauds, and vespers. Some combine certain of the hours, like vespers and compline (the last two of the day) into a single office. Others allow monks to pray the little hours privately. This dispensation usually accommodates work and/or schedules that make it difficult to reassemble the community in church.

A few Trappist monasteries make it a point to go through the entire Psalter, all 150 psalms, within seven days. Others do it in two weeks. Some exclude what many monks refer to as the "raging" psalms, those that are dominated by anger and calls for violence.

The psalms have been a spiritual mainstay since before the time of Christ. They were and have remained an integral part of the Hebrew liturgy and Bible. Christ and Mary frequently used the psalms to express themselves, especially on significant occasions. In the early Christian church, the mass was celebrated only on Sundays. During the week, the community would gather in church twice each day to recite the psalms.

The desert hermits gave similar priority to the psalms. Like them, many Trappists have memorized the psalms and can often chant them by rote. While familiarity does lead to distraction at times, they find themselves relating to the psalms on ever-deeper levels with the passage of time.

"It's all there," said Mac. "The whole gamut of human conditions, including despair. I think their effect depends on the degree of the reader's ability to be honest.

"To me the psalms are archetypal. Jung himself said they are just swimming in archetypes. That's where people live. The collective unconscious. I like the unity of the race that that notion embodies. For years, whenever I pray the psalms, it's been as though the human race is praying with me."

Father Matthew Kelty calls them strong meat and believes a certain degree of courage is necessary for anyone who would pray the psalms regularly. In a chapter talk titled "The Psalms as Prayer" (included in his book, *Sermons in a Monastery*), he explains, "If I say that the psalter is not too popular, perhaps here is the reason.

> "People do not know and they do not want to know themselves. They much prefer to live on a fragile surface with a workable bundle of adjustments they pass off to themselves and others as to who they are. Hand such people a psalter and they will be ill at ease with anything except pretty ones about the glory of God and the beauty of nature. But turn to some of the wilder psalms and they find the words inappropriate and the sentiments unchristian. As undoubtedly they are. But until you have penetrated with Christ into your own depths, much of you also is unchristian and will remain so.
>
> "The psalms can teach us much of this, of the conflict with evil within us. Bring us face to face with the traitor in our own heart: the two-timer, the time server, the false friend. Who has not met the demon of envy, of jealousy, of greed, of hatred, lurking in the dark shadows of his depths, a side of himself that rarely comes into the light? And what appropriate elements of hell within us! Christ descended into hell and we must descend there with him, into the infernal regions of our own heart."

Like the psalms, certain traditional prayer modalities may be found in use at most monasteries. Along with choir or, as it is generally known, Opus Dei (God's work), Lectio Divina, the practice of reading and reflection on scriptural texts, is another mainstay. The hours between the end of vigils and the beginning of the monastic workday at eight o'clock, are usually reserved for Lectio.

It is reactive reading. Essentially, the reader moves along slowly until a word, phrase, or passage strikes a chord in his mind, imagination, or heart. Then the book is laid aside and the reader gives himself to the thoughts and feelings the text has inspired. Some find it helpful to read the passages aloud, treating them as though they were mantras. Selections can be from the Scriptures, the writings and lives of the Saints, or a book suggested by a spiritual director.

Most monks also use the early morning hours for a half hour of private meditation. Some add another period of meditation in the afternoon or evening. When I stayed at Gethsemani, I found it helpful to join a group that meditated together in the chapter room immediately after vigils. Chapter rooms have been a basic part of monastic structures since their beginning in the Middle Ages. Monks would assemble in them and, seated primarily on benches that ran around the room's perimeter, listen to the abbot each week as he shared pertinent information and preached to them about the spiritual life.

The room was darkened, lit only by a lamp at one end, and as I would pick my way to a bench, I could see other monks arranging themselves for the meditation period. Several had grown fond of Zen methodology and knelt using prayer stools that straddled their lower legs and allowed them to sit back, their torsos erect, hands folded loosely in front of them. One or two sat in full lotus, the Buddha posture. I had tried those postures, but found they placed too much stress on my knees.

I was pleased to see that Mac, who took his place each morning at one end of the row where I sat, must have shared my preference. In the dim light, I could just make him out: his eyes closed, head erect, apparently deep in prayer.

Meditation seemed so simple and yet could be vexing, even for monks who had been practicing for years. The basic notion was very similar to meditation techniques that have been popularized in recent years. The monk cleared his mind of thought and remained receptive to God. In theory, God knew everything and anything one might have to tell him. All that was necessary was the act of will by which one chose to be present to God for the moment.

The competitor in me presumed I would get better with practice. I patiently endured and often struggled with the distractions that flooded my mind. At times, they would include the most marvelous ideas—clear solutions to problems I had been trying to solve for days. Mac had recommended I try using a one-syllable word that conjured up thoughts and experiences of God. Silent repetition of that word might foster concentration. When I became conscious of distractions, all I had to do was quietly and calmly to repeat that phrase and return to the centered prayer.

It did not seem to help very much. I found myself not only distracted, but growing more impatient with my inability to manage this important prayer. When I told Mac about the trouble, he cautioned me: "Stop trying to make God happen according to your image of him." "Just give the time to him, without strings or expectations. That decision alone, reinforced every time you let go of distraction and bring yourself back, is enough.

"Remember too, that God's communication comes in ways that may not be readily apparent. If you want to look for the effects of the prayer, look in your life for its fruits. Are you growing more patient, aware of others? Are you loving more? Then the prayer is taking hold. Relax; let God have his way.

It didn't seem to make any difference on some mornings. One random thought would follow another. I would catch myself and begin thinking of my prayer word. I would repeat it once, twice. A rhythm would set up and for a brief moment, a split second, everything would grow quiet, still. It seemed as though I could hold it, keep it secure from distraction.

The next thing I knew, my mind would be racing with plans I had made for the day: perhaps an interview, or the photos I wanted to get of Brother Conrad doing farm work. Sometimes my ruminations would be as earth-shaking as deciding if I should try the granola I had helped Brother Anthony make in the kitchen earlier that same morning. Then I would think of how he's really into meditation. He and several other monks took part in an annual Zen meditation workshop, conducted at the monastery by a Buddhist monk. Those attending would go off into a separate guest house for two whole days and concentrate on learning as much as they could about Zen techniques.

At this point, I would realize my mind had wandered off again. I would begin repeating the prayer word and a small gong would sound, signaling the end of the meditation period. I'd reassure myself with Mac's counsel. Don't rate the meditation, he had said. Whatever took place was enough—all it needs to have been. Distractions were there because I was human. All I needed to do, all I had to remember, was to avoid involvement with them.

"Treat it all as though you were on a river bank watching," Mac had said. "As boats come into view, you see them, but nothing more. You don't begin to focus on them, drawing them close, examining their detail. Just let them go by. Remember, every time you return to the prayer, you make an act of will; you choose to put yourself in the presence of God. That intention is what counts."

Mac reminded me again about the desert hermits and their conception of prayer. There is no such thing as one way, just as there is no typical person. While everyone prays, one's prayer reflects one's unique identity. Few things in monastic life get the priority given to pluralism in prayer.

"People are different," Mac said. "Watch them and you'll see what I mean. The way they change is different. How long it takes them varies. It is conceivable that a prayer I would find useful and nourishing at one time, would require changing or replacement as I myself grew and changed with time."

Each Trappist reviews his prayer life during the meetings he is required to have regularly with his abbot. Overall, the purpose of these meetings is to monitor each monk's life and to make certain it has all the necessary elements for continued growth. However, ask an abbot what and how he expects every monk to pray, and he is most likely to answer, "It depends"—on the monk, his makeup, and the relationship between him and God as he can describe it. It depends.

Prayer is the monk's priority. It enables him to achieve the purpose for which he entered the monastery: to get closer to God. In a strict sense, everything he does, confirmed by his decision to enter the monastery, and presumably reaffirmed often during the days, months, and years that follow, is a prayer.

The primary purpose of a monastery is to make God as accessible as possible. In that sense, monks are like athletes. While training for their particular athletic event, they repeatedly put their minds and bodies to the movements that said event will challenge. Training brings their bodies and skills to peak levels, so that their ultimate performances will be as close to perfect as they can make them. In the same way that athletes choose their diets and every other circumstance of their training to custom-fit their bodies for a single performance, so too do monks prepare. They practice, again and again, what they hope to do once, to the best of their ability, for all eternity.

Eternity is the monk's "event." He does now, on earth, in this life, in the monastery, what he hopes he will do forever. The sacrifices others see him making are in reality no different from the athlete's recognition that certain elements detract from one's performance. That is the difference between the monk and the athlete. While the former's notion of victory is restricted to a future possibility, the latter knows victory takes place now—the result of everything one does.

If anything should be remembered about the Trappist's life, it is of its communion. "Where two or three are gathered in my name," Christ said, "there am I in the midst of them." The Trappist monk, unique and different as is every human being, expresses that destiny in company with others. His prayer is the sum total of everything he does, but especially that which he does with others.

I met with Saul one afternoon in the tiny room he uses for his work as the monastery's cellarer (business manager). It was as cluttered as his own room, except that there were no clothes to be seen. I told him what Mac had explained about the relationship between people and prayer and asked how that squared with his own ideas on the subject. This is how he answered.

"Maybe our life does resemble an athlete's. I guess then, I'm in the process of changing my workout routine. Right now, I need things to be simpler. My job is making me hungry for more simplicity in my life. It's as if I'm up to my eyeballs dealing with the complexities, the world. That's driving me to simplicity.

"A cellarer really has a lot of responsibility. He takes care of the temporalities. Like in marriage, you have the kids and school and the job and taxes and the dentist's bill and the car and insurance—you name it. A ton of paperwork. Endless phone calls and running around. It's all time-consuming and takes energy. That's what the cellarer is ultimately responsible for.

"If those things are not there, and well done, the spiritual life isn't going to be good. People will get anxious, nervous, distracted. If I do my job, people leave us alone, bread's on the table, heat's in the pipes, and everybody has a fair share of work to do. It's like those things are out of sight and they don't have to worry about it. So people are able to go about the one thing necessary, because they aren't distracted.

"Brother Cornelius, the guy who had my job under Dom James, really ran a tight ship. This place was humming. Probably why he's done so well since he left. Some of our priests gave him a really hard time. He was only doing his job. But in order to do it, [he had to have] everybody work a little more than they felt was necessary.

"We had a meeting with the abbot after Cornelius left. Those same guys who gave him a hard time asked the abbot just how many hours we needed to work to keep the place solvent. Turned out we could do it if we rented most of our land and closed down everything except the cheese and fruitcake operation. Done, said the abbot, and closed it all down.

"There's still a lot to do. This is one of the biggest houses in the order. I could be buried by the paperwork alone. Maybe that's the part that gets to me. It seems like everywhere I turn, there's something I have to do, or some place I have to be. I try to get off and walk for a while each day, just to have some quiet time by myself. That's what I really miss, what I really would like more of—space, a simpler existence.

"I feel the tendency very strongly. That was supposed to be one of the hallmarks of the Cistercians. Our old laybrothers would be in the tradition of Cistercians. Up until the sixties, they were a real alternative.

"When I came into the order, everyone who joined the choir became a priest. I really like the chant, the liturgy. But if you went into the brothers, choir was not part of your life.

"There were two distinct groups back then: the brothers and the choir religious. The only time the two groups came together was for Sunday mass and every evening at compline. The choir religious had stalls up in the front of the church. The brothers were in the back under the balcony. They couldn't sing. Not allowed to. Funny—if they had, they would have drowned us out. There were 140 of them. They were quite an impressive group, with their dark brown habits and beards.

"The brothers were separated from us in most things. They had their own sleeping quarters, their own scriptorium. They had their own spiritual formation program, a continuing thing, unlike ours which ended when you made solemn vows. Every time the choir monks went to church, the laybrothers met to say a special breviary they had, or the Paters and Aves—ten Our Fathers and ten Hail Marys.

"If they were out in the fields when the bells rang for a choir office, they'd stop and pray their Paters. They'd come up into our section of the church at night for the Salve, after we chanted compline.

"I think the changes after Vatican II took a lot of starch out of [the brothers]. Most left. I think they really loved the old life-style. They had very deep values, a real sense of camaraderie, and probably more solitude than we did. The old work routine must have functioned as a prayer form for them. Agriculture, working in the fields, gave them an intimate sense of God at work in the universe. You were aware of it, part of it. The brothers shared that.

"Most of them were macho guys. They really dug the penances and sacrifices. Their work was affirming. Their self-esteem got a constant boost. They could see what had come of their work. They kept this place going, just like laybrothers made the first Cistercians commercial wizards in medieval times. I think that's why the life appealed to them so much. No matter what you had been on the outside, in here you were the obedient servant, but you were important. You knew you were a hero.

"As a choir monk, I had a lot more time than the laybrothers. They worked eight hours. We worked four and the remaining time was for reading. When you made simple vows, that was reduced to two hours, because that was when you started studying for the priesthood.

"I was into my theology studies when a movement began in the mid-sixties. Started in Europe. The main idea was that monasticism was a lay movement. I remember the article that really pulled it together for me. It was the text of a conference given by the Dutch theologian, Schillebex, at our monastery in Holland. He was saying that theologically there was no basis for monks being priests. They did no pastoral work.

"Here we had all these priests in the monastery saying masses without congregations. They hardly heard any confessions or dispensed any of the sacraments. The whole purpose of the priest is to minister and they were not doing any of that. Schillebex also had a lot of difficulty with private mass, which is what most of our monk-priests did. A private mass was almost a contradiction. We had a lot of monks who didn't function as priests did, or maybe as they should.

"That got me to thinking. I was caught up in the purity of monasticism: I couldn't think of mixing it up with priesthood. It kinda appealed to my original [wish] to be a plain monk. It was a revelation to me—that I could be a monk and not a priest.

"I talked to Louie [Merton] and he was very encouraging. He had been my novice master, my idol even before I joined. When I was still at NYU, and beginning to think about the religious life, I talked about it with one of my professors. He was a pretty devout guy. Made regular retreats down here. Well, he gave me Louie's book, *The Seven Storey Mountain*. It really got to me. That's how I came down the first time.

"What I didn't know was this professor was a friend of Louie's and he wrote to [Louie] about me. I nearly fell over when somebody tapped me on the shoulder while I was eating in the guest dining room. I turn around and there's Louie. We had two or three really long talks and that's what pretty much convinced me to sign up.

"Anyway, after, when I spoke to him about my feelings regarding the priesthood, he told me privately that if he had to do it over again, he wouldn't have been ordained. This was in the late sixties, just before he died. I just don't think he would have said that in an attempt to be nice.

"So, I had him backing me up. [And] it helped [build my resistance] when the other priests in the community found out and started giving me flak. What clinched it for me was a retreat we had with Dom Jean LeClerq. He's a highly respected French Benedictine. I had a talk with him and he told me he had been forced into the priesthood. His superiors just kept insisting that someone with his education [had to] go on for ordination. But, he said, he wished he had resisted. He would prefer not to be a priest.

"He was talking to a lot of monks in Europe and they were thinking the same way. He told me, 'If that's what you want, that's what you should do.' About the same time, Vatican II was coming along and they were switching everything from Latin to English. I spoke to our abbot and said I needed time off from theology studies to work on our music. (I was doing the translating.) I just never went back to them.

"I've always felt the Catholic church is very schizophrenic, between clerics and laypeople. The priests were the church. The laity were the compliant, docile audience. I think the biggest hindrance to the development of the church is its clericalism. They really have an old boys' club.

"I remember a priest who made a retreat here once. He was really turned off. Young guy. His pastor got to him one time. Urged him to cultivate 'priest' friends, as though laypeople were a subspecies. Told him, 'Don't you realize we're part of the most exclusive club in the world?'

"I think you see this when they talk about ordaining women. That club isn't about to open its membership. Not unless some of the people in the power center make the move. We laypeople can't do it.

"I've got nothing against priests or theology. I've kept up the studies on my own and I read a lot. But the simplicity of the brother's vocation is really attractive. The old laybrothers, I mean. Some of those who are left still follow the old way—working and a pretty simple prayer life. No way are they dummies, though. A lot of them are pretty holy guys. You know how you can tell? They get along with everybody. I mean, everybody loves them.

"If you stick around here long enough, you'll tangle with one or another of our not-so-lovable brothers. I don't have to mention names. I think you already know who I'm talking about. You run afoul of one of them and you'll see these old-timers swing into action. They are very caring. They can bandage a battered ego better than Florence Nightingale.

"In one sense, my job has been a blessing. I have to deal with people in here and out there. The work brings me into contact with them a lot. Really opens you up. You do business with someone and you get to know them. In a way, it makes you responsible for them.

"I think though, the contact outside has done me the most good. We hired this one young guy, a neighbor. He's just moved down with his wife and two kids. He's having a tough time of it. His wife's not too well, I hear. We needed some work done with the backhoe and he could handle it. Gave him the job. Couldn't thank me enough. Sent a lovely card to the community. What a nice guy. I think he used to be Catholic. I mean, he seems to know what we're all about. Makes me wonder.

"People get easier with time. That's my experience. You get a bigger perspective. You don't get threatened as easily. We don't rub shoulders with that many people, ordinarily. You do it through reading, as I've done with that book on AIDS, *And the Band Played On*. It exposed me to all these people: the scientists, the politicians, the doctors, the patients. Gave me a new perspective of them—people in that situation. I try to stay up on things. Right now, I manage to read *The Economist*, another mag put out by *The Christian Science Monitor,* and a couple of business journals and trade magazines that deal with our work here.

"If my life is a prayer—and I try to make it that—then the people I meet every day have to be part of my praying. I mean, what comes of me meeting them? I think that's what it's all about. Remember what they said about the early Christians? 'See how they love one another.' Christ doesn't go into formal praying a whole lot in the gospel. But he sure spent time talking about love and brother and neighbors.

"It's toughest with people who are close to you. Some of the brethren can really get under your skin, regardless of the job you have in here. I found that tough, being an introvert. I bottle things up. I have trouble contradicting people, or saying something that I think will make them angry or upset them. I'm impatient.

"Take Bede. Some guys have all the answers, right? Well, he's the one with all the questions. He'll come in and just go on and on and on, as if I have nothing else to do. He's meticulous and scrupulous, and he really has the interests of the place at heart.

"He does have the background for certain things, but he throws his two cents into everything. I've got an engineering background, but it was in electrical, so he'll catch me out in the open and that's when it's tough. He'll just stand there and keep banging away.

"The guest house was a real scenario. 'The contractors aren't doing this right,' he'd say. 'They're not doing that right.' I'd check and find out they were. I mean, the contractor was on top of things. So, I'd have to make a choice. If I choose the other guy, Bede will say I'm prejudiced against him. Course, he doesn't hold a grudge. Meet him an hour later and he's forgotten it completely.

"I found that if you try to walk in the other guy's moccasins, see his perspective, the difference, you get more patient. Don't give me any medals, though. I slip. You know, your own shoes get more comfortable as you get older. It's tough to give them up, put on moccasins that are a little too loose or a little too tight, and walk on.

"I keep trying, though. Old Brother Leo never came to choir when they gave him the chance. He really has a thing about priests. Now he's confined to a wheelchair. Guys like him seem to get into an acedia, the dry time in spiritual life. They don't get nourished much by liturgy. So I go over to the infirmary once or twice a day and say the Paters and Aves with him. Maybe someday soon, I'll find a way to relate better with Bede, learn to appreciate him for what he is, as different as that is from me. God, I sure as hell hope so.

"The hardest part in here is getting close to somebody. You do that and one day maybe you wake up and they're gone. They go out into a completely new world. You're left to walk around in one that's filled with their memories. That happens and it makes you gun-shy. You're pretty cautious about letting people get in close after that. Then there are the ones you can't get far enough away from.

"There used to be a guy here, really gave me a hard time. I was praying once, real angry, after we had a big blowup. I prayed extra hard, trying to get the thing under control. I asked myself, 'How can God let a guy like that stay here?' I could pray for him, like I knew I should, and at first I prayed—selfishly, I have to admit—that God gives him the grace to make him more lovable. Or that [God would] open my eyes so I can see what he loves in him. I lost it at that point.

I remember I almost yelled out loud, 'How can you love that son of a bitch?' Like a telegram, the answer came right back to me: 'He loves that son of a bitch so much, he sent you to show him just how much.' Try that pair of shoes on for size."

$\mathcal{S}$ection Three

DARKLY IN A MIRROR

Of the many thoughts written about love and loving, few were as eloquent as those the Apostle Paul chose for his Epistle to the people of Corinth in A.D. 57. Possessed by the most extraordinary of gifts but lacking love, he told them, he was as sounding brass and tinkling cymbal. Given all knowledge, present and future, but lacking love, he would be nothing.

Love is all—patient, kind, scorning self, he explained. "It bears all things, believes all things, endures all things." It is eternal. In life, love is flawed, imperfect even as it will one day be perfect. Now, he told the Corinthians, we see as though through a mirror, in an obscure manner, but later, we will see face-to-face. "Now I know in part, but then I shall know even as I have been known."

Or as Mac, no less eloquent, once phrased it, "We will stand, one day, before Infinite Love, known and knowable only to the degree that we have been loving. For the time being, here in this life, our grace is to reach out to all that is different, to grow by our act of affirmation, to love what we can only see as though darkly in a mirror."

13

The Unavoidable
Christ

DURING MY second visit to Gethsemani Abbey, I was assigned to work with my old seminary classmate, Father Dan. His seniority didn't earn him or me any special status when it came time to parcel out the work that needed doing.

Although a monastery might at times seem to be ignoring a monk's particular talents or skills, the fact remains that most of its work is as ordinary as it is necessary. Bathrooms need cleaning, potatoes must be peeled, and somebody has to cut the lawns. Monks may have some special job, as did Thomas Merton, the well-known Trappist writer, but even he had to cover a regular share of the ordinary, day-to-day work.

Those jobs that carry authority or the semblance of territory change hands often. No monk owns a position and most abbots take pains to make that point. Anyone who shows signs of territoriality is likely to find himself evicted posthaste. In addition, during the peak season of any abbey's particular industry, everyone helps. This is true in New Clairvaux, during its fall prune and walnut harvest. Likewise at Gethsemani during those months immediately before Christmas when the abbey ships the largest percentage of the fruitcakes it sells annually. Everyone takes a turn wrapping and labeling packages, Dom Stephen included.

So I was not surprised to find Dan working alongside me at eight o'clock in the morning, as we harvested corn in the monastery's five-acre farm. It was a bumper crop, which meant the community would be served corn in an endless variety of ways for the next few days. I asked the cook, Brother Edward, how the monks took to culinary monotony after we had deposited full crates in the walk-in cooler adjacent to the basement kitchen.

Depending on the cook's relative creativity, they might never notice, he said. But there had been times when even the most creative chef was unequal to the challenge posed by certain customs.

At one point in Gethsemani's history, an aging benefactor had come to live out the remainder of his days in the monastery guest house. His business career had given him some familiarity with the local market to which the area's farmers brought their produce for sale. He therefore insisted on shepherding the cellarer on the weekly trips to buy the monastery's provisions.

The trip, the benefactor had sagely pointed out, was best made on Thursdays, the day before the market completed its weekly cycle. Since new fruits and vegetables arrived on Friday, vendors were more than willing to bargain on materials they had not sold during the previous six days. Bargains, he exultantly told the cellarer. There were bargains to be had for a pittance.

Unfortunately, Brother Edward said, the bargains were most often to be had in a single item, left over in so great a volume that the vendor was more than willing to sell it for "a pittance"—or often to give it away. "You had to be here some days," Brother Edward said, "when all of us would be sitting around searching through cookbooks to find some way of dealing with several dozen crates of fast-fading sweet potatoes, or an equal amount of broccoli, cauliflower, or cabbage. It may not have cost us much money, but only God knows what our collective dietary tract had to endure because of that blessing."

Strange things happen when a community is intent on economizing and has a pool of free labor at its disposal, Dan pointed out, as we walked over to the bakery for our next assignment of the morning. Keep in mind, he told me, that the people who plan things like the monks' menu or their work aren't bound by the same considerations as they might be in the outside world. A monk learns to accept his portion. "As a matter of fact," he said, "if we can save a few bucks on food and labor and bring our egos into line at the same time, we've got a pretty good thing going."

I reminded him of that observation fifteen minutes later, as the sweat poured from us. We had both been assigned to clean a corner of the bakery's storeroom, where two wooden pallets had been stacked with plastic pails of corn syrup. The pails had been piled too high and the weight had forced open the lids of the bottommost layer, spilling their sticky contents onto the floor. It had oozed beneath the pallets, under the door of the adjacent closet, and after several months, had hardened until it was only slightly less dense than the concrete floor that it covered.

The storeroom had only one small window, hardly sufficient to ventilate against the day's heat that had already begun to build. By the time Dan and I had moved three dozen fifty-pound pails, our shirts and pants were dark with perspiration. The crystallized syrup then had to be softened with hot water and pried free with a scraper. Finally, its residue had to be scrubbed away with a stiff straw broom and more hot water. Slowly, the mess yielded to persistent effort.

There was an unexpected dividend waiting when we finished at half past eleven. It was Friday, and on Friday morning, the bakery devoted itself to preparing the community's bread supply for the coming week. After Brother Timothy, the baker, had inspected the now-clean storeroom, he expressed his gratitude by urging us to help ourselves to the freshly baked, hot whole wheat rolls.

"Getting enough to eat?" Dan asked, as we sat on the bakery steps, munching the fresh rolls. The question pricked my curiosity. Dom Stephen had asked me the same question two days after my arrival. He also wanted to know if I was getting enough sleep. Aside from the first day, when my body clock had to adjust to an early bedtime, the schedule seemed manageable. Besides, there was something special about rising so early to pray. My mind seemed clearer, less open to distraction.

I thought any concern about my starving was even less justified. The food was plentiful and I had yet to have my dreams haunted by giant Big Macs. Why were they all so concerned? I asked. What was it about their diet and their schedule that they felt was so impossible to manage?

"You're right," Dan said. "You'll probably never feel the pressure. Everything's still a novelty. It takes time before you realize that it will never change. Basically, the commitment a monk makes binds him to a deadly boredom. Everything will repeat ad infinitum. The monk has to come to terms with the fact that nothing and no one may ever change.

"That's what's going to make your job harder. Right now, you're a novelty. All we see are your good points and that's all you see of us. It's a first-date situation and we're both on our best behavior. You don't really have to accept those parts of this life you don't like."

"That's not true," I protested. "I'm doing everything you monks are doing. I don't want any special treatment."

"But somewhere in the back of your mind, you know this will end. You won't have to get up at three in the morning some day when you're tired or you have a headache. You can hop in your car and go into Bardstown anytime you want. Our vow of stability binds us to this geography until they plant us in it."

"Some critics claim that vow insulates you from the problems the rest of us can't escape," I countered.

"Think so? What about our commitment to the people here—people we didn't choose, who we have to accept as though we did?" When most people in the world talk about finding God in their daily lives, they overlook their immediate circumstances, Dan said. "Charity comes easy with complete strangers. You never run up against their differences, those nice little sharp edges of their personality.

"Try accepting somebody you'd like to change," Dan suggested. "Try resolving that you won't even try. Try accepting the world and everything in it as it is. Try limiting yourself to contributing rather than controlling it."

The degree to which a monk is open to his world indicates the degree to which he has opened himself to God, Dan explained. Openness is a function of poverty and obedience. Openness is freedom. It is the alignment of the individual's will with that of God. It is the path to authentic identity.

When a Trappist monk vows to be poor, he does not simply forgo ownership of things, Dan said. He promises to stop wanting. He resolves to wean himself from the pull and the call of possessions and of power.

There is an aspect to the Trappist's vow of obedience that warrants notice. When Saint Benedict explains this virtue to monks in chapter 5 of the Rule, he cautions them. Obedience will only be acceptable to God, he says, "if what is commanded is done without hesitation, delay, lukewarmness, grumbling, or objection." Even if the monk obeys but murmurs in his heart, his obedience is worthless.

It is one thing to obey your superiors, Dan pointed out. It is another to be obedient, without grumbling, to circumstances that unfold with each day. "I think the most inspiring thing I've seen in the monastery is the monk who opens his arms to terminal sickness or debilitating old age," he said. "Brother Leo may still be contrary, but since he got Parkinson's, no one has ever heard him utter one word of complaint. For a guy who was so tough to live with, he's showing real class right now. It's as though this illness has freed him and allowed a part of him to come out that was always there but hidden."

Vowing to stay in one place with the same people for the rest of your life is a commitment to appreciate unending beauty in the simplest elements of existence. It makes the Lord's Prayer come alive, Dan said. "Not my will, but yours, on earth as it is in Heaven." A monk opens his life to God—on God's terms. He recognizes that every one of his brothers was brought to this place by God. Their presence in this place is sacramental.

" 'I trust and depend on you,' the monk tells God. 'I know you love me. You will be present to me in whatever a day brings, whomever I meet. You will be present when the ovens overheat. You will be present when my brother who can't stand me overheats. I know you will be there. I will look for you and if only because I do, you will be.' "

14

What Martha Knew

"For then they are truly monks," wrote Saint Benedict, "when they live by the labor of their hands as did our Fathers and the Apostles." For all his compassionate understanding, the man whose Rule has been the bedrock of countless religious orders had no use for anyone who would not work. "Work and pray," became his rallying cry, one he himself had heard in the voices of his predecessors, the desert hermits, after whose lives he modeled his own, and those of the hundreds of monks whom he formed.

If Saint Benedict is the father of all monks, then their spiritual grandfather, Saint Anthony, proves his lineage by having given similar priority to work. Anthony did so, he reportedly told his followers, because he took Saint Paul quite seriously. He who does not work should not be allowed to eat, the Apostle had told the early Christians. Anyone who doubted the importance Saint Anthony gave to work, had only to listen as he gasped his dying words. After more than one hundred years of life, he was happy, he said, because he had never troubled anyone, living instead by the labor of his own hands. In the centuries after Saint Benedict's death in 547, his followers were drawn away from manual labor, although it can hardly be said that they spent their time at leisure.

During the Middle Ages, religion counterbalanced the gross inequities of the class system, which were further aggravated by the greater susceptibility of the poor to plague, famine, and war. War was society's principal occupation and pastime—the enterprise that franchised monasticism.

As godlessly as medieval man might live, nothing equaled his fear of the God he believed would call him to an accounting after death. God, sin, penance, and salvation, in that order, were the axioms of his existence. If he sinned and died without atonement, he would be eternally damned. He had to do penance.

Penance was a serious affair in the Middle Ages. If sin could damn a soul, only proper shriving could save it. Fasting was one of the more usual levies. After the Battle of Hastings in 1066, Norman bishops fixed the penance for every member of the victorious army: one year per each man killed. That restricted every soldier in the Norman Army of Occupation to bread, salt, and water during three separate forty-day periods for each penitential year. However well shriven the Norman soldiers might be, they would also be effectively scratched as an army.

Feudalism had a solution: scutage. People fulfilled their military obligations by hiring others to serve in their place, or by paying their liege lord a tax for that purpose. God was simply another suzerain. Just as the medieval citizen needed someone to fight his military battles, he needed someone to take up the cause for his soul. Enter monks, the spiritual knights. The local parish priest, living on land given him by his baron, often married, barely literate, was hardly perceived as a likely spiritual counselor. Whereas his credibility (and often that of the bishop who ordained him) was compromised by allegiance to civil authority, which in all likelihood had appointed him to his office, monks were professional pray-ers. Unbreakable vows bound them to their purpose for life, and woe to anyone who disturbed or distracted them.

In the course of time, this function shaped monastic life. The monks were freed from anything that would keep them from praying and their prayers became both public and elaborate. Choral chanting of the psalms was organized into specific periods, spaced throughout the day much as they are at present. Since mass was deemed the most perfect of prayers, good sense (and the stipends such liturgy commanded) dictated that it be celebrated every day.

By the eleventh century, monks in certain of the more prominent Benedictine abbeys were reciting 138 psalms each day, almost the entire psalter. The liturgy of chief festivals would often consume the night and the following day as well.

The composition of the monastic community changed in response to this increasing obligation to liturgy and the Divine Office, as psalmody was called. Their caste was distinguished by minor orders and ultimately, toward the latter part of the Middle Ages, priesthood, which was eminently practical, given the premium its powers commanded.

Monks had to be literate to cope with their liturgical responsibilities and so they were drawn almost exclusively from the ranks of the nobility. It became common practice for nobles with large families to arrange monastic careers for late-born sons whose claims might have complicated the division of an inadequate estate. Gifts and benefactions to monasteries ensured that these monks would live comfortably in the company of their peers.

As monasteries grew rich and powerful, the monk's life was so completely monopolized by public prayer, he had no time left for individual meditation or study, much less for manual labor. Consequently, a support group of tenant farmers, craftsmen, and artisans took its place in the monastery's ranks. They tilled the abbey's lands, produced whatever material goods the monks needed in their daily life, and saw to the construction and maintenance of a structure that was as appropriately awe-inspiring as the prayers that took place within its walls. This state of affairs reached its culmination in the Abbey of Cluny. Cluny was founded in 910 by a dozen monks, to whom William the Pius donated a small farm with a chapel in the French valley of the Grosne. By 1132, its monastic community had grown to more than three hundred.

Cluny is said to be the grandest enterprise produced in the Middle Ages and the largest monastery ever built in the West. No abbey ever attained its lavishness and scale. The monastery proper could accommodate more than twelve hundred fathers and brothers in its halls and dormitories. The church could hold thousands. There were workshops for every trade and craft necessary to the abbey's self-sufficiency, as well as provisions for enamelers and goldsmiths.

Cluny would ultimately control more than fifteen hundred abbeys and priories in every part of Europe. Its abbots would achieve princely status—some powerful enough to be compared to kings. Monks would profess before them rather than before their own abbots. The abbots of Cluny were the counselors and judges not only in the monasteries adopting their reforms, but also outside the cloister, where emperors, popes, and kings sought their verdicts.

Cluniac monasticism still predominated when the Commercial Revolution began spawning the changes that would stimulate the birth and extraordinary growth of a new monasticism. Stability and relative peace returned to Europe in the eleventh century, a period that witnessed the rise of medieval cities, the guilds, and international trade and commerce. Perhaps most important, as far as monasticism was concerned, was the growth of personal freedom. A middle class was emerging, strong enough eventually to break the grip of feudalism, as well as to loosen ties that bound serfs inextricably to the manorial soil for life.

Commerce brought about a fluidity in society. It predisposed the minds of those who financed the Crusaders, whose stated noble purpose only thinly hid their dreams of plunder and riches. Their conquest of the Holy Land gave impetus to the growing phenomenon of the pilgrimage.

Christians made these faith journeys, primarily to shrines, for several reasons, such as to petition, to do penance, or to gain remission from their sins. In some cases, the pilgrimage might last a lifetime. The more fervent of these pilgrims were likely to evolve into hermits, a development that grew prominent in the tenth and eleventh centuries and that made concrete the laity's desire for increased spirituality.

There is a striking similarity between Christianity's circumstances in the tenth and eleventh centuries and those in which it found itself in the time of Constantine, more than five hundred years earlier. More than ever, the Christian faith, which had once been persecuted to death by the world, was now being strangled in a worldly embrace.

While there were many popes, bishops, priests, abbots, and monks who did honor to their offices, there were far too many who arrived at their stations by way of payment of one kind or another. Emperors had seen to the installation of popes who were to their liking. Episcopacies and abbacies were currency in a ruler's purse. Clerical marriage, especially among priests, was common. In fact, since the children of priests were considered bastards and thus disinherited, many were offered (with suitable donation) to monasteries while still young, thereby securing these youths some degree of comfort.

In short, "the world" had become an encumbrance, a problem that eluded control. And while Cluny had undertaken a reform of monasticism, notably successful in its attempt to remain free of civil interference, its overemphasis on corporate, public prayer left monks longing for solitude and periods for personal prayer and study. The hermits of this period, like those of the Egyptian desert five centuries before, seemed to have achieved the greatest degree of success. Attempts to reform monasticism followed that trail.

In 1098, eight monks began one such experiment in the north of France, in a swampy area known as Citeaux. There they would stay beyond the reach of society, its contaminating riches, and its solitude-destroying interference. The members of this small band were the first Cistercian monks, the religious order from which Trappists would later evolve.

Their aim was to return to pre-Benedictine monasticism, which they believed was the purer expression of the ways of the desert hermits. Toward this end, they forbade all self-indulgence—with food, housing, and clothing. Their's would be a centralized order which would mandate and maintain a universal rule and monastic life-style. Every abbey would be subject to visitation to ensure this observance. Neither abbot nor abbey would ever be allowed to attain the primacy or power that Cluny once enjoyed.

The search was for greater solitude, poverty, and austerity. The monks would be bound to their monastery. They would be poor like the poor Christ, living as he did from the fruits of their own manual labor, grown on land they bought, far from all intrusion. Two years after its foundation, the fledgling order secured a papal bull, known as "the Roman privilege," which placed it under the protection of the Holy See and ensured its freedom from annoyance of any kind. Donations to the abbey were to be "free alms," gifts without strings or conditions of any kind. The Cistercian monk's energies and attention would be focused on God. Simplicity became his way of life.

The order's struggle against all display was fanatical. Only their poverty was to show. The monks would wear unbleached wool, without the coloration of black. Their liturgy would use unembroidered vestments of light linen, wooden crosses, and iron candlesticks. Their monasteries would be similarly unadorned, with unplastered walls, towerless churches, and windows displaying only colorless patterns.

They competed in asceticism. As more monks came under the Cistercians' white mantle, a spirit of unrelenting self-sacrifice prevailed. They ate two meals daily from Easter Sunday to 14 September. Thereafter they ate only one meal each day, at about two o'clock. There was never any breakfast. The rigorous asceticism reduced their mean life expectancy to twenty-eight years. Considering that the average youth was fifteen years old when he entered a Cistercian monastery, one concludes that the life was supportable only for about a dozen years.

The first Cistercians' determination to avoid involvement with the world made them forswear all parochial services, tithes, and pastoral duties. The severity of their life, devoid of ritual, carried on in the plainest surroundings possible, offered visitors and guests little in the way of encouragement—if they were persistent enough to find their way to the monastery gate in the first place.

Cistercians placed their monasteries in the most remote places, frequently on what were the frontiers of uninhabited Europe. They sought primitive, virgin, uncleared sites, always hidden, preferably tucked deep in valleys—never atop a mountain, by a lake or a sea, on an island, or by a big river. Unwittingly, they performed a singularly vital function for an expanding society: they became the outposts of advancing civilization. Corporate prayer, the liturgy of the Divine Office, was central to their notion of prayer, and enclosure an essential precondition to solitude.

Agriculture was the principal means by which they could support themselves, and yet it was an implacably jealous master, one that would not be subordinated to the hours of choir, nor satisfied with an enclosed site that could never provide sufficient land for cultivation. They might have hired help, as monks had done for hundreds of years, but that would have brought laity into the monastic enterprise.

The Cistercians solved their dilemma by making their helpers members of the order, the first laybrothers. These laybrothers were to manage and work those distant granges which would be a necessary source of income for the monastery. The laybrothers would be allowed to remain outside, to deal with the world and its contaminating influence. They would be in the world.

But while they would be members of the monastic family, they were not to be seen as the equals of the monks. Once they took vows as laybrothers, they remained so for life. They were forbidden to read any book and could learn nothing but the Lord's Prayer, the Creed, the Miserere, and a few other prayers which they were to sing from memory. They were not even allowed to look at any text.

The laybrothers were strictly segregated. They were not allowed in the cloister. Special buildings were set apart for them in the monastery, with their own dormitories, refectories, and latrines. They used special pews in the church, where screens hid them from the monks. Even their access to church was through another, separate door. Only in death did they use the same door at one end of the nave, which led to the cemetery where they were buried as members of the community.

Although some members of the nobility and clergy did seek this lesser, humbler state, the majority of laybrothers were serfs, who flocked to the opportunity. The rapid, dramatic growth of Cistercian monasticism and its extraordinary success in the very society it initially spurned, was largely due to this component of dedicated manual laborers.

There is no question that for many of them the desire to escape poverty and insecurity by entering a great abbey was a powerful incentive. In a world where starvation and calamity were daily possibilities that dictated short lives, monastic affiliation could be considered a sinecure. The fact that their lives and work might also be directly applied for credit toward an eternal reward was a bonus as well.

Citeaux's scions were nothing if not prosperous and great, the self-denying intentions of its founders notwithstanding. The twelfth century belonged to the white monks. By the turn of the next century, there would be five hundred Cistercian monasteries, spread across known civilization. In virtually every case, laybrothers outnumbered choir monks by as much as four to one.

The Cistercians became a corporate powerhouse whose centralized organization was ensured by a chain of command and a single, unchangeable modus operandi by which every abbey had to abide. Cistercian organization and simplicity became a nuclear reactor in which the fissionable power of the laybrother was unleashed. There were no systems extant that could compete with the Cistercian juggernaut. Given an abbot with normal intelligence, a layer of educated choir monks for his executive cadre, and an endless supply of dedicated, obedient laborers, monasteries quickly dominated the economic system.

Time and seclusion enabled them to observe, experiment, and take note for future improvement. Although the first monastery farms were lands considered worthless, hardworking monks transformed them into verdant pastures and productive acreage. Since Cistercians were prevented from embellishing their living conditions, all profits from their enterprise were put to purchase of more land and expansion of those industries in which they continued to acquire expertise. The level of their education led them to hand down experience in farming and forestry that accelerated their growth. Cistercians became the best agronomists, stockbreeders, vintners, and foresters of the later Middle Ages. They discovered the mode of pruning vines that French vintners still use. They became skilled in animal husbandry and their small herds multiplied. When that success gave them more milk than they needed, they began to make cheese.

Gethsemani's monks can trace a line to this last-mentioned effort. At first, the monks made cheese for their immediate needs. Then they noticed that changes took place when the cheese was stored in the monastery's stone cellars. As it aged, cheese advanced through stages that were distinguished by texture, taste, and aroma.

They learned that the flavor of cheese also changed, depending on characteristics of the animal from which the milk was taken. Even the pastures upon which a herd grazed at different times of the year produced a difference in taste. This experience became part of the order's store of knowledge that was passed on to the monks who founded the monastery at Port Salut, near the city of Laval in 1815. They shared the recipe for their unique cheese with monks in the neighboring abbey, Notre Dame de Melleray, who took it with them when they left to found an abbey in Kentucky.

Cistercians were just as methodical and successful in other fields. They were experts in fisheries and in the use of water. They pioneered in mining and smelting copper, silver, and other metals. By the thirteenth century, Cistercian monasteries held extensive estates, leased farms, and possessed whole villages, sawmills in the woods, and mines.

In England, the Cistercians became one of the largest producers in the wool industry, with abbeys that owned not only flocks, but also mills in which their wool could be processed, and ships that could carry it to markets abroad. In 1194, a year's clip from Cistercian flocks paid ransom for the release of Richard I from his Saracen captors.

The flood of Cistercianism crested toward the end of the thirteenth century as pestilence and war brought about the decline of vocations to the laybrotherhood. An estimated twenty-five million people died after the Black Death began taking its toll on the European population in 1347. The Hundred Years War between England and France began less than ten years later and further reduced the manpower pool that had invigorated the first century of Cistercianism.

Lekai, in his book *The Cistercians*, traces this decline in laybrother numbers within Cistercian ranks, noting that laybrothers ceased to exist in many abbeys by the fifteenth century. It was only the advent of Trappists in the eighteenth century (when that reform was formalized as the Order of Cistercians of the Strict Observance) that brought about a resurgence of the laybrother vocation.

Laybrotherhood continued as a separate category of religious expression but did not experience marked growth until after World War II, when laybrothers constituted a majority of the increase in vocations to Trappist monasteries in the United States particularly. (European Trappist abbeys did not have a similar increase in vocations.)

After almost a century of existence, during which vocations had trickled through Gethsemani's front gates, the monastery was inundated with applicants. They were relatively young, most often educated, and perhaps most notable, mature as only a man can be who has watched death stalk senselessly among the very young on a daily basis. At an age when men would normally exult in time that seems to stretch endlessly before them, these veterans had been forced to ponder the meaning of a single moment of existence. At a time when men find a surplus of ambitions with which to fill their lives, only one ambition made any sense at all to these laybrothers: put all your energy and talent at the disposal of the Almighty; let him decide what is to be the meaning and purpose of your life.

In an essential vision, the men who chose the laybrotherhood in the twentieth century perceived the benefit of Trappist life as the outgrowth of simple manual labor, the deprivation of sensory pleasures—of which total silence and perpetual fasting were the most obvious—and the erasure of any outward signs of identity. To the laybrother, these were not demands so much as they were time-tested means.

The army, navy, and marines had done their job well. The monastery could have been another branch of the service. For these veterans, unquestioning obedience was an accepted mode of existence, in which the potential of their youth and skills could be properly realized.

Their coming filled the monastery to overflowing. By 1954, Gethsemani had a total of 233 members, of whom 144 were laybrothers. When no more room could be found for their straw-mattressed beds in the abbey dormitories, tents were pitched on the enclosure lawn. They formed an elite inner circle that retailored Trappist life to their measure. Whatever distinctions history had made between laybrother and choir monk became rallying points for the group. Choir monks had their Divine Office, but laybrothers had their work, which for them constituted as distinct a badge of honor and as unique a prayer as singing did for their brothers in choir. Skills they had developed outside the wall were rediscovered in a monastic world that was ripe with opportunity. Tools and machinery were extensions of their bodies—extra fingers, hands, and muscles. Pray? They could swing a sledgehammer for hours on end. Pray? They were as comfortable dismantling a tractor as they were running it precariously sideways to a sloping hill. Each could work harder, longer, and more efficiently than any two choir monks. The Rule may have stilled their tongues, but their facile fingers were soon tracing new signs, creating still another bond among them even as they expanded existing boundaries of communication.

Democracy demolished their millennium. With the advent of Vatican II and its sweeping changes, Trappist monasticism changed. By decree, a general chapter of the order's abbots ruled in 1964 that everyone would simply be a monk. The laybrother's distinctive brown habit would no longer be worn. The community's prayer was the Divine Office and former laybrothers were to be encouraged to participate.

The move was well intentioned, part of an overall change in which externals were made to surrender to essentials. Customs that had been followed blindly and faithfully for centuries were discarded. If the monk ultimately took part in a dialogue with God from the core of his individuality, then only the individual monk could determine in good conscience the rightness or wrongness of any prayer.

Silence was no longer a Trappist absolute. Interior silence, the type that grows rich in private space and time, the kind that manifests itself in sensitivity to others, replaced the exterior observance that had often made a sham of communal charity and the gospel mandate of brotherly love. No longer could one pull the cloak of the Rule around a flawed personality. Neurosis could no longer masquerade as sanctity. Both the introvert and extrovert were expected to grow, to balance their personalities, to mature into people who could ignore reflex reactions long enough to develop appreciation for their polar opposites. One not only had to pray for one's brother in secret; one had to pray publicly in deed.

Fidelity to vocation now allowed for changes in it—recognition that personal growth often mandated new career paths, new directions for one's life. Some found their new direction in a richer monastic observance, the essence of which was a greater self-respect born of the assumption of responsibility for personal decisions. But some clearly were discomfited by the change in established customs. Still others were troubled by a definition of the monastic charisma that too closely specified the notion of prayer (i.e., the Divine Office).

"We missed the boat," said Mac. "Manual work was the laybrother's equivalent of choir. We stepped into the same trouble on the laybrother issue as we always do when we try to define God. It's the old story of the blind man describing the elephant by his sense of touch alone.

"What's important for all God lovers is to express that love and grow by its expression. We must do that with others. We must give when— especially when—giving isn't comfortable. The monk who wants to stay out in the fields and plow till the sun sets is saying vespers in his own particular way. Do you doubt that it's acceptable to God?"

"But if everyone goes off and does his own thing," I asked, "then what becomes of this loving community of faith? How is communion going to be for that monk who loves to sing the psalms but can't find someone to sing with him? If no one comes to choir, where is that special something that Pete found here?"

"That's funny," Mac said.

"Nobody coming to choir?"

"No. You, the outsider, arguing for the status quo and winding up in the same camp as the monks who don't want outsiders participating in things like choir."

"I like choir. At this point in time, it allows me to be present to God and him to me in a way I can't imagine happening otherwise."

"Good point. Now take a look at what happens in that very situation. As sure as we're talking here, there's at least one monk who probably is getting zilch from choir at the same time as you're getting everything. His participation is his gift to you in community, in love. He is the agent of God's love, the way God is present to you.

"But that goes both ways. When you and Dan cleaned the storeroom, you both gave to the community. You affirmed them by that work. You told them they were worthy of God's love by your willingness to do a dirty job that needed doing if this place is to continue as a community. You prayed like a laybrother.

"Work is as necessary to this place existing as a community as choir [is]. If I can't sing a note, is my participation in choir any less a prayer than if I can't fix a carburetor? Have you ever heard someone described as a gifted mechanic, or a gifted teacher? It's the act of giving that makes us a community. That's how we realize our role as partners in creation. What we do, how we do it, is the not-so-simple outgrowth of discernment. That's where poverty and obedience enter the equation. Remember? 'Not my will, Father,' Christ said in Gethsemani on the night of his giving, 'but thy will be done.' What can we do to make the other guy—Christ in disguise—become more of what God designed him to be?

"It might do some of us a lot of good to ride a tractor when the sun's setting, or listen to an engine purr after we've tuned it. I know there've been times I've stood back and looked at a room I've just painted and the sense of me re-creating fills my soul. I wonder what praying in that way does for the worker's self-esteem, to know he has grown, that he has increased the universe by giving. I wonder what it would do for the brother who teaches another to do those things and who grows in our esteem by that sharing."

15

Bums
and Saints

ALTHOUGH TRAPPIST monks are notably long lived, they are not exempt from mortality. The debilitation of aging simply intersects with their lives at a later date. And like every other human, some of them are cut down by diseases that prolong their dying over years of increasing dependency. It is in these instances particularly that the monastery distinguishes itself from the society outside its walls.

I became aware of this when I first noticed two lists that were posted each week on the monastery's bulletin board. Each listed the days of the week and provided blank spaces where volunteers could sign their names. One list was for those who would feed Brother Leo his meals. The other was for those who would go to his room at one o'clock in the morning to help him get to the bathroom and avoid lapses of continence.

Unless a would-be volunteer got to the bulletin board very soon after the new lists were posted, the slots would all be taken. As a matter of fact, after two unsuccessful attempts to get on the list, I finally coaxed one monk to let me take his turn. He agreed reluctantly, and only when I argued that the experience was necessary to my research.

Brother Leo was clothed, drowsing in a rocker alongside his bed, when I arrived one day at noon to feed him dinner. After helping him to the small desk where he ate his meals, I began cutting the food into bite-size portions. As were all aged and infirm monks, Leo was excused from the Trappist regimen of vegetarianism. That particular day, his tray included a small pork chop, along with apple sauce, mashed potatoes with gravy, and stir-fried broccoli.

The old monk craned his neck and carefully scrutinized the tray as I tucked a white napkin under his chin. The pork chop rated an approving "mmm, pork," even as the broccoli drew a scornful "yuck, bunny food." He obediently began eating from each of the portions after I reminded him that all of them were necessary for his continued health.

He ate slowly, chewing each mouthful, and paused only once, turning to me as he swallowed. He had not seen me before, so he concluded I was a new man and, without waiting for me to confirm or deny that, said, "Good. We need some new blood." At about that time, he noticed the dessert, butterscotch pudding. He wanted some. He wanted it now, he said, and proceeded to inhale several mouthfuls, until I reminded him that he hadn't eaten enough of the basic meal.

"Only a few more mouthfuls, OK?" he bargained, and let his mouth fall open like a trapdoor, without waiting for agreement. He allowed one more bite than he thought the bargain called for and then gestured to the half-finished pudding. "The Lord wouldn't have me wasting good food," he said.

When the meal was over, he asked to be helped to his bed and to have his shoes removed. He stretched out, folded his hands behind his head, and asked my name. When I told him I was a guest and revealed the purpose of my stay, he asked me to linger. If I was trying to learn about Trappists, I had come to the right man, he said. I didn't have to edit out my questions when I transcribed our talk. He never gave me the chance to ask any.

"YOU'RE talking to one of the last of the Bums," Brother Leo began. "That's what we laybrothers named ourselves in the old days. There were all the choir monks, walking around with their eyes lifted to Heaven, pious as could be. They were the Saints.

"Talk about a two-class society. Back then, the laybrothers did all the work. We ran the place. Sure as hell we did. The choir monks, they had to study theology and sing the office. So they only had a short work period in the afternoon, maybe three or four hours. Laybrothers started work at about seven and didn't finish until maybe five or six in the afternoon.

"I joined in the late thirties. I was thirty-two, working as a waiter in

Manhattan. I used to stop into Saint Francis Church down on Thirty-first Street, near Penn Station. I became friendly with this guy I met there and would you believe he tells me I should be in the monastery? God knows what gave him that idea. I sure as hell wasn't a model Catholic. Anyway, he takes me with him to visit this place one time.

"The place grabbed me—dammed if I know what, or why. But this friend tells me to give it a try. So I come up and they let me in. First day here, they feed us four ounces of plain bread and a pint of hot barley water—that's what passed for coffee—and when the sun's barely out, I find myself out there in two feet of snow, chopping and hauling wood. With only sandals and socks, my feet are wet and freezing.

"Along about lunchtime, out comes the brother who's in charge of us, [who's] no more than twenty-two. He begins to give us hell for not getting enough done. When I tell him my feet are freezing, he starts telling me about grace and me earning some by offering up my suffering.

"You should've seen his face when I offered him the chance to earn a little of that grace by trading me the galoshes he was wearing for my sandals. It was love at first sight, it was. You know, I'll never believe he didn't try to run me over once with a truck. When I got the chance, I grabbed him and put him up against the wall. 'If you've got any idea to try that stunt again,' I told him, 'you better not botch the job, because I'll have to show you how to do it right and you won't be needing any more lessons after the first I'll give.'

"He was a 'Saint' if there ever was one. Thought a lot of himself. When they gave us brothers the chance to join the choir years later, he fell all over himself switching. He even went on for the priesthood, and tried to get in the running for abbot after that. Thank God, everybody saw him for what he was. The phony left and got married. Good riddance.

"That was in the late sixties, when guys were leaving in droves. All those changes. The Saints really grabbed control of the place. I remember one of the other brothers coming to me and telling me in sign language that they were going to let the laybrothers vote. 'They want to make us equal,' he signs to me. 'They're going to free the slaves.'

"What they did was take away our vocation. They made us get rid of our brown habits, 'invited' us to come to choir, and they allowed us to work less. Who the hell asked them, anyway? We came in here because we wanted a simple life like the old brothers had. Hell, [the Saints] thought we were a bunch of dolts anyway.

"You know, at first, the brothers used to be in the back of the church in a separate choir. We weren't allowed to sing with the Saints. We used to

sing our own, shorter version of the office, in English, in another building. But there were twice as many of us as them. So, even from across the
yard, our singing used to drown them out. They made us close the
windows.

"You see, in those days, if you didn't have Latin, or weren't good at it,
they almost automatically put you into the laybrothers when you joined.
You weren't expected to do the reading and studying the Saints did. It was
a carryover from the Middle Ages when the laybrothers were peasants
they brought in to do the work the bright boys in choir couldn't handle.
Those days, the monks used to be in choir seven, eight hours a day. No
way you're going to get a herd of cows that needs milking to wait for some
fairy to finish singing.

"I remember I wasn't here more than six months when I went to the
novice master. I used to read a lot before I joined. But laybrothers weren't
supposed to go to the monastery library. So I went to ask permission. The
novice master then was an old-timer from France. I knelt down alongside
him and he said, 'Yes, my child?'

" 'I'd like permission to get some books from the library to read.' "

" 'Books, my son?' he answered. 'You have books, no? You have the
sacred Scriptures. You have the lives of Saints. What more do you need?'

" 'Literature, Father. Classics, like Charles Dickens, Edgar Allan Poe,
Shakespeare.'

" 'Those do no good for your soul. You are a laybrother. You gave that
up when you came to us.'

"But no one told me I wouldn't be able to read.'

" 'And so no one is telling you that now. Read what you have, ponder its
meaning and be happy with your portion instead of grumbling and
seeking to question heads much older and wiser than yours.'

"We got our licks in though, me and a few other of the Bums. Like the
time one of the Saints decided that the poor choir monks were cold in
their scriptorium. So he asked us to run a line from the main heating pipe
and set up a new radiator.

"We gave them their radiator all right, but that was all they got. We put
a disk the same diameter of the pipe into the connecting valve. It had a
pencil-size hole in it. The hole let just enough heat through to keep the
new line hot to the touch. But the radiator could have been turned off for
all the heat it gave.

"We finally got the privilege of using the library, but not because of
the goodness of their hearts. When the local fire marshals insisted the
monastery have a fire watch round the clock, they gave the job to the

brothers, of course. So, three of us were assigned to divvy up the night and early morning hours into shifts. And they gave us keys to everything. Before you knew it, us Bums were reading everything.

"But the librarian figured books were missing. He's a priest, of course. So, what does he do? He makes us build a wall around the stacks. No kidding. Pity was, when we do the job, there just isn't any lumber long enough to reach the ceiling. We had to finish it with three feet between the top of the wall and the ceiling—which turned out to be just enough space for a guy to squeeze through.

"We fix it so the first shift has enough time to bring a ladder to the wall. The second shift goes over and gets the books and the last guy put the ladder back in place. It took the librarian a little while to figure out what was happening. He was waiting inside the wall one night when I climbed down. That was when the abbot decided the time had come to bring the brothers a little bit further into the twentieth century. It was the only way he could keep from having a war on his hands.

"After Vatican II, the brothers started leaving. Once the Saints had their way, there was nothing left of our laybrother vocation. It was tough watching guys leave after twenty, thirty years of being close. Some of the guys went into choir. Not me. I had my work—at least until this dammed sickness hit me. But if that's what the Lord wants to send, well, I guess he's got his reasons.

"To tell you the truth, I wondered if I was going to be hung out to dry when this thing hit. It's bad enough not being able to take care of yourself, but the monastery is already short on people. Everybody's doing two jobs. Now, when I see these guys giving up their free time and their sleep, I'm a little embarrassed. Then again, maybe the Lord is finally giving those Saints a chance to appreciate old Brother Leo before he takes him home to Heaven."

BROTHER Leo's willingness to tell me about his experiences was a surprise. He was one of the monks who were opposed to the work I was trying to accomplish. Mac had cautioned me about them. The polite ones would refuse, he said. Others might be direct enough to leave some bruises. "It'll be a miracle if you don't step on at least one land mine," he said.

I tended to doubt that possibility. This was the place where God had come back into my life. I had taken the trouble to explain that to the community in a note I tacked on the bulletin board the first night I arrived. I considered the work I was doing very special, I told them. It was not just another piece of work for me. Its genesis obliged me to do the best I had ever done. It was my prayer and sharing that fact made me confident that the monks would set aside any shyness and help me. I told them I would not be able to do as well as I wanted if they did not.

Up to that point in my second visit, I could not have asked for more cooperation or a more genuine acceptance. The reception I had gotten on my first visit had touched me so much, I was genuinely saddened when it came time to leave. I had come to know many of the monks very well. Their trust had reinforced the feeling that I was living in a very special place. It was a feeling I had only experienced when I was with people I loved and who loved me. The monks had made Gethsemani come alive as though it were one such person.

The experience had made me eager to return. In fact, I decided to drive straight through when the time came for my second visit, rather than split the sixteen-hour trip with an overnight stay en route. I catnapped in the back of my truck when necessary and grew more and more excited as the miles flew by. I felt as though I were going home to a reunion with another family God had given me.

Father Bede was the first monk I saw when I got to the monastery. He was walking by himself around the utility buildings, near where I parked. He extended his hand in greeting and I thought I felt him stiffen when I exuberantly hugged him instead. He asked how long I planned to stay and whether I would be staying in the guest house. I appreciated the concern such consideration represented, I said, but I much preferred living with the community. I told him about my experience the first time and said I was looking forward to a similar one on this second visit. I took his wordless nod for agreement and his smile for the first of many greetings I would get that day.

I wondered why Mac's face grew serious later the same day when I described Father Bede's reception. "Why the frown?" I asked.

"Bede's never been Gethsemani's welcome wagon hostess," he said. "I get worried when people change very much very quickly." I had the feeling he laughed to allay any anxiety I might have, and I was eager for the reassurance of the remark that followed. "Maybe after all these years the Holy Spirit is going to use you to get through to our brother Bede."

I thought of Mac's comments after I had interviewed Brother Leo. He never talks to outsiders, I'd been told. I felt my breakthrough warranted a try with Father Bede. I wrote him a short note, asking if he would set aside some time to meet with me. I knew he had a different view of the monastery, I said, and I felt it was important that my research include it. I slipped the note beneath his napkin in the refectory and waited for a reply.

I was walking from the refectory one evening soon after my interview with Brother Leo when Father Dan motioned me to follow him outside. He found it hard to believe that Leo had been so forthcoming. "I heard he bent your ear for a couple of hours," he said.

Was it possible that his bite had grown more terrible in memory? I asked. Though Leo was given to exaggeration, I thought he was pretty likable.

Debilitation had done that, Father Dan said. "He's dependent now and he knows what a brother he used to be. He's humbled by the care and concern."

Of all the priests in the monastery, Leo had singled Dan out for praise during our interview. He was one of the few "real" monks, he had told me. "Dan would have made a great laybrother."

"What earned you so special a place in his heart?" I asked.

Dan smiled. "Let me tell you what it was like before I smartened up."

DAN began his story more than fifteen years in the past, a few months after he had made his solemn vows. He was jogging one day when he noticed the abbot running along a road that would converge with his own. He slowed and ran alongside Dom Stephen after their paths met.

The abbot was curious. He asked how everything was going with Dan's new assignment as assistant to Brother Leo. It was a question Dan was eager to answer. He had found the way to deal with Leo. When he was first assigned, he had been uncertain whether he could even have persevered as the old laybrother's assistant.

At the time, there was no question about Leo's feelings toward Dan. Dan was a priest, and as Leo had said more than once, the monastery would be a much better place without priests. Leo wasn't shy about his enmity, and he had already gone out of his way to make his feelings for Dan quite clear.

As Dan spoke with Dom Stephen, he thought about how long a road it had been to final profession and how the difficulties he had encountered along the way had made that event all the more precious and meaningful. He had left Maryknoll to join the monastery and had stayed almost five years, right to the month when he would have been eligible to make his final vows. In the intervening time, he had begun theological study and the presumption was that he would one day be ordained.

But the prospect of remaining in the monastery for life had unsettled him. That was not unusual. The moment of solemn profession is a predictable time of crisis. The monk is promising to remain in the small Christian community that comprises the monastery and to live the life of the gospel. He takes an oath that he will never stop trying to grow into the person God made him to be. He asks the merciful acceptance of God and his brothers so he can keep that vow.

Not all of Dan's brothers had been that lovable in the years leading to his profession. Even God had become somewhat distant. The emotional highs that had permeated every spiritual practice had long since vanished. When he looked at the years he had already spent at Gethsemani, he saw endless days in which he had been put to a series of seemingly trivial tasks: cook's helper, farm laborer, assistant librarian. The only challenge took place within, and after sampling some of the truth about himself, Dan lacked the taste for further self-revelation.

None of this was uncommon to monks at that stage of their monastic existence. But yet, Dom Stephen was the slightest bit surprised when Dan yielded to the pressure and asked for exclaustration, a leave of absence. He and the abbot had entered in the same year and they had become close friends. Dom Stephen knew Dan as a man who was honest, albeit a bit too intense, a perfectionist.

That tendency could make monastic life more difficult than it had to be. One does not force God's hand. One does not work at being a monk in the way that one works at being a doctor or a carpenter. The monk's job is to make himself available to God's grace as it comes through his brothers. It was that simple and in the talks the abbot had had with Dan, he had tried to help Dan see that. When Dan left the abbey, Stephen wasn't certain he had succeeded.

Since Dan's only remaining relative, a brother, had moved to Chicago from their native Connecticut, Dan went there to live. For a time, he drove a cab. By his second winter, he had joined the city's public welfare department as an investigator. It was then he began dating, and for a time he had an exclusive relationship with a co-worker.

But something was missing, he felt. There was no support for a spiritual life—no silence. Except for the woman he was dating, people seemed reluctant to become involved. He had even been cautioned about that at work. The poor had been around a long time, his superiors told him. No one was going to change that overnight, or even within his lifetime.

Workers who got involved, as Dan was doing, ran the risk of losing their objectivity. It was unprofessional.

After Dan had been cautioned for a third time, his supervisor suggested he take a week off—without pay—to try to think a little more about what he was trying to do versus what the department needed done. The silence of a nearby church had beckoned and there Dan did all of his thinking.

He had been out of the monastery for six years. Dom Stephen had kept in touch by mail and had met him for lunch when he changed planes at O'Hare on his way to Europe for a general chapter meeting. The door was always open, the abbot had told him. He was still on the community's roster. In the silence of the church, Dan found himself remembering his former brothers. Faces came to mind, both those he missed a great deal and others with whom his dealings might always be difficult. He resolved to visit the abbey and was only slightly surprised when he decided to return for good.

He had to do a second three-year period of temporary vows, but when the time came for solemn profession, Dan had not the slightest hesitancy about voicing his determination to make a permanent commitment and to accept ordination to the priesthood.

His emotions had begun to swell during the ceremony of his final profession. He remembered signing his name to the paper that legally bound him in the eyes of the church to the vows he had just made. It seemed Dom Stephen's smile ran out of space when he accepted Dan into the monastic family and helped him don his seamless white choir robe, the outward sign of the step he had taken.

Then it was time to greet his new brothers and Dan could feel the tears flowing on his cheeks, mingling often with those of the monks as each in turn embraced him heartily and welcomed him. He had almost completed the circuit of the community when he glanced at that portion of the church sanctuary where most of the old laybrothers waited.

It is doubtful that anyone but himself caught the movement, since all faces were turned to him. But from the back row, Brother Leo quietly slipped out the door. And so Dan was accepted by his brothers—all, that is, except one.

Therefore, it came as no surprise when within a month of Dan's solemn profession, he was assigned to work in the carpentry shop, where Leo had held forth for several decades. During that time, a succession of assistants had been apprenticed to the laybrother. But while the monastery clearly could use another monk with carpentry skills, the community had yet to produce an apprentice with the patience to persevere long enough to become proficient. Most monks believed Dan might easily set a record for the shortest tenure to date.

Dan saw things differently. He had been in the job for five months by the time he and the abbot chanced to meet while out jogging. In his opinion, he had solved the problem, Dan told Dom Stephen. Since he did not have to rely on Leo to learn the necessary skills, he could function on his own from the beginning. That was the secret to success, he said. Slowly, he had let it be known that the other monks did not have to put up with Leo's sour personality. If they needed something done, they had only to see Dan. It was a perfect demonstration of the free-market system in action, he said. Leo was now trapped. Either he must change his ways or he would find himself without any work to do.

It sounded as though Dan had everything under control, Dom Stephen said, as Dan finished his impromptu report. The abbot said nothing more, his face expressionless, and as the pair reached a fork in the road, Stephen turned and, with a wave, ran off alone.

Dan knew his abbot. Dom Stephen normally had little to say, but what Dan had just received fell into the category of a pointed nonresponse. Dom Stephen wasn't delighted, that was for sure. But unless Leo reported Dan as outrightly disobedient, the abbot would do nothing more than he had just done. There was no question that he knew exactly what had been happening before Dan had told him. Very little, if anything, happened in the monastery without Dom Stephen's knowledge.

Where, Dan began asking himself, is Christ in all of this? There was no question that he was handling Leo, getting him to clean up his act. But there was some question about Dan's own "act." Where was he changing, growing? Or was he simply causing change to suit himself—making another monk adapt to his way of doing things?

If Leo was acting out of insecurity, from a need to control, what was Dan doing to reduce that insecurity and allow the monk to regard him in a nonthreatening way? Was either of them growing by the experience?

The answers were no more comforting than the decision Dan made. Beginning the following day, he referred all requests for carpentry to Leo and followed the monk's direction insofar as his own duties were concerned. He left no doubt in anyone's mind that Brother Leo was in charge.

He did that until the day two years later when Dom Stephen called him into his office and gave him a new assignment. This time, an unambiguous smile relaxed the abbot's face, appropriate to the compliment he offered Dan. For once, he said, Leo had found a priest who behaved differently from his expectation. That may well have been the reason why he had protested the change in assignments. It took him a long time to train a new man, he had told the abbot. And, he emphasized, in most instances, those the abbot had assigned were not too good at learning—especially the priests. Dan had demonstrated real ability, in Leo's opinion. "He's turned into a helluva carpenter," he said, "and if you had let me have him a little longer, who knows how much better a monk he might have become?"

AN alarm should have gone off in my head after Dan told me his story. I was making the same mistake he had made. But things were going too well. There was no questioning the warmth with which most of the monks had greeted me as soon as we met. Customarily, they only nod in greeting as they pass each other, which made the reception they gave me all the more noticeable: they went out of their way to say hello. Even at places and times when the rule of silence was in force, they were walking up behind me or crossing the cloister to shake my hand. Two old brothers even whispered a welcome as they walked past me to get to their stalls in choir.

But James always looked straight ahead as he walked by. You can't win them all, I said to myself. However, I was not so philosophical after Brother Bernard and I renewed our acquaintance. I had interviewed him and he had cheerfully posed for a portrait on my first visit. I needed to double-check some of his information and dropped him a note, asking when he might have the time to meet with me.

I still had not received an answer when I spotted him walking toward me in the cloister two days later. I stopped and motioned toward the outside of the building, where talking was permitted. He scowled, shook his head emphatically, and walked on. I wrote the response off to the bad days that sour everyone's existence at some time or another. Previously, we had met outside the refectory after supper, so I decided to try again at that time the next day.

I was waiting when he walked out of the refectory. He glanced toward me and immediately shoved a hand forward, palm out. It clearly said, "Stop." "Keep away from me," he said angrily. "Understand?" I stood there, dumbfounded. I hesitated, searching for some way to defuse what was obviously becoming a bad situation.

Brother Bernard was in his mid-forties and built like a light heavyweight boxer. He spent the largest portion of his Vietnam tour as a Green Beret, teaching unarmed combat techniques to Montagnard fighters behind enemy lines. I was very much aware of those facts when I saw the fingers of his one hand stiffen. He slowly waved me away with the other. "I'm not fooling around," he said. "Now you get lost. Right now."

But I had gotten through to Leo, I thought. I never doubted I would have the same success with Father Bede, up to the very moment when I found his answer to my request taped to the outside of the door to my room.

"Dear Frank," it read, "With regard to your request for an interview with me as part of the research for your book, I think you must know by now, that I am one of a number in the community who are strongly opposed to your presence among us.

"During my earlier years here, what you are doing, living with the monks of a strictly cloistered monastery, was unthinkable and out of the question for a layman. I am all for according every degree of hospitality that Saint Benedict desires for the guest—but his stipulation was that the guests should always be kept in separate quarters and not mix with the monks.

"I am sure that you have certain places in your own home, or times/events in your family that would not be shared by outsiders or invited guests. It is so for the monastic family also, and the cloistered enclosure of the monastic family has always constituted that for us—and still does for a majority of us who came here for a strictly cloistered life separated from the world.

"I feel (and others with me) therefore, that your presence in the intimacy of our family life constitutes an unwarranted invasion of our family privacy (much as it would or should for you if a guest entered areas of your home restricted to family privacy), and a further compromise of our already-too-compromised-enclosure policy.

"This is not meant so much personally in your regard, as simply that I believe your place here is in the guest quarters, and your research should be done from there. I realize you feel the nature of your work requires what you're doing, but then I would say it's the nature of your work that should have been changed to conform to our life-style and privacy.

"For all the above reasons, I think it would be hypocritical of me to further endorse your work and presence within the community by allowing you to interview me. I must therefore decline your request. Fraternally in Christ, Father Bede. P.S. In the future, please leave any correspondence for me in my monastic mailbox and not beneath my napkin in the refectory."

Somehow I had wandered onto the land mine Mac warned me about. I wondered whether I had misinterpreted my reception. Maybe I saw only what I wanted and needed to see. I thought of sounding out Mac, but rejected the idea. My objective was to learn what a monk's life was like.

Friction was part of that life. If I were one of them, I reasoned, I'd have to fight my own battles and make peace however that was possible. I would at least try. Father Bede's allusion to those who were opposed to my presence indicated he was in touch with them. I decided to confront my opposition squarely in a written response to Father Bede.

"Dear Father Bede," I wrote. "One of the last things Saint Benedict shares with us comes at the end of the Rule. All his wisdom, insight, and advice are only a beginning, he says. We must go to the Gospels for further directions in our spiritual journey.

"So let me ask you, where in those Gospels does Christ qualify the love He gives or asks that we share with each other? As far as the desire of each monk to leave the world is concerned, I think Dom Stephen addressed that in the talk he gave in chapter this past Sunday. 'It is not the world we leave behind,' he explained. 'Rather, we forswear the ways of the world. When our life intersects with our brother's, we must not do as the world does. Rather, we must see Christ in our brother—as he meets us each day, needy, looking to us for God's healing peace and love.' There is no mention of geography in that mandate. The precincts of Christ's love have neither boundaries nor walls behind which we can hide.

"I was raised in a very traditional Sicilian household, and that's where I learned about family and the love that notion personifies. When we opened our door to anyone, we opened our hearts. If you came to my home, I couldn't think of a better way to honor our kinship in Christ than to invite you to our table and share whatever we had with you.

"Similarly, that kinship would include you whenever there was joy to be celebrated. When one of my daughters was married, my wife and I shared our happiness with all whom we counted as friends. How far does that sharing go? Obviously my wife and I hold places and times apart for our special intimacy. Aside from that, our home and our celebration of family represent the means by which we tell someone they are special. They are friends. They are Christ.

"When I first came to share your life and that of your brothers, I was deeply touched and honored that the community invited me to your table, allowed me to rest under your roof, to participate in your prayer. I can only try to tell you how rich an experience it was for me to stand as one of you in the early morning, listening to God speak in the psalms.

"Knowing I was welcome here made work which has not been easy, manageable. I don't know why God saw fit to call me to do this thing. There are a lot of writers who are better at this business than I, and nicer human beings to boot. But he called me. I am enclosing a copy of the introduction to the book I hope to write about this experience. Maybe it will help you understand why I believe I must use my skills in a better fashion than I have ever done before.

I wouldn't dare do less than that. That's why I'm trying to learn as much about your life as I can.

"God blessed me and my wife with five very beautiful children, and we tried to teach them the value of family as we had been taught. If at any time, they had made a guest in our home feel uncomfortable or unwelcome, as you and certain of your brothers have tried to make me feel, they would have been called on the carpet pretty quickly. They would have remained there until I was satisfied that they understood why their conduct would never be acceptable and they convinced me that they had learned a very important lesson.

"Michael, the youngest of them, could not let a day go by when he didn't find a way to share and love. If God made you, you were his family. He was killed in an auto accident not long after his eighteenth birthday. I am still praying and asking God to help me understand why he allowed death to take that loving person and leave behind people whose capacity to love and share would make a stone expressive by comparison.

"I am sorry you and the others have only been able to see my presence in a single stereotyped way. My request for an interview was really an attempt to open a channel through which more of the love I have found here might have flowed to others.

"As you can guess, I am also offended, and so will do as follows. I will withdraw from the community and restrict my movement among you to what is absolutely necessary for my work. I will no longer come to choir, meals, or any other community activities. I would take a room outside the monastery if I weren't certain it would make any further work impossible. As soon as I can, I will finish and leave. I am, nevertheless, your brother in Christ, Frank."

16

Seen in an Obscure Manner

I FOUND a note from Father Dan taped to the door of my room at the end of what had suddenly become an uncharacteristically bad day at Gethsemani. "Don't hang yourself from the chandelier. It would ruin all the good karma the monastery has managed to build up over the years. Meet me outside after compline."

He was waiting for me as I walked out the door that led to the rear of the monastery. He knew about my run-in with Brother Bernard and also about the letter Father Bede had sent me. He put an arm around my shoulders and squeezed. "Now you know you're part of the family," he said, grinning.

"Thanks," I grumbled. "I'm thinking of putting myself up for adoption."

He laughed. "Might be tough finding brothers who love you like we do."

"With brothers like this," I said, "who needs enemies?"

Dan's face was still relaxed, but the smile had faded a bit. "Look. You said you wanted to learn what happens in here, right? A lot of us have butted heads with Bernard."

"He's an incident waiting to happen," I said. That kind of mercurial personality made me very uneasy and I pitied the monks who had to live with it. "I'm dying to know what you guys do to avoid having him blow up in your face."

Dan screwed his face into a "do you really want to know?" look and when I nodded, glanced at his watch. Finally he took my arm and began walking back into the monastery. "C'mon," he said. "Let's see if we can grab a cup of coffee from the guest-house kitchen. Then we'll find one of the visitors' parlors where we can talk for a while."

The coffee urn was still on, the visitors' parlor available, and Dan neither dodged my questions nor tried to sugarcoat his answers. "Living this close to other human beings isn't easy," he said. "Not everybody can hack it. You've got to learn to look at things through the other guy's eyes. You have to remember, this is God's business. He's the one who's breaking down your chemistry and the other guy's. He's chipping away and challenging both of you at the same time.

"The devil has a hand in this, too. As much as God's trying to make us feel his love, Satan's trying to make it seem like nobody cares, like it's useless to keep trying to live this life. God's saying, 'I love you' and the other guy is whispering, 'Who do you think would be crazy enough to love the likes of you?' That's just what happens when things go wrong in your life. You feel helpless, abandoned, worthless. You certainly don't feel lovable.

"[Feeling lovable] gets toughest when you turn yourself inside out as we do here and you realize that you're not perfect, that you have faults and habits that are going to trip you up as long as you live. That's what we mean when we talk about somebody's brokenness. You come to terms with that in the monastery. You learn to live with what you are, because you find out that what you are is acceptable to God. You know that because your brothers here accept you, just the way you are—broken, real, no facade, no games.

"A lot of monks get to the point of saying, 'I can live here, if you guys can accept me.' Now that can mean some monks will be acting out their brokenness at times. They'll be trying to come to grips with their imperfection, maybe shake it loose. The rest of us have to realize we can't interfere; we don't have the right to intervene. If we do, we pick up the gauntlet and that guy's brokenness feeds on the both of us. We're just being co-dependent.

"So if we find ourselves getting angry at a brother who's running his old number, we have to ask what it is in us that's broken. What's in me that needs to get involved with that crap? That's what this life is; that's what it's about.

"All these guys are very simple. If you belong in the monastery, as you learn about yourself, you're able to live with your brothers, love them, accept them the way they are, and stop demanding that they become something that they are not, something you're comfortable with.

"You have to relate to them. You really learn a lot of tolerance and diplomacy. You have to learn to get along. You have to. That's why most people who come here leave. They're self-absorbed, insensitive, or they just turn their brothers off. They project their own hang-ups on their brothers. If God gives you the grace and you honestly face yourself, you realize you are the problem—that if you leave, you'll take it with you.

"It means not playing games. It means you stop trying to control, especially by fake giving. You do what you can for other people. When I was cooking, I tried to cook decent meals. Sometimes they worked; sometimes they didn't. But I began to watch for times when I got extra fancy, because I might have been angling for special attention. A game. Fake giving.

"You find peace when you can break free of those games. You begin to see what's around you, who's around you. You begin to see and accept you. Things start to come together. 'This is what I need to do,' you tell yourself. Not for any return or ultimate end.

"That's our work. We've got a lifetime to do it.

"You find God in these people. As long as they're here, he's here. If you live with them, you live with him. Every guy is different—another face of God. If you don't give them false sympathy, or stereotype, you see them as they are. You see God's design. There are moments when you see us all together, as one, functioning as one, working as one.

"You realize there's a someone, my special God, here, for me. It's all these guys together as a single someone. That's real community. There are moments when that comes through. There are a lot of people on this earth of ours who never experience that.

"You see it in choir. We're together there five hours a day. It brings out everything. All sorts of things happen to you there. Year after year, day after day. After a while, it's very subtle what happens. The psalms can be very deep and sometimes they're like sawdust in your mouth. You have all these guys around you. Each of them is grappling with God and the devil. So one sings this way; one sings that way.

"I remember one day [choir] was awful, really terrible. I mentioned that to Brother Saul and he thought it was great. It was completely subjective. I was out to lunch. Saul obviously was there. Whatever you bring, you get. There's a lot going on there.

"If you're there for the show, it's not going to last. You're in here six months and then they give you these robes and it's great and fancy. But nothing has changed. Then you make vows and they put a black scapular on you and it's still the same. The time comes when you just go and do it. It's a public thing. You have to keep going back. It won't leave you alone.

"The community exists as a single entity in choir. You can really feel it—which means you accept what is there as an expression of each person, as they are what they are, different, broken, growing. That includes the times when each of us couldn't and didn't go. You can't judge why the other guy does or doesn't. Maybe he needs space, just the way you do sometimes. Maybe God's giving him a breather by allowing him to be less demanding of himself.

"This is a very simple thing that we do here. It's harder and harder for me to keep remembering that it is very simple. The joys are simple. There's an awful lot of suffering. That's part of living. Very real, very strong. Often we find joy in just getting away alone, with nothing to do, just to think or be. We have a lot of that. You see guys just wandering along on one of our monastery roads. Just spending the time of day. Just being, letting their life happen to them. It's not a real high. It's very simple.

"You find all of this makes you communicate differently in here. There are certain people I can communicate with easier. Like Bede."

I was shocked and it showed.

"That surprises you? Well, it surprises me too. He and I couldn't be more different. But on a nonverbal level, we get along. Just eye contact is a big thing. It's very joyous. Sometimes he'll just bump into me accidentally on purpose. Something like that, spontaneous jostling, something physical. But it's also very affirming and supportive. And very simple.

"It's like he and I are telling each other, 'Hey, you're here. I'm glad. Isn't it great we're both here?' That sort of thing. That's where the joy is. I've seen people who look for more and it doesn't work. They want more interaction and it's not going to happen.

"Of course, there are close friendships. Saul and I are close. We talk and share what's happening to us. But you can't come here and demand that someone be your friend just because you think they're neat and [they] like what you like or something like that.

"There are people who come here looking for contact, like an addiction. They have a hard time, unless they realize that what you are demanding is not what you're here for. God is going to reach out to you through other people, through your brother monks, but unexpectedly, on his terms. You can't be a child and throw a tantrum because it doesn't happen according to your schedule, or somebody doesn't roll over when you clap your hands. Most of the guys here will just tell you to go take a hike.

"Some people just can't make use of this life. They're fine to meet, briefly. They're just wonderful. But day in, day out, they're a burden. They're the people you have to tiptoe around all the time. They always want their own way. They're just psychologically dependent. They can't or won't do this or that.

"Every family has them. You have to carry them. Overly dependent personalities like that can suck the place dry. There's a real limit to the number of those any community can handle.

"Not that any of us are perfect. All of us have our moments, when we're in one or the other category. Mac likes to say that 'We all have our bad days. Thank God we don't all have them at the same time.' You learn to spot people who are having a rough time. You give them space. But the ones who are always on edge make it difficult. They can fool you, blow up when you don't expect it, like Brother Bernard chasing you the other day. He can do a lot of harm to the community. That kind of thing destroys trust.

"Guys like that used to act out their aggression in the old days. They'd break into another monk's room, tear it up. That doesn't pass nowadays. It's not allowed to continue unchecked. If the monk's not in solemn vows, it might be goodbye time. If he is vowed, he might be sent away for a time, maybe to another abbey.

"Sometimes they can be helped by therapy and in those cases, we've got an outside professional who has worked with us for years. [For] the monks who have to live with a brother who's working out that sort of problem, well, it takes an awfully big person not to be hurt, not to react to the slights, the humiliations, or the memory of them. It takes someone who's acting off the God life.

"You'd have to be here about six months to pick up all the tensions. Then you see the little feuds, maybe become part of one yourself. Maybe somebody turns you off, gives you the cold shoulder, and you decide not to look at him or talk to him either—kind of an 'I'll get even with you, brother.' It's surprisingly easy to play into the devil's destructive little game. You fool yourself into thinking it's no big deal—you're only teasing the other guy.

"And it rarely is a big deal. Maybe one of the brothers is in a crappy mood and he simply won't let you get in front of him. I remember the time one monk took a whack at another monk in choir. We're all bowing to pray the doxology and we hear him yell, 'Knock it off' and before you know it, he swats the guy. Turns out the other guy had been teasing him, twisting his tail, just because he thought he was such a stuffed shirt.

"More and more people are coming here looking for a community that is really an emergency room, where people are going to be good to them, patch their wounds. Love is something else. You have to be able to stand alone. You get healed when you heal others. You don't love to get love. You can't go around as though you have a right to sympathy. You can't have a shopping list and call it loving. If you try that, things will get tough and you'll find yourself saying, 'Hey, God, what's going on? I gave up everything to come here. Now you gotta be nice to me.'

"That's when you're going to hear God talking through the monk who tells you to get lost. That's not because we're self-involved; it's because most of us realize that if we respond to superficial friendship, it's going to perpetuate behavior that doesn't belong in here. Eventually, [you'll] have to leave.

"All that matters is how we go through this life—completely free of ulterior motives, letting God have his way, obeying what happens as a manifestation of his will. If you don't try to set things up, that's what you'll see. Talk to anybody who has been involved in spiritual direction, counseling monks, and that's what they'll tell you happens all the time around here.

"If you try to fake it, like put on a show, you're going to have a very hard time. There's one guy here who still has this notion of piety. He's going to learn that that's not what life is about. Humanity is here, not holy pictures. If you really want to live life directly, you can do that here.

"A moment comes when because of the simple daily life, you reach a point where you have to say you're willing to let the real person live this life and the 'show' person has to go. It's painful. You have to be willing to say, 'I'm weak and vulnerable.' And you realize that everyone is going to see you like that. You're going to stand naked. But you also know as sure as you exist that these guys will accept you as you are—real, weak, vulnerable.

"You replay a lot here. Like constant therapy. The more I talk about it, the more I can see my own patterns—where I've hurt people, where I've fled from them. I see the things I've developed in my life. If you're here and you're serious, you say, 'Hey, I'm supposed to be loving and I'm not and what are we going to do about it?' You just continue and live the life.

"A while back, I asked Stephen if I could work with our therapist on some of my stuff. I really wasn't letting myself go. I think I was afraid that maybe I'd really like someone—you know, fall for the guy. Well, that's something I've got to confront, and I'll never do it by holding back. You're living with these guys twenty-four hours a day. You have to like somebody. It's tremendous to see yourself breaking open and trusting to something you've never let happen, not knowing what's going to happen.

"I have a greater and greater sense of being someone I never knew I was. I told the abbot it's amazing to me that I can talk about this. He said it's about time I cracked and became myself.

"All of us have had some part, some change that has made [us] authentic. But you can't demand that the other guy open up, or see a shrink.

"There are guys who are superprivate and it's very sad. Without their wall, [life is] very painful and frightening. This place is supposed to be about loving. Well, you find out that you have to love the guy who may not love you back and you have to be able to withstand the temptation to stop and not try again.

"Love is really a one-way street. If you really appreciate someone, you do that, and you do it without saying, 'I really appreciate you. Why don't you appreciate me back?' You can't do it as a bargaining lever, because then you haven't done anything at all—just developed a new wrinkle in an old game. That doesn't work. If you're lucky, you'll get kicked in the teeth like you deserve.

"You have to learn. We all struggle with it and we hurt each other in the process. But there's a lot of charity here. A lot of people have been through a lot of this stuff. If you can touch them, they turn out to be very human. They've had deep hurts and loves. Very real.

"You'd have to be here a long time to see how God moves through the brothers. You see it in the manifestations of a real life-giving friendship—instances where two people trust one another to be intimate, share their lives—'Hey, this happened to me.' It happens enough to allow people to be human and to keep their spiritual senses open to others.

"There are those inspired moments, too—when one monk sees another having a hard time and realizes that his brother needs someone he can trust and open up to, when the perceptive monk can step up and be just the brother someone in need can trust.

"It's a delicate thing, the need for real love and the ability to give it. How do you hold someone, just listen, be there? How often can you move into someone's vulnerability and come away clean, certain you didn't exploit the circumstance or set up a dependent relationship?

"Even though we live in here and sometimes ask ourselves, 'Where did we get this bunch of crazies?' we try not to be too hard on each other. There's a great shyness here. It takes compassion to understand that. Most monks are not high-powered. They're simple. I meant it when I said we walk around naked. You can't hide anything from people who see you twenty-four hours a day. There's a real absolute necessity for aloneness. Some monks are really concerned that we'll lose the solitude that's preserved by enclosure. People coming and going can be distracting. Solitude can get torn down. What we do as Trappists could get lost.

"The world outside values social interaction. It's a priority. There are people out there who can become very holy by social interaction. But we're called to be Cistercian monks. Solitude is our priority. We need that. We're protected by this setup. It's because we're weak that we need that. If we didn't have it, we'd probably be disreputable.

"That's why people like you get a negative reaction. You're a typical New Yorker: high-powered. You're outgoing. That can overwhelm a lot of monks. They don't have big gifts. They have very little ego, few gifts. They live with insecurity. That doesn't go away overnight. Sometimes it never leaves. That solitude helps people become very real and direct here. People come in from the outside and they sense the effects of that solitude. They experience something from the place.

"Those are the people we allow to come all the way in. Stephen has a real touch for that. It's like a spiritual radar. He senses who will be part of the prayer here—those who can benefit from an opportunity to live like us. They come to choir, work, attend community events. That's an experience, but you have to realize it's not the same as it would be if they came for life. It's different when you commit yourself to live here for the rest of your life.

"That's taking on an experience you can't resolve. You commit yourself to living in flux. It's unfamiliar, disorienting. It's supposed to be. The whole thing of shaving the head, changing the clothes. They say it's like marine boot camp. But the Marines are finding people collapse when you tear down their identity or what passes for an identity outside. We're experiencing the same thing. People get disoriented, they dig down, throw out the facade, and find there's nothing else there. People come here with great veneers. Depending on what happens, you lose the veneer. If it gets too bad, you can crack up.

"You get drawn in. You begin the spiritual journey. We tell them, 'It's going to hurt.' Stephen tells them they can get burned. You can. We try to discourage guys. We tell them, 'You have to want to go through this thing. Are you sure you want to? Why don't you keep your job? What would happen if you waited another year outside?'

"The ones God calls can't let it go. They want to do this. They want to confront themselves. They come here and begin to live life from moment to moment. No games. Simple. They stop reading the spiritual literature for directions and standards and somebody they can imitate. They realize you don't have to do that. You just *be*. That's very liberating. Just being. Doing what you have to do. You go to choir because that's what we have to do. It's having a secret that no one wants to hear and you don't have to tell.

"Nobody really knows what's deep down inside somebody. Even you. That's what happens in here; that's what the solitude allows. You turn inward. There's nothing to distract you, so you begin to look at yourself. You never stop. You go deeper and deeper. There's always something new you learn.

"I remember hearing one abbot say that everybody comes to us wounded. It makes sense. When you figure that about 96 percent of people grow up in one or another sort of dysfunctional setting, then everybody's got some wound that needs healing. That's what this place is about. It provides the circumstance in which people can become whole. It helps you work on your wounds, your dysfunction. It calls for a real selflessness, orientation toward others.

"This is a very serious business. Who are you before God? Are you prepared to stand there and hear the answer? Can you let whatever happens happen? It's hard work. That's what we do. It looks romantic. The trappings, the sight and sound of all those holy monks praying in choir. But it's simple. You get up and pray when you're tired and the psalms bore you and then you clean a bakery storeroom with hot steam in the middle of the summer. Very simple. But it can drive you up the wall. And if you give it half a chance, it can also bring you face-to-face with God."

17

Called
by God

My LETTER to Father Bede had made him confront doubt and uncertainty that had been accumulating for some time. The Rule and authority had always been paramount in his life, beyond challenge, a taskmaster for whom the best effort was never enough. But life was supposed to be difficult. One carried one's cross, pausing only to add to the load. That was the path to Paradise for miserable sinners. Happiness in this life was simply to be regarded as the seduction of pleasure, the fork in a road that led to perdition.

It all made sense; it had always been logical, provided Bede lived in a vacuum. What challenged his thinking was the realization that his modus operandi inflicted the pain he sought for himself on others. He could readily take up Christ's cross if it relieved his Lord of the burden. But there was something wrong when his choice of pain and hardship served as a portion to the Christ who came suffering in the person of Bede's brother. Christ, hanging from his cross, asked for drink and Bede offered him a sponge soaked in vinegar.

It had happened again. From the beginning, when he had first felt called by God to give his life as a monk, Bede had begged to have his vision made clear. "Let me see you," he had prayed over and over. "Do not let me pass my brother, lying wounded in the road. I believe, Lord. Help my unbelief."

There was no question in Bede's mind that he had been blind. He glanced again at my letter and then at the copy of this book's introduction, which lay in his lap. *God called this man and led him to you,* he said to himself. *And you would have turned him away.*

"But good Father in Heaven," Bede said aloud in anguish, "would you have me substitute my miserable judgment for that of others, so many others, who formed this way, who set its rules according to your inspiration? Me, the man whose choices have never added to anyone's happiness? How can that possibly be pleasing to you? What kind of God needs a sacrifice of suffering?"

Frustrated, pushed finally to that point where logic can no longer indemnify inhumanity, Bede began to weep. And his tears were those from time past as well as the present, for all the moments when suffering had no meaning, when he had to stand powerless in the face of pain, when the powers that be seemed to scorn the offering of himself as a substitute sacrifice.

He had been abandoned as an infant. A priest at the Catholic orphanage thought the name Christopher most appropriate when he baptized him. Even then, the weight of the world seemed concentrated in his large, sad eyes. That overly serious expression proved a marked disadvantage. Childless couples quickly turned away from a stare that grew ever more judgmental as years passed. A sturdy frame may have redeemed him in 1930, when Tom and Mary Powers carefully picked the seven year old as their first foster child. Later the same year, another boy, five-year-old Martin, would join him and five-year-old Patsy, the couple's only natural child.

The income Mr. and Mrs. Powers realized from the government subsidy for the keep of their two foster children enabled them to manage when many of their unemployed peers were often homeless as well as hungry. Aided by Christopher and Martin, Mrs. Powers was also able to cover many of the superintendent's chores that earned the family rent-free lodging in the basement of an upper middle class apartment house in Sunnyside, a predominantly Irish neighborhood in Queens, New York. The bulk of the family budget came from Mr. Powers's position as a patrolman with the city's police department.

Leisure and laxity were synonyms to Officer Powers, who saw to it that his foster sons were not exposed to either. "Spare the rod," he would say to the baker, nodding. He rarely completed the phrase. Like so many others, the baker had heard the sermon that followed many times. His head bobbed obediently as he filled a bag with day-old rolls and bread each morning. He had children of his own. He well knew that the poor unfortunates the Lord had placed in the burly policeman's care needed an even stronger hand than most. Discipline was the yeast of sound citizens. It also made for an unusually soundless household, where men who worked the early morning hours might get their sleep when the rest of the world was awake.

A dollar moved slowly through the Powers household and Christopher was surprised when he was allowed to finish high school, with the proviso that he retain his job at the neighborhood delicatessen. By the time he was a sophomore, conscientious performance had earned him a promotion from general helper and delivery boy to counter clerk. By then he had come to know Kathleen Loughlin well.

She had been the smiling, friendly face that greeted him when he delivered groceries to her family's well-appointed home. Though two years younger than Christopher, she seemed able to help him forget his shyness. Their doorstep pleasantries grew longer and longer, until Christopher found himself sprinting back to the grocery store to make up for the precious minutes they spent chatting. By the time he began his senior year in high school, they were meeting regularly, albeit without her father's knowledge.

Mr. Loughlin deduced the extent and direction of the friendship from Kathleen's frequent mention of Christopher. After a brief inquiry, he made what he felt was a critically important point. It was one thing to be polite to the delivery boy, he told his pretty daughter, but she should keep in mind the plans her father had made for her. Those did not include any degree of serious relationship with an Irish orphan who at best might end up a New York City civil servant like his surrogate father.

It was Mrs. Loughlin who risked her husband's wrath by encouraging the relationship and keeping its existence secret. He was such a quiet, polite young man, she told Kathleen. And those lovely eyes—they did make you want to get a smile out of him, didn't they?

Christopher's eyes drew no smiles from Patrolman Powers—merely a pointed observation. "Enough's the problems I have with the likes of him looking down their noses at me all day. Mind you don't add to them because you're not man enough to control yourself."

Patrolman Powers's tone was understandably different on the afternoon of 7 December 1941. Patriotism guided his remarks that day, with only an allusion to the fact that Christopher's eighteenth birthday would come in a week's time. The government subsidy for his keep would end on that day. But duty weighed more heavily on Powers's mind, he said. Any real

American knew where duty lay. Besides, the smarter of them, those who volunteered, stood to gain over the yellow bellies who waited until they had no choice. In the army, Christopher would also begin to earn a man's salary early in life, which would allow him to show gratitude, in the form of monthly allotments, to those who had been the agents of his government's benevolence toward him for so many years.

Christopher's enlistment in the army materialized the war for Kathleen, as it did for anyone who became party to its jeopardy. She and Christopher had been prepared to overcome whatever obstacles might lay in the path of their marriage. But military service and certain combat were circumstances before which their determination was as nothing. Those circumstances precipitated despair that was fiercely manifested when they met to say goodbye on the day before Christopher had to report for basic training. It took their strongest resolve not to step over the line beyond which passion pulled insistently. Only the assurance that they would see each other again in six weeks' time saved them.

The letters they sent each other almost every day further charged the atmosphere for the farewell both knew would be coming, when he would be sent overseas. Somehow they would find a way, they promised each other. God would not ignore the plight and prayers of two people who loved each other so much and yet had managed to resist such strong temptation. But such hope and faith seemed in short supply when Christopher came home for two weeks' leave. When he returned, his unit would be headed overseas, almost certainly to combat.

Mrs. Loughlin discovered degrees of creativity even she didn't know she possessed, while screening Kathleen's whereabouts during the two weeks. A feigned illness won time off from school and hours of daytime for the couple, but Kathleen still had to be home for dinner. When business called Mr. Loughlin out of town two days before Christopher's leave was up, the three conspirators figured a providential God as a fourth hand in their game. It seemed so until the final evening, when a dark future seemed to shadow all hope. Then the unanticipated time alone became part of the message they discerned in their circumstances. Surely God understands, they told each other. He who was love had to understand theirs and the affirmation they gave each other in its physical consummation.

Christopher was training with American troops in England by the time Kathleen became certain she was pregnant. She pledged her mother to secrecy, thereby sentencing the poor woman to perpetual fear and anxiety as the time approached when it would be impossible to conceal the situation. Kathleen's weight gain finally prompted her father to question her and Mrs. Loughlin closely. A medical examination confirmed his suspicions and Kathleen was forthwith dispatched to a private clinic. She would remain there until the child was born. Then she would surrender for adoption the occasion of her shame and return home.

The last letter Christopher received from Kathleen was cheerful, but still told him nothing of her pregnancy. She had transferred to a private school on Long Island, she wrote, thereby explaining the postmark. She was worried about him and begged him to be as careful as possible. She had read of the North African invasion and guessed that he might be among the troops who were fighting there.

Her guess was correct. When Christopher received the letter in the last week of November, he was lying in an army field hospital in North Africa. Doctors had just removed two small pieces of shrapnel from his leg. The battle during which he had been wounded had claimed the lives of half of the eight men in his rifle squad.

By the time Christopher waded ashore in the Sicilian invasion the following May, he was a sergeant in charge of his own squad. He and Johnny Baldisari, Johnny B., were the only ones left of the original squad that had landed in North Africa. Their lone survival was a circumstance that would repeat itself in the three-month Sicilian campaign that followed. By the time the pair slogged wearily away from the deadly Salerno beach landing, Johnny B. at least had become superstitious. He accepted a promotion to sergeant and command of his own rifle squad only if he could remain close to Christopher.

Superstition did not begin to answer the questions in Christopher's mind. The men under his command were getting killed, even though he followed orders and procedure as closely as possible. They were his responsibility, a large one now that he was a platoon sergeant, the ranking noncommissioned officer in charge of three squads, twenty-four men in total.

He resolved to exercise even greater care in the combat that faced them as American forces battled their way toward Rome. He had to supervise the men more closely. Obviously, he and Johnny B. had survived because they stuck to the book. He had to see that the men did likewise. That had to be his objective. He had to concentrate and give it his full attention.

Concentration had become difficult—at times, impossible. Christopher had stopped receiving mail from Kathleen. When he finally managed to persuade Patrolman Powers to check into matters, he learned that the family had moved away and left no forwarding address. He would do well to put the matter out of his mind, Powers advised. He had to avoid situations where feelings controlled him. There was no place for that luxury in his life. "Stick to business and stay alive," he wrote. "Congratulations on the promotion to first sergeant. No doubt about it being important. The increase in our allotment check says that plain as day."

Christopher's mood was only slightly less bleak than the conditions that plagued Allied forces in the closing months of 1943. The coming of winter brought cold rain that turned the fertile black soil of southern Italy into a quagmire. The mountainous terrain gave the enemy further advantage. Crack, seasoned German troops dug into position; their artillery and automatic weapons zeroed in. All roads may have led to Rome, but the men who fought alongside Christopher paid a costly toll in lives for every inch they traveled.

Few portions of the journey were as costly as their passage through the Liri valley. When Christopher's outfit arrived at the entrance, early in January 1944, they were confronted with the Rapido River, a stream that, though narrow, was deeply dredged and rapidly flowing. A buddy of Christopher's in the engineers shook his head pessimistically when he described the job he saw ahead. "We ain't paid nothing yet compared to what this one's gonna cost," he said.

Crossing the river would be only the beginning of their trial, he added. High on the mountaintop to the north stood what would soon be perceived as the living embodiment of their enemy, the ancient Benedictine abbey of Monte Cassino.

Saint Benedict himself, the man regarded as the founder of Western monasticism, had fled to that mountaintop in the sixth century. There he saw to the organization of the order that would nurse Western civilization through five hundred years of history. The Rule Saint Benedict wrote while living in that lofty retreat would govern monks to the present day, its words and maxims repeated until they became like daily bread.

By the time American GI's saw it glistening in moonlight, Monte Cassino had already been destroyed and rebuilt three times. Christopher remembers thinking that its walls had no beginning. They seemed to be the smooth extensions of the rocky slopes that led to them. The five-story structure was the mountain's top. Four levels of windows looked like sockets through which the enemy's eyes monitored every movement in the valley below.

Rumors already in circulation indicated that the abbey was not to be touched by gunfire. Seasoned veterans like Christopher shook their heads in disbelief. They had already been bloodied on the peaks and slopes of southern Italy's mountain ranges. Such an order, if it in fact were issued, would concede the enemy an incalculable advantage.

Everyone could feel German troops watching, gloating, as the Americans tried to cross the Rapido for the first time on the night of 20 January. Christopher had added his own private briefing to that given by their company commanders. Their orders were to cross the river and hold on at the other side at all costs. He reminded each of his squad leaders to double-check the men under them. Intelligence indicated the enemy was dug in not far from the points where the squads would emerge from the river.

Christopher knew the luck he had experienced in the previous months could not possibly survive the coming engagement. He punched Johnny B. on the shoulder as they stood in the darkness after Christopher's briefing. "Hell," Johnny B. said, playfully, "it's about time we both took a bath anyway."

Nothing seemed to go right, from the beginning of the operation. American artillery drew immediate answering fire when it began trying to soften up the river's opposite shore. Christopher's platoon lost its first members to uncleared mines even before the men reached the river. Those who made it across buried their faces in the muck of the opposite bank, while mortar rounds and machine gun bullets methodically scoured the earth around them.

By dawn, only the remnants of two companies held on at the other side of the river. Johnny B. had a flesh wound where a bullet had grazed his leg. He alone survived from his squad. He and five others were all that remained of Christopher's platoon. They huddled in foxholes during the two days that followed, as additional attempts were made to reinforce their position. As darkness closed over the battlefield on 22 January, Christopher and Johnny B. slipped into the icy cold waters of the Rapido. Somehow, they made it back. More than two thousand American GI's were not so lucky. Saint Benedict's Abbey had drawn its first blood.

Christopher watched, becoming ever more confused in the weeks that followed, as men continued to vanish from the ranks beneath him. Some fell when the river was finally crossed; others died on the lower slopes that led to the abbey. Christopher was always wet and cold; the rain seemed to fall almost as heavily as German shells. He and Johnny B. were part of the assault team that made one last attempt to reach the monastery during the first days of February. Fighting was especially vicious. Where the terrain was not slippery, it was blocked by barbed wire or seeded with antipersonnel mines.

Their attack had advanced within a half mile of the monastery when they had to stop. Christopher used the lull to check on the men under his command and found that he had become the ranking officer. The platoon's lieutenant was among those killed. The deaths never seemed as meaningless, or his survival more mysterious, than on that night. The abbey, where men gave themselves to God, appeared so empty and impersonal. Worse than that, it had become an active weapon in the destruction that lay all around on the rocky battlefield. Still, its status as a venerated shrine protected it. The enemy was holding God hostage.

All of these thoughts swirled in Christopher's tired mind—questions he could not answer in a world he could no longer control. People were dying and he was alive. A church became a fortress and was respected as though it had not. He was relieved when he crawled to the lip of a small crater and found Johnny B. huddled with one other member of his friend's dwindling command. "Hey, Sarge, you're late," Johnny B. said, as he slithered over the edge of the crater and rolled down beside his friend. "I was wondering when you were going to get here."

Christopher relaxed, eager for the joke he knew was coming.

"It's Friday, Sarge. If we can make it up to the monastery by Sunday, we'll be in like Flynn. Those guys up there were Italian before they were monks. I'll bet they still eat like kings. If we get there in time for dinner, they'll roll out the red carpet. You'll eat like you never did before."

Rain had turned to snow when New Zealand troops fought their way to the American position a week later, on 11 February, and relieved them. Christopher was one of the few men able to walk down the mountain. Most of the others, including Johnny B., started that retreat on stretchers. Enemy fire tore and taunted them. As Christopher stumbled along behind the men carrying Johnny B., he was embarrassed by a feeling of utter helplessness. Nothing worked—not his care, not his concern, not even the force of right. Lives had slipped through his fingers like sand. What had he done wrong? What had he left undone? Why had God abandoned him?

Enemy spotters in the monastery had noticed the movement of Christopher and his men. Their shattered condition had confined them to well-established trails, funneling them through a merciless gauntlet of death. Whatever price they might already have paid would not buy them safe passage. They were the leftovers from a macabre meal. Efficiently, effectively, enemy gunners were picking their bones.

Christopher had fallen back to the rear of the column, checking his men as each passed. They had to hold on, stay alert. They could not surrender to the numbing fatigue. As the last man passed, Christopher paused and looked back up the mountain for stragglers. Death was reaching out greedily from the house of worship that it had perverted. When he looked back, the first mortar rounds were exploding on either side of his men as they cleared a bend in the trail. He raised an arm and began to scream a warning that froze in his throat. It took only a moment for fragments to scythe the column.

Johnny B. was still alive when Christopher reached his side, but he was struggling to finish words he could only whisper. Johnny's eyes were glazed as Christopher knelt beside him and bent his head close to listen. "Firmly resolve . . . help of thy grace," he heard his dying friend say, "to confess sins . . . do penance . . . amend my life." He coughed and then smiled as his eyes focused on Christopher. "Hey, buddy . . . you ever get to monastery . . ." He coughed again. "Ask for prayer menu . . . order for me . . . all the trimmings." Christopher thought he felt Johnny's hand squeeze his just before Johnny inhaled deeply, as though in relief. Then the eyes and smile froze and the only sound was the silence that marks life's departure.

Three days later, Christopher watched as wave after wave of B-17 bombers destroyed the abbey with six-hundred-pound bombs. Whatever satisfaction that gave his cheering buddies dissolved when they learned that the New Zealand troops were thrown back when they attacked in the wake of the bombing. Enemy troops had found even more impregnable positions within the monastery's ruins.

Major Griner, the Catholic chaplain assigned to Christopher's regiment, made it his business to talk with each of the men as they were taken off the line. Christopher worried him. Although every soldier had watched at least one of his buddies fall beside him, combat had stripped very few as it had this particular sergeant.

He was holding it all in. That was what bothered the chaplain. Christopher had politely refused to talk. He was OK, he said, and only wanted to get back into combat, where he was needed. He did not like being idle. He requested a new combat assignment. Major Griner intervened and saw to it that Christopher was assigned, at least temporarily, to a supply unit. That work kept Christopher in the Monte Cassino area.

He was ferrying supplies to the front lines when the Abbey passed into Allied hands on 18 May. The victory could not have been more hollow. Early in May, the Allied high command had decided to try bypassing the mountain, as had been suggested months before. Alerted to the almost certain success of that strategy, German troops had slipped away from their positions during the night. When Polish troops crept cautiously into the abbey, they found it empty and in ruins. The destruction had been as unnecessary as all the death that had preceded it.

A week later, Major Griner was on his way up to the abbey to say mass for the Polish troops. When he asked the commanding officer of Christopher's unit if Christopher could drive him, he learned that the sergeant seemed to be having trouble. He had become even more reclusive. He never spoke. He did whatever he was asked, then returned to his bunk and lay there, staring up at the ceiling. The chaplain found him there when he stopped by.

He needed a driver to take him up to the abbey, Major Griner said. Would Christopher be able to spare the time? Christopher's eyes flickered toward the chaplain and remained staring at him. Then he reached into his pants pocket, took out a folded sheet of tissue-thin, pale blue paper, and offered it. His eyes never left the chaplain's face.

It was a piece of V-mail, postmarked from New York, January 1943, addressed to *Corporal* Christopher Powers, United States Army, North African Campaign. As vague as the address was, the army's postal service had refused to give up. The letter, worn from handling, was waiting for Christopher when he and other weary veterans were temporarily removed from combat. "I hope this will reach you somehow," the letter began, "and I pray God will give you the strength to accept my sad news. Kathleen loved you very much and I gave her my word that I would let you know what has happened if anything prevented her from doing so."

Mrs. Loughlin had written the letter. She had urged her daughter to write and tell him when Kathleen first found out she was pregnant. There was some way out, she was sure, but both she and Kathleen were still trying to find that door when events sealed it closed. Kathleen had died giving birth to the baby, which had been given up for adoption immediately afterward. Mrs. Loughlin wished she knew more, but as it was, she had risked her husband's fury to smuggle the information out. "My greatest fear," she wrote in closing, "is that our lovely Kathleen may have died without the last sacraments. I pray for her soul every day and hope you will join me in that effort. God watch over you. Mrs. Martha Loughlin."

"Why?" Christopher asked, as Major Griner finished reading the letter. "Why has God taken everyone he placed in my care and left me behind? Please. Tell me why."

The chaplain would try to answer, but first he wanted to pray over it. "Men have been finding answers up in that abbey for hundreds of years," he said. "Come with me. I'm sure we will, too."

The trip to the abbey was eerie. Burial details had removed the dead, but the terrain itself had not healed. Craters and foxholes were intermingled with sandbagged emplacements. In some instances, spring wildflowers had begun to sprout innocently alongside abandoned weapons. Portions of walls outlined what was once the most imposing abbey in Christendom. The statue of Saint Benedict inside the principal cloister had been decapitated. It was there that Christopher had served as altar boy for the mass Major Griner celebrated for Polish troops. It had been the feast day of Saint Bede and Christopher followed the liturgy in a small missal the chaplain had given him.

Saint Bede had been an English Benedictine monk who lived in the eighth century and was renowned for his scholarship. Christopher read the gospel slowly and continued thinking about it as the chaplain went on with the rest of the mass. Christ told his disciples they were "the salt of the earth," the medium through which men would be brought to their God. They were to use their lives for lights, setting them up high on stands so they could illuminate surrounding darkness. "What light has my life been able to shed on those around me?" Christopher asked himself. "I've been of no help to anyone."

There is a purpose to everyone's life, Major Griner said to him after mass. Saint Bede, hidden for his entire life in an English monastery, made knowledge available to men for hundreds of years after his death. However productive his life may have been, though, he died, as all of us will one day, the chaplain said. "For everything, there is a season, Christopher. All those men, the woman you loved and who loved you, they all had seasons. We must believe it was sufficient for God's purpose, and that he still has something in mind for your life."

Johnny B.'s act of contrition came to Christopher's mind. He had asked for Christopher's prayers, just as Mrs. Loughlin had done. There was no question about that. That was his purpose. He would make it so. There was nothing to go back to in New York. God wanted him to do penance somewhere else. He would find that place.

THOSE events were distant memories, ones Father Bede had not thought about for a long time, until he received my note. Gethsemani was a place for penance, he had always believed. God found the means to bring people there. The Almighty did not need publicity. "But who am I to question?" Bede now asked himself. "I've been like the centurion, ordering others, so blinded by my pride that I left no room for my Lord who never orders but only loves. I have hidden behind the letter of the law, fixing creation at what it already is and ignoring my purpose: to help it become so much greater."

Bede felt the need to be as close to God physically as he could imagine. He needed tangible affirmation—the sight and sound of God's house. He got up and walked down to his stall in the abbey church. It was time to listen, he felt. He tried to quiet his thoughts, but images from the past crowded his mind, always dissolving into the face of Kathleen. Smiling, laughing, reassuring him of the power of their love, she seemed so present, nearer than ever before.

He wanted to weep and was about to surrender to that desire when the sound of someone else weeping caught his ear. He had thought he was alone and now he looked around. It was late afternoon, so the church was dimly lit by the setting sun filtering through the tall windows.

There was someone sobbing in the new guest area beneath the old balcony. The sound called to him, even as an instinct reminded him that to respond was forbidden. The cloistered area was separated from the guest pews by a velvet rope. The pain reached him from across that wall of velvet and Bede knew he had to go to the Christ who hung sobbing from a gibbet made of everything that had always crippled Bede's efforts to love. He got up and walked toward the figure. When he reached the velvet cord, he grabbed it almost in anger. He knew now that love was never meant to be bound. Unhooking the rope, he half-flung it to the floor and moved toward the pew.

The young woman who sat there had not heard him approaching.

"Please," he asked, "is there anything I can do?"

She brushed most of her tears away with the handkerchief she held in one hand and as she turned to face the figure beside her, she heard him draw in his breath sharply. There was no explaining the resemblance, but the face that Bede saw was Kathleen's, more beautiful for its indisputably real presence before him. For her part, the young woman, Betty Ryan, was no less stunned. The Trappist monk standing in front of her looked exactly like her father.

18

Faces in the Mirror

THE DAY had been long and had left Dick Ryan weary and wondering whether his effort had yielded any fruit at all. He was sitting on the edge of the bed in his Manhattan hotel room, alone, far from home, and only a little closer to solving a mystery he wasn't certain he wanted to unravel.

When he was in his late teens, his parents had told him he was adopted. Not that he cared. They had married in their forties and the opportunity to adopt Dick came when they were convinced their age was an insurmountable obstacle to having the family they both wanted. They treated their infant son like the miracle they honestly felt him to be. The resulting love had formed a bond that transcended biology. They had died of heart failure, within months of each other, Dick's mother first.

Upon learning that he might himself succumb to cancer, Dick began rummaging through his important documents, trying to put them in order, in preparation for the worst eventuality. His adoption papers were among them, still in the envelope into which his mother and father had placed them. A paper clip held a small handwritten note from his father. If Dick ever wanted to locate his real mother or father, it said, Holy Innocents Children's Services in New York City might be the place to begin his search.

Dick had finished one phase of treatment for his cancer and a close friend had urged him to be evaluated by specialists at Memorial Sloan-Kettering Cancer Center in New York City. After his tests were completed, Dick had phoned Holy Innocents and spoken to the authorities. They could not give him any specifics over the phone, they said. There was a possibility, however, that the people who had surrendered him for adoption had left instructions that might be helpful.

They had indeed and Dick quickly followed the trail they blazed to a private residence for the elderly in a Westchester suburb. The supervisor who had spoken with him had not been very optimistic. Mrs. Loughlin had an advanced case of Alzheimer's disease, she said. Although doctors had had great success treating many such patients, Mrs. Loughlin had not been one of them. She stared into space for most of her waking hours, virtually catatonic. When Dick and the supervisor found her, she was sitting in a wheelchair, where she was held upright by the harness. Sunlight from the wall of windows at one end of the dayroom washed over her, making her white hair glisten.

She had shifted her gaze and smiled when the floor nurse crouched down in front of her chair. She showed few signs of recognition, beyond the simple smile. She always smiled, the nurse said. She was one of the happy ones, smiling gratefully, sometimes even thanking those who fed her and helped her into her wheelchair each day. Mrs. Loughlin's world had finally become a happy place, one where people always did nice things and only the brightest of memories ran like an unending motion picture.

The smile vanished when Dick got down on one knee beside the nurse. Mrs. Loughlin looked puzzled. She focused on Dick's face and then looked at the nurse. She seemed to be asking for help. Then the smile returned, noticeably brighter, and the old woman leaned forward against the restraining brace and reached out. Very gently, she touched Dick's face.

"Christopher," she said. "You've come back. Kathleen will be so happy." Then she turned to the nurse. "He's a monk, you know. Went to the monastery after the war. To the Trappists—the ones who never speak."

He must have closely resembled someone from the elderly woman's past, the nurse later told Dick. Images from the past had often stimulated patients like Mrs. Loughlin. Use of such images was the principal form of therapy, in which the staff used old songs, photographs, and vintage motion pictures to help patients recapture their memories. Any success was therapeutic, a hedge against the disorientation that often terrified the elderly. Although retrieved memories often scrambled past and present, the experience made the patients happy. They had remembered. They still had some control.

The floor nurse told Dick that Mrs. Loughlin often spoke aloud, mentioning her "little girl, Kathleen" and "that nice young man." It was an unvarying stream of consciousness that would leave her frowning and sadly wagging her head. "Such a nice young man," she would say. "A Trappist monk."

Mrs. Loughlin had left instructions when she entered the residence many years before. If someone—specifically, a man—ever came searching for her by name, then he should be allowed to see her. She was still reasonably coherent when she detailed those wishes, a widow with sufficient means to arrange for her care until she died.

It was she who had left similar instructions with Holy Innocents Children's Services, where Kathleen had been sent to await Dick's birth. When Mr. Loughlin had surrendered Dick for adoption after Kathleen died in childbirth, he had insisted that all records of the birth be sealed. His wife had successfully countermanded that order after his death. She had given her name, and permission to disclose her identity, to a New York State registry, to which Dick was referred by the staff of Holy Innocents. Mrs. Loughlin had laid a trail that led to her, so her grandson could follow it one day.

But debilitating effects of aging had betrayed her good intentions. After her brief reaction to Dick's appearance, she had lapsed back into her blissful catatonia. The cryptic information she had provided about Dick's father could only allow for speculation by the New York Archdiocesan Vicar for Religious, to whom Dick went later the same day.

The vicar's best guess pointed to Our Lady of the Valley Abbey which, at the time of Dick's birth, had been located in Rhode Island. After a fire destroyed that monastery, the community had relocated to Spencer, Massachusetts, where it was now known as Saint Joseph's Abbey. That would have been the logical choice for someone who came from New York City, the vicar believed. The only other two abbeys in existence, Gethsemani in Kentucky and New Melleray in Iowa, would have tended to draw members from their immediate vicinities.

The vicar had cautioned Dick not to get his hopes up. Hundreds of ex-servicemen had become Trappists after World War II. Armed with only a baptismal name, which the Trappist would have abandoned, it might be extremely difficult to find a man who had entered a monastery, even if one assumed that he had stayed. Religious orders in general had experienced a mass exodus during the late 1960s. Dick's father might have been part of that ebbing tide.

The meeting at the archdiocesan offices had ended a long day, one that had drained Dick's reduced energy levels. He had learned just enough to fuel further inquiry. One part of him was afraid of what he might discover. From the beginning of his search, something inside had warned him to leave well enough alone. People had told him stories of adopted children like himself who were turned away by natural parents who preferred to let the past lie dormant. Besides, a man who had become a Trappist might not be the most sociable of human beings.

His daughter Betty's college study group had covered the Trappists and she had spoken briefly about them with her parents. The Trappists had changed a great deal since Vatican II, she had said. They were not quite as reclusive as they had been before. Then Dick remembered. Betty was at Gethsemani, the Kentucky monastery, at that very moment. It was the wrong one, of course. The last clues he had about his father pointed to the monastery in Massachusetts. If he was still a monk, that was where Dick believed he would find him.

Maybe he should wait a while, an internal voice advised. Maybe he should let the matter rest. If the doctors finished with him tomorrow, then he would have no more business in New York. He didn't like being separated from his wife, especially now that illness had made life so tentative. That thought reminded him: he wanted to phone her and share what he had found.

She was happy to hear from him and relieved to learn that so far, his prospects for recovery looked good. She grew quiet when he began to tell about his search. Dick expected that. She had not been enthusiastic about his decision to trace his natural parents. Who knew what would turn up? In an effort to allay her fears, Dick tried to lighten the subject. "You'll never guess what I've found," he said. She continued listening quietly as he told her about meeting Mrs. Loughlin and he half-expected her to say, "Oh, my God" when he related the old woman's words.

"It's incredible, isn't it?" he said. "My father may be a monk. But it may take some doing to find him, if he's still there."

"I think it won't take much doing at all," she replied.

"What makes you say that?"

"Betty called me today from Gethsemani. She said she met a monk who could easily be your twin if you were twenty years older."

Breakfast at three in the refectory of Gethsemani Abbey.

Ring the morning bells, traditionally, at New Clairvaux Abbey.

Twentieth century habits.

Genesis for Trappist jams at St. Joseph's Abbey.

With psalms and palms,
the Sunday before Easter
in Gethsemani's cloister.

Gather round the Lord's
table to celebrate at
Snowmass Abbey.

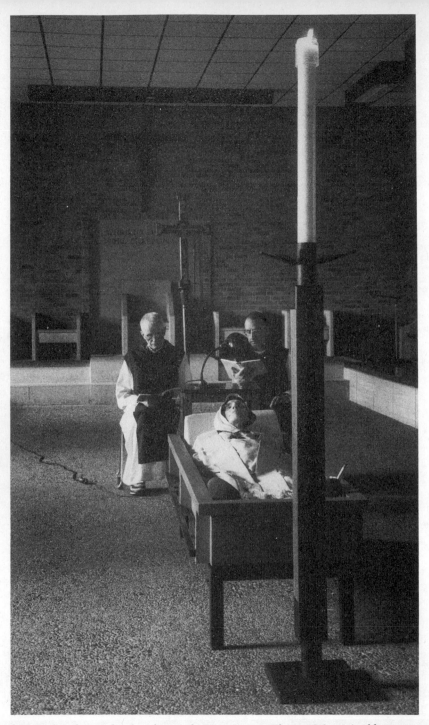

Sing psalms for our brother departed, Dom James, Thomas Merton's abbott at Gethsemani.

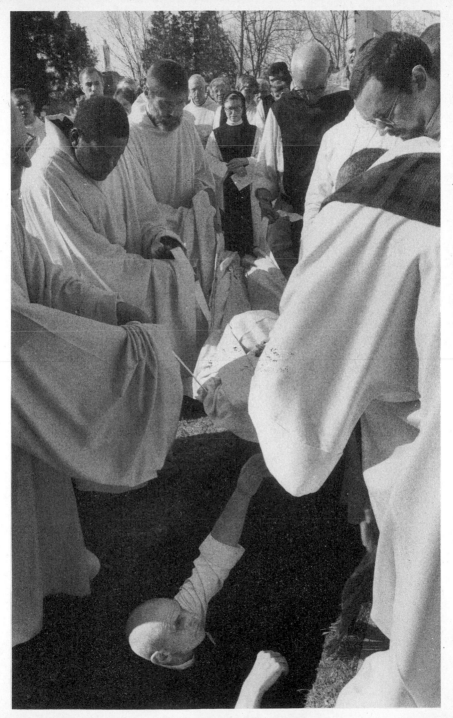

Gently lay my brother down for final rest.

Sleep, monks of Gethsemani, for the prize your perseverance has won you.

Section Four

A TINY WHISPERING SOUND

In the first book of Kings, chapter 19, the Prophet Elijah had been reviled and rejected as he tried to do God's will. When he searched for meaning, an angel told him to go stand on the mountain, for the Lord would be passing by.

When Elijah did so, there first came a strong and heavy wind that rended the mountains and crushed the rocks, but the Lord was not in the wind. After the wind, there was an earthquake, but the Lord was not in the earthquake. After the earthquake, there was a fire, but the Lord was not in the fire. Finally, after all these phenomena in which Elijah had expected to find his God, there came a tiny, whispering sound, as small as if it were nothing at all. There, in the silence, God revealed himself to Elijah.

19

Scaling the Mountain

THE SURROUNDING hillsides were clothed in the rich colors with which fall blesses the Kentucky hillocks that surround Gethsemani Abbey. The autumn air enveloped the three Trappist monks as their combination tractor/wagon moved through the open field, harvesting hay. The day was pleasantly warm, the hay fresh and fragrant. A summer of farm work had tuned their bodies, allowing muscles to respond readily, barely tested by the continued effort.

When the trio had collected all the hay from a particular area, Brother Simeon drove the tractor, while Mac and Dom Stephen rode atop the bales of hay that were stacked two-high on the open wagon. Rather than sit, they stood erect, cockily shifting their weight from one leg to the other as tractor and wagon rolled gently over the uneven field. Their ability to keep their balance was one small part of the pleasure the work gave them.

The abbot and Mac shared similar feelings about the farm work. Given a choice, both would have done it exclusively. They also agreed that the hard physical labor made them feel good. Mac had always relished the sense of vitality from the days when he had worked on his parents' ranch as a child. The abbot was a newcomer to that feeling of satisfaction, having grown up in an urban setting. He had once told Mac that he sensed a need to nurture his physical being, to allow it growth and expression. That was why he had taken up jogging. Every evening after supper—which he normally kept to a light snack—he would don sweat-suit and running shoes. His technique was quite good, especially given that, by his own admission, he had not been inclined to athletics before entering the monastery.

Both monks made special effort to take regular turns at the work schedule, insisting that they be assigned rather than choose, and that their preferences be subordinated to the regular cycle. It was just as likely, therefore, that the two abbots might find themselves cleaning toilets or mucking stalls as naturally as they might be found performing a preferred chore.

Aside from getting positive feedback from the work, both Mac and the abbot believed it allowed them to maintain and deepen their contact with their fellow monks. They readily admitted that they felt naturally in-clined to solitude, but were convinced that the essence of their vocation was to be found in communion with their brothers, relating to them in work which was as much a part of their daily prayer as any other activity.

Although a few more bales remained to be gathered, there was very little time left until the monks had to clean up in preparation for vespers. Brother Simeon had, however, resisted the temptation to drive faster, aware that his two brothers were somewhat precariously perched, despite their evident self-confidence. Nonetheless, he would later fault himself, believing he should have at least spotted the depression before the tractor rolled into it and caused the hay wagon to lurch sharply.

Mac, who was standing in the middle of the wagon, tumbled out one side to the ground. Dom Stephen was not as lucky. He had been standing toward the front of the wagon and as it shifted suddenly, he was thrown forward, his body nearly landing on the wagon's tongue. He had managed to twist himself almost completely out of that path. Almost completely. He had extended his right arm to effect the maneuver, sacrificing its wholeness. It struck the tongue and the abbot knew immediately that it was broken.

THE abbot. Spiritual leader. Father Stephen sat in his office and turned the phrases over in his mind. In his opinion, the power those words conjured up could not adequately represent the reality. The problem with thrones was that they were single seaters—a person could get pretty lonely traveling that way. The abbacy set him apart from his brothers. He worked hard to counteract this effect; thus, he still signed his name on all internal documents as "B. Stephen." "Just one of the monks," he said when questioned. "Plain Brother Stephen."

He looked at the plaster cast covering his right hand and forearm. Another barrier. It would be six weeks before he could get back to the regular routine—hard physical work with other members of the community. He consoled himself with the thought that he could at least continue running. Given the reduction he had noticed in his metabolism, the last thing he wanted to hazard was physical inactivity. He did not fancy the prospect of ballooning into a fat friar. He felt it was incumbent on him to lead by example as much as any other way.

Abbatial office had never particularly beckoned him. Not that his election was a complete surprise. He had served as undermaster (assistant) to Thomas Merton when Merton was Gethsemani's novice master. Merton had told him then to get ready. "The abbot's prepping you," he had said. Dom James had sent Stephen to study in Rome and was trying him in one of the abbey's important posts. Stephen would very likely take over the job of novice master if Merton got his wish and retired to be a hermit. "Someday you're going to be abbot," Merton had predicted.

Merton. His books dominated the double-shelved bookcase on one wall of Stephen's office, and by extension, the entire room. They had to. The only other items in the room were three chairs, one of which was positioned behind the walnut desk, whose top was always clear. Stephen wished the memory of Merton was that uncluttered. He had watched the various groups as they made their pilgrimages to Merton's hermitage, or as they held what one monk dryly described as the Saint Thomas novena.

The pseudocanonization made Stephen uncomfortable. It reminded him of the Elvis Presley hysteria. Too often, such movements missed any real contributions the man might have made. Stephen was absolutely certain that if Merton were alive, he would have perceived the movement as nonsense and discouraged it.

He had never wanted disciples; he dropped them the moment he saw stars in their eyes. In his opinion, mimicry was the enemy of personal identity. The hero-worshiper wound up playing a role, which in Merton's view was as counterfeit as making one's profession one's entire life.

Stephen was convinced that honors and offices were a potential trap. One could do as the world did—define oneself by what one did. It was easy. When someone asked who you were, you told them what you were. Easy—exceptionally so for an abbot. He could get caught up in his own vision and become blind to all that God meant him to see. In his own time, he had had the unpleasant task of telling several abbots that their vision—and their eyesight—had failed. It was time for them to resign.

That was the hard way. Stephen tended to agree with Mac: avoid the problem by limiting an abbot's tenure to six years, with reelection possible only after a successor has served for an intervening term. That way, no one would get too comfortable, neither the monks nor the abbot—who would remember all along that he was just one of the guys. Dust to dust and ashes to ashes. It was easy to lose sight of that.

Stephen was wary of the temptation an abbot's office presented. He did not want to forswear his own creativity any more than he wanted to trespass on a monk's God-given identity by ordering him to do what Stephen thought was best. In fact, what the abbot saw as "best" could easily represent the limited range of his vision, his experience.

He believed that deeply. But he could see now how that belief might tend to oversimplify the challenge every man receives when God calls him to be the agent of his love for other men. The temptation to push people in the direction you thought best was strong. It was made even stronger by people who would forfeit responsibility by letting any superior call the shots—if the superior let them. As the bewildered ruler sang in the musical, *The King and I,* "Is a puzzlement."

Often monks and retreatants would go to Stephen for counseling and come away grousing, "He just sits there and shrugs his shoulders when you ask him a question. He laughs and doesn't say a word. I'm going down the tube and he treats it like it's a joke." That perception could not have been further from the truth. As far as Stephen was concerned, the man's anguish, his problems, required self-examination. Only rarely did the Holy Spirit need assistance. Honesty was all that was needed.

That was what the monastery provided: an atmosphere of honesty. Stephen could not see any point in coming or remaining if one was not prepared to look at oneself and one's life honestly. That was why God had touched their lives and called them apart to be monks.

Stephen believed Christ was every one of them, but most of all, he was the one who turned you off, the guy who was different enough to make you turn away. For that reason alone, Stephen bent over backward to make room for anyone who knocked, no matter how difficult the person seemed to him. Somehow, though, ever since he had made that principle the bedrock of his policy, he had begun to see how everyone belonged. Moreover, he began to realize that the monastery was like an oasis. No one owned it, no matter how long he lingered, and every pilgrim had the right to rest in its shade.

The meeting he had just concluded with the Vocations Committee (Saul, Robert, and Father Michael, the prior) supported that philosophy. The monastery had a half-dozen men in the pipeline, so to speak: one monk on leave, three in the formation process and two applicants. There would have been three applicants if Robert's suspicions had not been confirmed. When Saul, as vocations director, had asked for medical records, the man had admitted that he had Kaposi's sarcoma, a cancer common to AIDS patients.

During the first review, when the committee learned the man had "terminal cancer," they generally supported his desire to enter the community, despite the fact that he would become helplessly dependent during the short time he claimed was left to him. But interviews had revealed the man's homosexuality. That alone would not have prevented his acceptance, but coupled with the presence of terminal cancer, it had made Robert suspect AIDS.

Stephen had departed from normal procedure on learning that the man was an AIDS patient. He agreed with the committee's decision to reject the application, but proposed that Saul maintain contact with the young man. He was to be encouraged to visit as often as he wished. Saul was specifically authorized to see that the man had adequate care and if there were any financial problems, he was to be assured that the monastery stood ready to aid him in any way. The proposal received unanimous approval.

The committee had been somewhat more hopeful regarding the prospects for the other two applicants. Both were in their late forties. One had come directly to the monastery from the Marine Corps, retired after twenty years, with the rank of colonel.

Stephen had seen determination in his day, but not to the degree the former marine displayed. "This is where I belong and whether you people want me or not, I'm coming in," he had said. It had been amusing to observe the man standing in choir during his visit. Ramrod straight, chin tucked, hands at his sides, he looked like a marine shavetail standing in front of his platoon for the commandant's review.

His posture epitomized his expectations of the life. He and Stephen had met for the final interview that capped an applicant's initial visit to the monastery. The life could get quite ordinary, Stephen had said. It would sharply contrast with the colorful life he had led as an officer of Marines. Was he certain he wanted to trade one for the other?

No life lacks excitement, the former officer replied. Especially not when the certainty of Christ in ever-changing circumstances came with each day's dawning.

"Wrapping cheese for that entire day?" Stephen prodded.

"Especially wrapping cheese, because it still bugs the hell out of me to put my brain on hold even for four hours a day."

One marine flyer's survival as a Vietcong prisoner illustrated his point, he said. Since the marine was the ranking officer among the Americans, the Vietcong made special efforts to break him with torture. The worst involved tying his hands behind him and raising them with a rope until his body was almost suspended. The pain in his upper body was excruciating, unbearable.

Presumably, he survived, Stephen said. How?

"He learned to love the rope."

No matter how bad it got, the prisoner believed he would be ever so slightly stronger after each session. That growth in strength became his goal. Similarly, the retired marine perceived God as most present when some aspect of the monastic life became distasteful. "If God's will has me cleaning toilets, then that job becomes something entirely different. I know for certain it's my doorway to him," he explained. "The more something I'm asked to do bothers me, the better I like it."

This recognition of the opportunity for grace—the catalyst upon which every monastic life depended—was delightfully unique, in Stephen's opinion. It was much the same with the second candidate, an old friend of the monastery, who had actually joined the community as a twenty-two year old. He had left after six months and in the intervening years had earned a doctorate in theology, taught on the college level, written several books on the spiritual life, and at one time had taught meditative technique.

Wasn't there a certain godlessness in some of the meditation modes? Stephen had asked as a point of curiosity—and a way of gaining insight into the dimensions of the candidate's faith.

"Only a foolish person blithely opens himself to a transcendental experience," the applicant answered. "Gods and goddesses live there, as does good and evil, Christ and the devil. I go there with Christ as my guide and God as my goal. So far as I'm concerned, without God, I risk wandering in an empty wasteland."

The Vocations Committee had been as pleased as Stephen was when he reported the substance of his interviews with the former marine and the second applicant. There was always the possibility that an applicant saw the monastic process—essentially aimed at healthy integration and growth—as simply a variety of psychological therapy. The monks knew that God had to be in the picture and unless they saw clear recognition of that fact in a candidate's life conception, they saw no point in granting entrance.

The committee also agreed that maturity was evident in the success the two applicants had made of life. They had not only achieved career goals, they had fed on the fruits of their achievements. Life was no idyll for them, but neither had it been a failure. They had experienced its joys and pain and explored its options. They were coming to the monastery as people came to the best of marriages—not to fill a need at the expense of another, but to share of their fullness and thereby enrich others.

Such vocations had generally worked out. These two held as much promise. In the opinion of the abbey's consulting psychologist, the results of their tests and interviews recommended their acceptance as postulants.

The tests consistently succeeded in identifying dysfunctional personalities—people who might be dependent, dishonest, or unstable. The psychologist could confidently predict the outcome of the postulant's first four months. After that, both the psychologist and the Vocation Committee agreed that everything depended on grace and God's will.

All of the Vocation Committee's members were convinced that the screening process had to be rigorous. They saw wisdom in Saint Benedict's admonition that applicants actually be tested to the point of being discouraged. The monastic journey was not for the faint of heart, nor for the religious hysteric.

It was a rare postulant who could withstand the pressure of self-revelation and the disintegration of the facade. The regimen was the abrasive that stripped away the mask, primarily due to the emphasis on self-discipline and obedience.

The unvarying schedule burdened a monk. He had to do the work assigned him, go to choir, obey the Rule. He was accountable. Any absence or failure had to be explained. As Father Robert was fond of saying, the routine made the monk-to-be "shell out." It made him look at himself, question his motives. "Figure that our regimen is nothing less than God himself," said Robert, "and he's pounding on you to do what you're told a hundred different ways, a hundred times a day. He calls out to us, hour after hour that we spend praying the psalms, in the Gospels, in the words of the best spiritual writers.

"If the Rule is no more than a pain in the butt, the candidate will leave to get away from it. But if he doesn't, if he believes God wants him here, then he has to confront his observance or lack of it. That brings him to himself.

"No one really knows what is deep down inside them," Robert explained. "In the first six months especially, there is nothing or no one to distract them or serve as a crutch. No one will play their games." That was not to imply that monks do not sometimes slip, Robert said. But the tendency to be honest with themselves reduced those possibilities and their duration to a minimum. Loneliness turns every monk inward, into the solitude that can only be found in the monastery. They begin to see themselves and as long as they remain in the monastery, they never stop. They go deeper and deeper.

The process was unquestionably artificial, Robert admitted, but its effectiveness had been proven over more than fifteen hundred years of monastic life. The solitude forces people to open themselves up to God and his healing love. Very soon, Robert predicted, the monk hears himself saying, "I never told this to anyone before," and that was when God had him.

"If you're 'normal' and can live without bumping off people, or being affirmed, you'll grow in the life," said Robert. "We know who is thriving on the life and who isn't by how generous they are. It's not hard to figure out who are the community builders and whom you have to watch.

"The first month—maybe the first two weeks—is really crucial. If you last that long, you're usually OK for a year. Nobody escapes the effect of the solitude beyond that point. Then the fireworks begin. The monk confronts the possibility that maybe he is responsible for what happens between him and other people. It's a tough time.

"Some of them show the pressure by rushing into me, moaning and groaning about how wasted they feel. 'What am I doing here?' they cry. 'Me, a writer, making cheese?' Or they may complain about being ignored or getting pushed around. We really have to watch them. Some of that's normal and they'll grow out of it. Some can't or won't."

Some of those who could not were "the tough nuts, the sleepers," Robert explained. They scored well on psychological tests and usually could resist the pressure for a year, maybe two, but not longer. Their neurotic needs were so great that they collided with the rule, which resulted in major infractions. At that point, the monk was confronted by his superiors and either began to change or left the monastery.

It was also possible that God might call people out of the monastery, Robert added. They might see their difficulty with the demands of the Rule as an indication that they did not belong, that the life was not for them. Or God might bring them to a point where they could not go any further. They just were not ready or willing and they had to leave, because as long as they stayed, the process would continue. "Once God takes the wheel, you can only be sure of two things," said Robert. "The trip will never end and only God knows where you're going next."

Stephen felt that Robert had articulated one of the monastic axioms. In his obedience to his superiors, and especially in every act of acceptance—of change and difference, of the unplanned and the unknown, of himself and others as they were—the monk acknowledged God. He found freedom when he acknowledged not only that he was dependent on God, but that he could depend on God.

In his talks to the community, Stephen often returned to the same message: For God, to know us is to love us. "If God cared for every bird, every blade of grass, and clothed the lilies in beauty," Stephen would ask, "how much more does he care for every one of us?" That was what the monk gave up when he entered the monastery—his "cares." The thought always amused Stephen. The monk "gave up" the thing he never had control over in the first place. He acknowledged the existing order. In so doing, he came to appreciate the priority God gave him in that order. Freedom (and peace) resulted.

There was only one small problem, as far as Stephen could see. If monastic life made so much sense, why aren't more people pounding on the doors to get in? Aside from the former marine and the professor, the monastery had three men who were finishing their postulancy. Two could go either way and the third looked so good, he worried Stephen. Too often in the past, the monk who looked like a sure bet was the one who walked away.

Micah had all the makings of a monk and yet the fit between him and the monastery was an uneasy one. Saul had been strongly opposed to his continuing. The novice had yet simply to do as he was told. He always had an objection; he always could see a better approach to things; there was always a good reason for him to be an exception to the Rule.

When he was assigned to scrub the newly laid tile floor in the monks' basement washroom, he argued for a delay until someone could get a special kind of vinegar with which he believed freshly laid tile should be washed. "He won't simply follow orders. He actually refused to do the work," Saul reported to other members of the committee. "He was convinced it was going to adversely affect the floor and his principles would not permit him to be party to something like that."

He could always justify talking when and where silence was the rule. While every monk recognized the need for flexibility in that rule's application, Micah bent the rule into a pretzel.

In effect, he was asking the monastery to go by his rules. He saw no reason to leave. How would the monastery ever shape up, he said, if guys like him always tucked tail and ran? "He honestly believes he can show us a thing or two," said Saul. "That's his biggest argument: He was sent here because we need his fresh approach."

At first glance, Brother Zachariah, the sixty-one-year-old former attorney, was not much different from Micah, Robert reported. But though Zachariah often objected, he eventually obeyed.

What about the matter of his mail? Saul had asked, referring to Zachariah's excessive correspondence. "Since we said three letters a week was the limit, he writes only three letters," Robert said. "But each of them is six to ten pages long—since there is no rule on their length."

The third novice, Gabriel, seemed to have resolved the difficulties that had prompted him to transfer from Snowmass. In Saul's opinion, something had clicked. Gabriel was decidedly happier, almost too much so. He had to be reminded that he was still a novice and therefore sequestered from too much contact with professed members of the community.

"Looks like he's in love with the rope," Saul joked.

"We don't want them discovering the secret too quickly, now, do we?" Dom Stephen quipped in return.

Micah was the only one who still troubled the committee. In a sense, he was breaking contact, refusing to learn to accept. It was one thing to fence with the rule, as Zachariah was doing, but quite another to refuse to do what was asked. Robert would have to confront him, everyone agreed. He would have to be told how unequivocally his opposition set him apart from the monastery.

The community was a social organization in which distinction was harmonized, but not extinguished. This harmony allowed for truer expression because it eliminated what was false. Saint Benedict had characterized the monastery as a school for service. That conception promised freedom to the monk. Micah had to learn how his urge to dominate might eclipse, rather than clarify, the matter at hand.

All three men were still trying to control their meeting with God and had yet to recognize that they could not. They had to discover the peace that came from accepting what each day brought, rather than compulsively trying to imprint themselves upon it. Lack of trust created an environment of fear in which love could never take root. Who can really say they know another person? Love grows out of trust that accepts and affirms what is unknown. Fear of the unknown made people balk and strive for control. It shackled them and made them try to set themselves over circumstances, over others. It precluded opportunities and thereby blocked God's graces.

Dom Stephen could see the struggle in the seemingly minor resistances each of the novices was making. They were as conspicuous as a battle flag with the motto, "my way." The abbot knew the trio would only see the changing wonder of their God when they reverently and respectfully allowed the world to be however and whatever God chose to make it. That was the ongoing process of creation. They participated in it whenever, by an act of will, they said, "I accept what is."

That was much more easily said than done and no one knew that better than Dom Stephen. He wondered what God intended when Gethsemani's roster grew steadily smaller. Every reduction in the community's size had a direct bearing on its life in a purely pragmatic sense. People were needed to run the place: to bake the fruitcakes, pack the cheese, mow the lawn, and fix the broken faucets. The monastery had to make enough money to pay its bills.

Although no one could remember an instance when Gethsemani's abbot might have allowed the shortage of manpower to influence him, he had been heard to joke about the temptation it posed. "I get nervous every time somebody talks about leaving," he said. He knew that the monastery as a corporate entity could only tolerate so much attrition before it felt the strain.

There were moments when he felt like a nineteenth-century New England whaling captain who shanghaied men to make up his crew. The monastery's manpower needs were sometimes just as desperate. Given the steady decline in vocations, it was virtually certain that Gethsemani and other Trappist abbeys might soon be critically short of personnel. The problem was a frequent topic for discussion when Stephen met with other abbots in the region.

According to one report made to the abbots in 1989, during the 1980s, the number of monks in the region's twelve monasteries had hovered at five hundred, but the median age had moved steadily upward until 1989, when it averaged 58.5 years. At that time, approximately 60 percent of the monks were over age fifty. Thirty percent were between the ages of sixty and seventy.

The abbots had long since noted that the ages of new vocations tended to support those statistics. Very few men below the age of thirty were applying for admission. The majority of new monks were men in their forties and fifties, so much so that many monasteries had abandoned their maximum age limit of forty-five years.

"It does make you wonder," Saul said, when I asked him to comment. "If we keep on losing men, where will this enterprise wind up? We have to consider the probability that certain of the smaller Trappist monasteries in this country might have to close down. They just won't have enough men to maintain the place, much less find an industry with which they can support themselves.

"The day could come when American monasteries are quaint museums, tour-bus stops, like many European abbeys. I'll be pushing up daisies in the graveyard and some tourist will be sitting on my tombstone, trying to figure out whether his trip—and mine—was worth all the fuss."

20

And the Lord
Was Not There

It was supposed to be Saul's annual retreat, a time for undisturbed recollection. He thought a change of scenery might help and had gotten permission to go to Snowmass Abbey. However, once he was there, he realized that the most beautiful location does not necessarily make for a peaceful setting. Not when there's work to be done and too few people to do it.

Snowmass had never been a big community and was not ever intended to grow beyond two dozen monks. For almost twenty years since its foundation, the abbey had underwritten expenses by selling eggs and hay, both of which the monks produced on their four thousand acres, high in the Rocky Mountains. But markets for both products could be calamitously uncertain, even at those times when the monastery had the manpower to cover the production.

The Abbey had dealt with that by switching to the production of cookies, which they test-marketed in their surrounding communities and slowly expanded into a mail-order operation. The success had not come easily. Finding profit-making work that seventeen monks could do without leaving their property was enough of a challenge. But the work also had to be profitable enough to pay all their bills—and only that profitable. Enough for bills, with perhaps a bit to help the local poor. Anything more might seriously compromise their vow of poverty.

Finally, whatever the monks did for a living had to take second place to their schedule of prayer and study. That was the priority. Trappist monks have been known to shut down production as soon as their needs are met, even when that means turning their backs on certain profits. Not surprisingly, that has often posed problems in a society that thinks of prayer as a way to make profits possible, and not the reverse.

At the time Saul chose to visit Snowmass, its cookie operation had grown enough to permit the dismantling of the abbey's eggery. There was just enough manpower to cover the hay growing and the cookie business, since the two peak seasons fell at different times. There were times, however, when every monk was needed to maintain the delicate balance of labor and personnel. One fewer monk could start the scales seesawing. Two fewer could tip the balance.

Manpower was not the only critical factor. As much depended on whether the work load remained constant. If a machine broke down and needed repair, Brother Arthur had to add that chore to his crowded schedule. He frequently had to say his psalms privately, often standing alongside a greasy engine, surrounded by its worn parts.

These circumstances had prompted Saul to ask Dom Stephen if he could stay at the abbey for a spell and throw much-needed muscle into the breach. On one particular day thereafter, he wondered whether his good intentions offset his lack of familiarity with a punishing work situation that often defied his efforts to master it.

The antics were pure rodeo, though the contestants lacked traditional costumes. The quarry was Jersey, a high-necked llama. Brother Arthur, mounted on a 250-cubic-centimeter, all-terrain motorcycle, essayed the cowboy's role.

Aside from the wool for which it is normally prized, the llama possesses natural, highly efficient herding skills. The abbey had decided to buy the animal on the strength of that reputation and the wisdom of that decision was quickly confirmed by Jersey's performance tending sheep. However, Brother Arthur soon found that his surrogate shepherd was quite adept at playing the lost sheep should someone leave a gate unlatched.

Jersey almost seemed to have a destination in mind as he fled rapidly across newly irrigated acres. Not that Arthur's skills weren't equal to the contest. His handling of the motorcycle would have earned respect from the best motocross pro. A rooster tail of spray traced his path as he closed in on the speeding llama, muscling the bike to his purpose, fighting the tendency of its rear wheel to slide as it alternately lost and found purchase on the waterlogged field.

Arthur had come abreast of the animal and had begun boring closer, to control the direction of Jersey's flight. He was revving the throttle, using it and his voice as prods as he moved parallel to the llama. "Get going," he commanded. "Move. Move, Jersey. Keep moving." He was using his own position and the fence to convey the llama toward the open gate, planning to force Jersey through it and then to the corral. The motorcycle began to fishtail slightly as the rear wheel spun loose from the watery earth.

The gate was ahead, looming close. Brother Saul waited alongside it, positioned to block Jersey from the open fields that lay beyond. But Jersey had his own game plan and now he set it in motion. It was as though the animal had a hidden turbocharger. Suddenly, he began sprinting ahead, beyond Arthur's reach.

Arthur was equally determined to avoid failure of his plan. If it worked, he might cut the loss of precious time; maybe he would even make it back to the monastery in time for a bite of supper before compline. The motorcycle's engine whined as he twisted the throttle to its maximum. He muttered his first "damn," as he felt the bike begin to slide out from beneath him. Desperately, he leaned away from the direction of the fall, trying to counterbalance and maintain control. A second "damn," annexed to a "bloody, bloody," came as he and the bike slammed abruptly into the sodden soil.

He looked up in time to see Jersey take advantage of the opening his misfortune created. Jersey flew past Saul, whose courage had disappeared, leaving him cowering, his arms wrapped protectively around his head. The llama decelerated after a short distance and stopped momentarily, kicking one leg scornfully backward toward the spot where his tormentor, the tall monk who curtailed his freedom every night, lay in a small lake.

"Damn. Double bloody damn," Arthur sputtered as he got stiffly to his feet. "C'mere, Saul," he said disgustedly, adding another string of damns, as he tried to purge himself of the water, the strain of overwork, and the force of a temper that was as difficult to control as was any fleet-footed llama. "C'mere and help me lift this friggin' thing."

Arthur moved awkwardly, grimacing with the discomfort of his bruised body, as he and Saul stood the bike erect and mounted it in tandem. They began to ride slowly away from the field, the acreage Jersey would own until tomorrow. Only then, and probably only after precious additional hours were expended, would the animal be retethered to rules that it seemed only Trappist monks were bound to obey.

HELP Wanted: Position available for bright, healthy male, interested in challenging career opportunity. Long hours; low pay. Benefits negotiable. Team players preferred. Start immediately.

Somehow, though this ad has never run, people keep answering it, eager for the challenge. Some choose to apply at Snowmass Abbey: one branch, so to speak, of the institution that might very well sponsor such an appeal. It is very likely that the Snowmass applicant will cross paths with a tall, thin man wearing dark sunglasses that contrast with his white, neatly trimmed sea captain's beard. A yellow baseball cap, faded jeans, and running shoes will seem no more casual than the man's way of introducing himself.

"Al," he'll say. "Name's Al. I'm the abbot." Despite the white beard, Dom Alexander will look far too young and behave much too informally to fit the popular notion of a Trappist abbot. His appearance and manner will seem more in keeping with the coffeehouses of nearby Aspen than with the cloisters of a monastic community, especially one that ranks as the most austere order in the Roman Catholic church.

Sixteen monks elected Al as their abbot in the mid-eighties, a choice they immediately ratified by kneeling before him and pledging their unqualified obedience until the day they died. According to one of them, the years have vindicated their choice. In his opinion, Al is a perfect balance of brother and, when necessary, the father whom they are convinced will always act in their own best interests.

When Al was once told of that characterization, his smile quickened with acknowledgment but soon gave way to embarrassment. He did not see himself in the autocratic mode associated with monastic tradition. Like Dom Stephen, he saw his role more as that of a facilitator, someone who helped each of his brothers to be the best monk he possibly could be.

Al had other concerns as well. For the most part, he and his fellow monks had chosen to keep their mountain-ringed abbey "open." They believed openness was necessary in order to share their spiritual life-style and, in turn, to be exposed to the Christ who came knocking on their door in ever-changing guises.

Men who came out of curiosity, or out of a need for the abbey's therapeutic solitude, were often attracted to the life. Many had joined the community. So the monks welcomed outsiders—"the other monks," Al called them—and took special effort to incorporate them into their ongoing prayer.

John Bonam was a good example. Unmarried and in his late forties, he had spent the greater part of his life as a peace pilgrim. Though often dismissed as an eccentric or fanatic—or both—he believed strongly in the value of witnessing to the call within him. For him, there was no possibility of compromise with destruction and war. His sense of the oneness of humankind did not admit of opposing forces. He had been jailed, beaten, and punished in all the ways an errant society tries to remodel its critics along politically correct lines.

Bonam had found his way to the abbey after one particularly exhausting campaign in the latter part of the Vietnam War. Though not a Roman Catholic, he found nourishment in the life of the monks and especially in their liturgy.

Initially, he respectfully observed the monks from an outer orbit, reluctant even to risk disturbing the integrity of their solitude. But the monks of Snowmass soon discovered their new guest's personhood. Like the wedding guest in Jesus' parable, Bonam found himself being called to a more intimate affiliation—a place closer to the head of the table. It became a regular practice of his to swing by the abbey whenever his work permitted.

And whenever he did, the monks welcomed him as a brother, opening their hearts and hearth. Often he was mistaken for a monk candidate as he chanted with the community in choir and moved freely through the cloister.

Bonam's case was only one example of the way in which Saint Benedict's Abbey was responding to people who wanted to share in the monastic experience. Like many Trappist abbeys, it had dramatically expanded its retreat program.

Originally, such retreats were restricted to weekends and retreatants confined to areas outside the cloistered quadrangle. The monastery offered a structured program that interspersed periods of prayer with individual and group conferences. The only other contact with the monks and their life came during those periods of choir when guests could watch and listen from balconies or closed sections at the rear of the monastery church.

After Pope Paul VI called on monasteries to explore ways in which they could further share their life, Snowmass was one of those that began to extend the lengths of visits and the degree of involvement in the monks' daily life. By the beginning of the 1990s, a small number of American

Trappist abbeys were allowing guests to stay for a month or longer and to live as though they were members of the community.

Snowmass was one of the first to try such a policy and Brother Gabriel (who later transferred to Gethsemani) had the distinction of being in its first such "class." For several years, the abbey also had a married couple living in a house on the monastery's property. The couple participated in the liturgical schedule, worked part-time for the monastery, and often joined the monks for meals and special celebrations.

Snowmass Abbey was especially distinguished by the way in which it made its liturgy available to people from outside the monastery. There were no choir stalls in its church. Instead, the monks sat in two facing rows of wooden armchairs. When the monks chanted their office, guests were encouraged to join them from their places on the stone bench built into the church wall, right behind the monks' chairs.

Once each week, the chairs were augmented and arranged into a large oval. At one end was a small wooden table, atop which was a single candle, a glass chalice of wine, and a basket containing large, flat, circular loaves of bread. This was the setting for the celebration of mass.

Everyone remained seated throughout the celebration. Only at the offertory did the monk who was celebrating mass leave the circle and go to the table. There were no genuflections, no elaborate gestures, no florid phrases—nothing that would detract from the vivid impression that this was precisely what Jesus Christ shared with those he loved on the night before he died.

Openness was a two-way street for the monks of Snowmass Abbey, who were freer to leave the enclosure than were Trappists in other monasteries. In Al's opinion, exposure of that kind was good for the monks. It allowed them to meet people of all ages and gender. Contact provided the monk with another opportunity to acquire experience.

Al believed the concept of openness gave his abbey a special charism and made it relevant to this particular period of history. However, there were critics of openness who found it threatening. Al's predecessor had been a monk for twenty years and a priest for most of that period. Then he had left the order and married. "Some people would like to leave that bundle on the doorstep of openness," said one monk.

"But that guy wasn't the first monk—or abbot—to bail out. And an awful lot of those who left did so when monasteries were closed up tighter than a drum."

21

The Spirit in Motion

THE MATTER of monks leaving had not particularly attracted my attention, but mention of abbots did. A monk's departure is always difficult for those who remain behind. It can safely be said that every monk is troubled by doubt at least several times in the course of his life, especially at those times when it is not going smoothly. Those doubts are triggered anew when another monk leaves. Said one monk, "When it happens, your thinking can get skewed, especially if you've been close to the guy. It seems like all the good guys leave and you get left behind with the clinkers."

An abbot's departure compounds that anxiety. He is the man the community has chosen to lead, the one monk they believed had lived their life so well that he was possessed of special charism, affirmed by God himself. The situation is not unlike the breakup of a marriage precipitated by one partner's repudiation of the union. The couple's children are apt to grow wary of the marital state. They certainly will examine the possibility of marriage much more cautiously.

I was not so guileless as to believe monks were immune to the same faulty judgment that could plague any human relationship. But the truth is, I expected more of monks. They had become heroes to me and I disliked learning they had clay feet like the rest of us. I said so to Mac one morning as we walked to work.

Whether I realized it or not, he replied, I had touched on one of the pivotal points of the spiritual journey. People who are devastated to learn that their heroes are human after all, probably were just as overwhelmed to learn that their first heroes, their parents, were fallible, he said. Most often, they are no less demanding of themselves. "Peel away the skin of a perfectionist," he said, "and you'll find an overidealized parent directing the psychic traffic."

People need to feel that somebody has all the answers, that somebody is in control. They spend the major portion of their lives and energy trying to gain and ("they think," Mac emphasized) keep control. "They're trying to prove they're perfect," he said. "It's a self-delusion that the devil himself bought. 'Let us be like God,' he urged all those poor angels who followed him into damnation."

Understanding required recognition of the existence of a loving God and an evil force that he allows to test the strength of our love. "Ask yourself," Mac suggested, "why you need to have us monks [be] perfect? Why are you disheartened to learn that abbots leave and get married? Did it shock you to learn that monks sometimes cope with their sexuality like pubescent teenagers and masturbate? It's not so much that you're unreasonably tough on us as that you're unreasonably hard on yourself. You still don't understand God's love."

Perfect love, he explained, can not even see imperfection. A perfectly white circle can not have the tiniest touch of any other color or else it isn't perfectly white. God is perfect love. Evil is self-love. It is philosophically impossible for God to even "think" of evil. He can not "see" evil. It is completely outside his orbit. That fact tells us what our final judgment will be like, Mac explained.

"We will come before all-perfect love (God), who can only recognize love. He will only see as much of us as has been loving. *That* he will take unto himself. To be condemned to hell is to be unrecognized by God. Just as the neurotic is tortured by the conviction that he is unlovable, hell will be an eternity of that torture.

"Sin and evil are nothing less than our inability to love. At those moments, it's as though we're invisible to God. He, the all-good, perfect lover, can only see the good in us. That's why he loves us just the way we are."

That notion of love stems from the enduring genius of Saint Benedict, who succeeded in articulating it in his Rule for monks. Inasmuch as it specifies virtually every aspect of a monk's daily life, there is a temptation to mistake it for the expression of a martinet's personality.

Saint Benedict specifies what a monk should wear, how he should eat, work, and pray. He describes the role of monks and of those superiors who will help him fulfill that role. In his determination to create a spiritual hothouse, he insists that any monastery be completely self-sufficient, equipped with whatever machinery, lands, and work as may be necessary to sustain the community.

Unqualified obedience overlays regulations that Saint Benedict ultimately subordinates to compassion. This is the key to understanding why the movement Saint Benedict started has endured, even though its particular expression may have changed several times.

He levies penalties against those who are late for the night office but also urges the monks to chant the opening prayer slowly, so that late risers will have extra time to make the deadline and avoid embarrassment. He details what is to be eaten but suggests serving two cooked dishes "on account of individual infirmities, so that a monk who cannot eat of one for whatever reason, will be able to make his meal of the other." He accommodates humanity again when he writes about the use of wine. "Nevertheless, in keeping with the needs of weaker brethren, we believe that a hemina of wine a day is sufficient for each. . . . We read, it is true, that wine is by no means a drink for monks, but since monks of our day cannot be persuaded of this, let us at least agree to drink sparingly."

St. Benedict did not want to give up on anyone. Of ten chapters that deal with transgressions of the Rule, seventy percent of them urge the abbot to admonish the monk not just once but twice and even a third time should it be necessary. Even then, he calls upon the abbot to pray and solicit the prayers of the community for a recalcitrant brother.

Monks are individuals, he writes in one of many cautions to abbots who will have to implement the Rule. An abbot will have "to coax one, scold another, persuade still others . . . a difficult and arduous task" that requires "adapting himself to many dispositions . . . according to each one's character and understanding. . . . Let [the abbot] know that he has undertaken the care of weak souls and not a tyranny over strong ones."

Several times, he counsels the abbot that he "must adjust" if he is "to avoid losing any of them." Adjust. Understand. Accept. Overlook? Yes, in the best sense of loving, because that was Saint Benedict's primary objective for monks: namely, that they grow in the love of God by loving as God does.

It is a theology of redemption, one that pivots on the notion of forgiveness as it flows from an act of loving. Saint Benedict knew that love was blind. A real lover sees the beloved just as a mother sees her child. He or she can do no wrong. Such love transforms the object of its affection.

Literature provides many examples of this dynamic force. Cervantes's Don Quixote sees not the sottish barmaid, but only his lady Dulcinea. His insistence, despite her protests, literally brings forth the lady of his vision. Who can doubt the power of such faith, which also kindles the cockney flower girl's metamorphosis into the well-mannered English lady in Shaw's *Pygmalion?*

In the theology of redemption, God is more than just a lover who readily forgives the faults and misdeeds of his creations. He never "sees" the transgression. The notion of perfect love can not admit of a nonloving act. God knows his creation, loves it, and recognizes it only to the degree that it loves and is good. He can not "see" the bad in his creations.

To be compassionate toward others is to love them (and see them) as God does, Mac said. But first we have to be able to give the same compassion to ourselves. "Remember what I told you that first day we met?" he asked. " 'Nemo dat quod non habet'—you can't give what you haven't got. If you're not happy with yourself, you can't be happy with others. And you can't be happy with yourself unless you can accept *you* the way God does.

"You begin to see how exciting it is to be your own person and you're able more and more to accept people as they are, to give them the same benefit of the doubt that your own difference deserves. You're able to back off from judging others.

"After all, how do you or any of us know what God's plan is for that abbot, who may only seem to have bailed out? Maybe, in God's plan, he hasn't at all. Or maybe if he did, God's waiting around the next bend in his life to nail him with another chance. They don't call God the Hound of Heaven for nothing. He never has any problem bringing order out of what we see as chaos and he never gives up."

What I also needed to understand—and accept—was the existence of a powerful catalyst, Mac pointed out: grace. I would never see the enormous potential of the monastic way if I considered it no more than good psychology. I would never know the dimension of humanity that went beyond itself to the level of the superhuman, to the level of the divine—not to the point of being God; rather, to the point of being like God.

In Mac's opinion, people had far too limited a notion of compassion, one that blinded them to growth and constricted their ability to contemplate. For example, he said, at various times in the history of monasticism, its numbers had soared. Though each boom spanned hundreds of years, they all seemed to have receded. "Not so," he pointed out. "Monasticism always pops back up again, appears essentially the same, fine-tuned to fit a different society's needs.

"We—you, I, everybody—have to remain open to the Spirit. The minute we start worrying about what's going to happen to Trappists, we're in real trouble. We're hanging on to what we know and have become comfortable with. That's neither obedient nor poor. We're trying to own, to control.

"It makes me laugh when I read about the big crisis in the church because of the dwindling number of priests. Baloney. We don't have a vocation crisis. We've got a vocation bonanza on our hands.

"Just stop and think about the great thought that's coming out of women in the church. Listen to the sermons lay deacons are giving. Look at the nourishing liturgy the laity have designed for themselves in the so-called priestless parishes. God's called them and they know it. They're realizing that they're not sheep. They all have the makings of shepherds. God doesn't want us to be perpetual children. He wants us to be full-grown, responsible adults—persons. The Christ that dwells in each of us deserves that degree of self-esteem.

"People are taking back the franchise Christ intended them to have when he established his church. They're searching for ways to make their lives meaningful. They want to be happy. The Holy Spirit is moving among us. Trappists might be losing numbers; they may even disappear as other expressions of monasticism have before them. So what? What's important is not how people get closer to God, only that they do."

22

Finding Peace

GETHSEMANI'S NEW guest house had created a ripple effect in the monastery's spatial arrangements, leading to the relocation of Dom Stephen's office. It had never been an imposing space, unless austerity is regarded as a decorating motif. The new office was even smaller and when I met the abbot there, I jokingly asked whether people who came to see him had to step outside to change their minds.

His resonant chuckle reflected a state of mind that was obviously untroubled. He shrugged his shoulders and said that less was really more in the monastery. The space he used could wind up owning him if he was not careful.

"There's a side to poverty that's really freeing," he said. "The moment you own anything—or anyone—is an instance in which you have really given away your freedom."

But, I objected, that theory, taken to its logical end, would discourage the simplest of pleasures. "I could no more love someone than indulge a fondness for ice cream," I said.

"No, no, you're wrong. The act of ownership restricts your ability to appreciate [something] by confining it to your use. If I personalize this office, I reduce its ability to be of use to anyone else. Think for a moment of the reasons why people grow jealous. Isn't it usually because they perceive something or someone of which they've grown fond is bringing joy to another?

"You are really open, really free, to the degree that you let go. If I hold on to just the simplest thing, I'm less available to the opportunity that the next moment of life offers me. Take the business of being a monk. If we're not careful, we could limit ourselves by retreating, confining our lives to a particular mode, or piece of geography.

"Maybe I limit my social contact with the world outside, but reading increases my experience and appreciation of people, of this world in general, even as it leaves that world free to be appreciated by others. That's what's so different about centering prayer. I allow God to be for me in whatever way he chooses. Really."

Dom Stephen finally clarified that concept for me. The problem I was having came from my continued insistence that centering prayer follow my preconceptions. I even became unhappy when I got distracted while praying. "We simply have to allow God to be, he said. "That's what it really is all about, isn't it?

"Not easy for people who have been taught to imprint themselves on as much of life as they can." Theoretically, the monastery is supposed to reduce those things that suck you in and prevent you from growing. We don't have to worry about housing, clothing, food, or health care. Do you know that only one one-thousandth of the general population enjoys that benefit?

"But people are people and even when you free them from those cares, they find others—"important" issues and concerns to occupy their time and energies. I call them the trivialities. Triviality can shackle monasteries. Everybody's got a few inside their head. So every once in a while, you can have a bunch of trivialities occupying a lot of people. Monasteries do that.

"Big monasteries do it more than little ones. Committees, meetings, debates accompany every decision. We spent months debating whether to allow non-monks to join us up in the church when we celebrate mass. I remember I was visiting Snowmass once and there were only a few monks for mass. The other monks had gone out to listen to Mother Teresa talk. We just turned around to the congregation and invited them to come up and celebrate with us. That was so nice and spontaneous. Like a married couple making love right when the spirit moves them.

"Monasteries are relevant but subject to distortion. It can become a case of 'me' and 'my feelings.' You can get trapped in that sort of preoccupation. It's a hazard of solitude, introspection. In the Tibetan tradition, the self-cherishing thought is the enemy. In Western monasticism, it's *the* problem.

"I remember Ed McCorkel (he was abbot at Berryville for a while) used to say, 'If we're not careful, we'll become a PBA'—a pious bachelors' association, all wrapped up in our own little worlds.

"We get a whole lot of self-preoccupation. 'As long as I got mine' is the battle cry. Goes on all over the place. Worrying about how many centimeters' space exists between me and you at table. We forget that everything in the universe is related. We forget we're all part of Christ's mystical body.

"You can have one monk bothered because another is so involved with choir, he won't come out and give a hand which in the former's mind makes him a workaholic. But on the other hand, those tensions, even the picayune crap, can be a healthy thing.

"Balance isn't static. It's the result of adjustments among values. Like a trip to the moon, it isn't a straight line. It's a whole lot of adjustments, going on all the time. It happens with people. I was a different person at each age and stage. There are things I couldn't do [when I was thirty-five that] I can now do and I'll do things differently ten years from now.

"There's balance between guys running out and guys wanting to close the doors. There's a danger in being too serious. There's danger in always being funny. Some monks have an inner strength that allows them not to be thrown by what people do and some have to develop it. It's all part of the diversity.

"The monk's life is really very creative. Like a painter or a poet, he is inspired. He listens, combines what he hears with his own uniqueness, and produces something beautiful. Great paintings and great poems can't be produced by an assembly-line process. Contemplation can't be scheduled any more than you can open your arms and catch the wind. You can only stand and feel it on your face.

"Monasteries are a great treasure in society, a very rich kind of place. There's a spectrum, a certain richness of personalities. There is space for a great variety of personality and values, art and work, approaches to God. You see that better in a bigger monastery.

"People who are shy or effeminate aren't ostracized in the monastery. Personal styles, different personalities, are honored in a monastery in a way the world won't allow. In a monastery, you can have and do have the hermits, the people whose style keeps them out of things. Solitude is valued in here. It gets priority.

"The art is to decide how much of that solitude you give away and how much you reinvest. The monk has to keep reinvesting in his withdrawing work. The monastery should have a variety of views about that art, that objective, how you do that. [That art] revolves around our relationship with neighbors, hermits, each other. The trick is to blend different monks' ideas of that—get the best each has to offer.

"For example, I believe a monastery belongs more to the people outside than it does to the monks. People outside are no less needy than we are. Our job is to look at each person who comes, diagnose their need, and give them the share of our life they require. Discernment—that's what it's called, and what it's all about. Listening to voices. In this case, to which voice is neediest.

"But that's a two-way street. The monks don't have a lock on holiness. At this banquet, we're all guests at God's table. Remember, people who come here bring Christ to us just as we bring him to them. They share with us in the same way that we share with them. As the words in the hymn say, 'One bread, one body, one Lord of all, we are one body in this one Lord.'

"It's hard to sustain that in light of the tendency to think of the monastery as 'mine.' Americans have a highly developed sense of privacy and property. People who think that way have to be reminded that the Son of man had nowhere to lay his head.

"The thing everybody has to remember is that the monastery is a place where withdrawal is honored and respected and, most of all, preserved. But it's a notion of withdrawal, not desertion. The monk is a lover. He may hate the ways of the world, but he loves the people. His prayer is not for himself. It's for—and with—everyone. How could it be otherwise? Each and every person, whether inside or outside the monastery, is something God created, another piece of God."

THE day was warming comfortably as I bicycled past the palm trees that dot the main road inside New Clairvaux Abbey. It was late April and northern California was shrugging off the winter that afflicted it like I never dreamed. "Makes the Northeast seem tropical by comparison," said Brother Michael, a Vermont native who was one of the monastery's founders. "We get out in January to prune the plum trees and the cold crushes you like a vise. Palm trees we may have, but Palm Beach this ain't."

The bike I was riding is one of a fleet at the abbey, a hallmark of its life-style. They're mostly clunkers—ladies' bikes that allow monks to pedal about the monastery's sprawling acreage while wearing their habits. Brother Benjamin, a block of a man whose sinewy forearms still bulge though he is in his late seventies, is the bicycle man. A gifted mechanic, he continually takes the cast-off bikes that the monastery buys at yard sales and police auctions and restores them to life.

His work is a form of gifted scavenging. Seldom are the "new" bikes usable. Wheels may need spokes; shift mechanisms may need rebuilding; coaster brakes may serve as mere reminders of what they once could do. No matter. Either the bike is recreated from Benjamin's small warehouse of parts or it is itself broken down for some future amalgamation.

There is something very satisfying about the work, Brother Benjamin said ("It's pieceable," he joked). He gets enormous pleasure from knowing that his mind and hands can rehabilitate something that has been written off, that he can draw from experience and synthesize new mechanical unions. These bicycles are a distinctive part of the life at New Clairvaux.

Every monk has one. They adapt the bikes as necessary to the work they may be assigned, and so one sees wooden platforms where a rack might normally be affixed, perhaps partitioned to accommodate pruning equipment or small pots. The ingenious configurations represent Benjamin's creativity matched with one of his brothers' needs or wishes. Pete rides one notable example.

On one of his daily errand runs to nearby Chico, Pete had passed the campus of Chico State College. One of the bicycles racked outside caught his eye. It was a recliner model. The frame had been reconfigured so that the rider reclined with his back against a narrow rest, his legs stretched out in front of him. Pete was fascinated. He left a small note, identifying himself, expressing his admiration, and inquiring about the bike's genesis.

Not very long afterward, he received a letter from the owner of the unusual bike acknowledging the monk's interest and rewarding it with a copy of the plans that had been used to fashion the bike. It took Brother Benjamin sixteen hours to produce a duplicate.

The recliner was now parked outside the one-story stuccoed building that Pete shares with Brother Adam's small bakery. The former has about 75 percent of the space for his pottery while Adam uses the remaining space to prepare the community's bread.

Pete had begun to work in ceramics only after he had become a permanent part of the New Clairvaux community. Serendipity distinguished his work. While he kept painstaking records ("I'm a 'Techie', remember?"), he constantly experimented with glazes, so much so that each time he fired a batch, the colors were unique. Only rarely did he replicate a color, preferring to see what might happen rather than be restricted to what he had already done.

There was a new lump of clay on one of Pete's wheels and he was preparing to work it when I walked in. The wheel's platform spun rapidly as he pumped the treadle beneath it and cupped the clay with both hands. Slowly, an amorphous mass took the graceful shape of an hourglass.

It was pure accident, Pete said—entirely unplanned. "I never sit down with something in mind," he told me, his gaze still fastened on the emerging form. "I just let it happen. It's an absolutely reliable insight into where my head is at on a particular day."

Tall, columnar forms, such as the hourglass, he explained, are decidedly masculine, whereas the round, squat forms, which he often fashions into graceful coffee mugs, are feminine.

"If the shape is masculine, I know I've got to watch myself with my brothers," he said. "I'm apt to be overly critical, maybe a little too aggressive. If I see a feminine form emerging, I can relax. That's a sign of gentleness, patience, the characteristics of a more submissive, accepting state of mind. For a guy like me who once thought macho was all, it's good to see the Holy Spirit coming across with the grace I—and the people who have to put up with me—need."

I was reminded of Pete's notion of balance as an essential objective of personal growth when I began studying the way monks balance work and prayer in their lives. Aside from being a source of income, it seemed to me that work allowed the monk to develop an appreciation of his body— physical self-esteem. But the change from self-sufficient agriculture to food products manufactured on an assembly line has decreased the possibilities for positive feedback that farming often provided individual monks. In one of their regional meetings, Trappist abbots agreed that the assembly-line nature of their current work tended to be boring and not at all conducive to contemplation.

Might it be possible, I wrote to Pete after I had returned home, that the Trappist of the future would turn to athleticism? I knew of many monks, including the abbot of Gethsemani, who jogged. Although many initially began running as a means of caring for their health, a good number of them admitted that they found the activity rewarding—that it gave them a good sense of their physical natures.

Pete agreed with my thesis and took the subject in an entirely new direction. "There is also one other balance I find necessary," he wrote.

"Work and play. Normally you don't hear much of 'play' in a Trappist monastery—and I don't mean football and baseball. What I mean by play is activity that is done for pure enjoyment, nothing else.

"Work is something done out of some need. That doesn't mean you don't enjoy your work—just that the only reason for play is enjoyment. For example: In the past I used to do pottery for fun. There was no work associated with it. Then I was invited to turn it into a business. So, for a few years now, it has been work. Not that I don't sometimes do it just for fun. But now it's different.

"You see, sometimes when I sense my balance is off (even with the work I'm doing), I go out and weed in my flower garden. Weeding in a flower garden is pure play—if you can believe that!

"In fact, yesterday (Sunday afternoon) as I was pulling out the weeds among the zinnias, I thought to myself: I think the real reason for the garden is simply to grow weeds so I can spend time pulling them out (when I need to play—or rather, when my balance calls for pure play!).

"What is important about play is that it is like prayer—we can only do it when we look to God. In prayer, we look to God for him to take care of whatever needs taking care of. In the spirit of play, we look to God to be taking care of what needs to be taken care of—otherwise we can't play!

"If God is not taking care of things, then we better be doing that. So, only when we have a sense that God is taking care of everything, are we free to play—like children can only play when they know that Mom and Dad are taking care of all their needs!

"So I trust that you are keeping a proper balance of play and work in your life and I hope your book will be a good mix of these elements also. And if you're looking for something you can do for play, try growing flowers. But make sure you leave room for the weeds. Bet you never thought of them in that way, heh? Why not?! You'd never appreciate the flowers if you couldn't compare them to the weeds—and God took the time to make them, just like he did with the flowers. Nice balance, no?"

Yes, I said to myself when I read the letter. Nice balance!

Pete's description of play as a necessary ingredient in a balanced life—everyone's life—reminded me of the point he had emphasized in our conversations: The Trappist's way of life was simply one way of answering God's call. It was nothing special, he had said repeatedly, and its essential practices were as available to people outside the monastery as they were to the monks.

Mac had implied the same point when he theorized that monasticism as it was known in the twentieth century might disappear. The essence of monasticism wasn't linked to a monastery. I had heard others echo that thought. Although people were increasingly interested in the contemplative life, they might not regard monasteries as relevant to its fulfillment.

That prognosis had been repeated by individual monks in virtually every monastery I had visited. They noted decreasing vocations and worried that their beloved monasteries might someday become museums. Some argued that the development was an inevitable consequence of changes that "opened up" the monastery and made the life "too easy."

While every monastery had moved in the direction of making its life more accessible, none had experimented in the way that Snowmass Abbey had. Dom Alexander and I had discussed their experiments while I was there, but I wanted to put this question specifically to him: Did he see an end to monasticism? If not, what role did he envision for it, given changes that were taking place? Dom Alexander's thoughtful answer indicated that he and his brother monks had carefully discussed the matter long before I posed my questions. His letter follows, slightly edited.

"Dear Frank: I hope they keep the place open long enough for me and my brothers here to finish our job, and somehow, I have a feeling monasteries will be with us for a while after that.

"I believe God invites each of us to come away at times in our lives, to join with him more directly. The monastery is one such invitation. It corresponds to a deep part of the human existence, a desire we all have to be in touch with self, spirit, God. It seems to flow from a willingness to forgo legitimate pleasures, options, material comforts. All of it comprises the archetype of monk that Mac so eloquently describes. People respond to it and find themselves in need of living simply, in the present, the moment, to be open and available to God.

"I think some of those who foresee an end of monasticism realize that we don't have to live in a monastery to do that. You can do it in all sorts of places, all kinds of life. But I think they are overlooking what seems to be a call to live that way of life in an environment that externalizes it, where effort is made to focus the environment into an ongoing opportunity. The monastery is a culture in that sense, a medium if you want to call it by another term, with parts and portions that aren't really different from what you'd find elsewhere. But here they become a sacrament—an outward sign instituted by God to give grace.

"People are stimulated and nourished when they come into contact with this medium, when they muster the courage to stretch into what is very different here from their usual environment. They grow. They come here on retreat, and they're touched by the sight and sound of our liturgy, by the silence we observe and in which we encourage them to participate. Those parts of our life trigger something in them. They carry it off. Some stay longer, remain in the culture. God calls them to that, just as I'm sure he calls others away from this place. But I think he's going to continue to call people to live this life, in this way, to serve as a spark, a reminder, a sacrament.

"Our experiment—allowing men to come for six months and be formed in the monastic way—is one of the principal ways we share our life. We respond to God's call by responding to others who themselves have heard his invitation. The way our monks here go out into the community and interact is another. Both of those represent ongoing efforts to give us opportunities to grow, and to give others the same opportunities. We're benefiting from their God life and letting them benefit from ours.

"You've got to keep that in mind when you try to project a future for monasticism, just as you have to include in your projection the fact that monks don't have a monopoly on the God thing. There are a heck of a lot of saints who were married, raised kids, worked in the world, and never saw the inside of a cloister.

"Also, remember that none of what we're doing is static, fixed. It's always open to adjustment, fine-tuning—depending on how and to what we believe the Lord is calling us as a monastic community. If we're to evolve to more sharing, individually or as a community, the Lord will show us.

"All of that is part of our monastic life. Each of us has his or her own process of growing through and to our own integrity. I'm sure it's back and forth. And it always involves allowing Christ to come into our lives by behaving Christlike to others. We never stop trying to find ways to make that more possible. Most of all we try to do that for each other right here, and thereby fulfill our mission to be the model, the witness for Christian life.

"For example, since you were here, we've begun to use a facilitator to help us dialogue and grapple with this process, help us learn to know ourselves better, relate to one another more honestly. So far, we've had several group sessions at the monastery. It's more than developing inter-personal skills. It's opening us up to the deeper levels. We're learning how we can get in touch with ourselves and share more honestly and lovingly. Hopefully, this will help us push a little further than some of the things we have done before, maybe lead to a deeper sharing on a community level. I see it as a push from God. Call it fine-tuning, a way to fill out the soul.

"Each monastic community goes at this differently. Each one has a personality that's comprised of the individual personalities of its monks. Some have a very different notion of enclosure than we do. Our life, the way we bring people into our liturgy, our experimental program, our use of outside counselors—that might not provide the nourishment some monks need. They share their life differently. But it's a sharing that is as nourishing for them as ours is for us.

"Being a monk is becoming more of what you are—stretching to appreciate what is different. Because whatever you learn to appreciate becomes part of you—not some antiseptic, sanitized robot being—but you, as you are the unique being God created and you grow into. The balance, the net result, is more of you, more of what God meant you to be.

"There's no doubt in my mind that you and your wife represent a unique expression of monasticism, one that incorporates the relationship you have to each other and to the family you raised. It's somewhere on that continuum I mentioned earlier, valid and unique to the degree that each of you expresses God's particular design.

"Keep in mind that God used a monastery to draw you close and has continued to use others of them to help you grow. I'll venture to say that your association with us and our life has had at least a little influence on people close to you, and those with whom your life continues to intersect.

"How much more alive—or relevant—could you want a monastery to be? I'd say the prognosis is quite good for our way of life, wouldn't you? In Christ, Al."

23

Then Are They Truly Monks

TRAPPISTS HAVE done many things in obedience to Saint Benedict's admonition that they support themselves. Only when they lived by the work of their hands were they really monks, the Saint once said. Farming was a mainstay until the bottom dropped out of the market. According to Mac, not every monk grieved its passing. Dom Jacques echoed that sentiment when he described Melleray's transition from farming to its computerized typesetting operation. The monks were far happier with computer-driven work than they had been when hitched to a tractor.

In most instances, Trappists choose work that is appropriate to the area, either because raw materials or a market for finished goods is nearby. That was the prime consideration when each Trappist abbey was founded in the United States. Very few have been able to stay with the original work they envisioned as an integral part of their monastery.

However, New Clairvaux Abbey still earns its income from its walnut and plum trees. Iowa's New Melleray Abbey does the same with corn farming, and Genesee Abbey, just outside Rochester, New York, does well baking bread for sale in that city and in Buffalo.

Scant regard for profit marks Trappist business ventures. Whenever Trappists offer anything for sale, it must be priced lower than the going market rate. In answer to the objection that such a marketing policy capitalizes on no-cost labor and cleverly (and unfairly) undercuts competitors, keep in mind that the monks limit the amount of profit they make. Production is pegged as closely as possible to covering the annual operating budget. Generally, any excess revenues are given to needy people in the monastery's vicinity.

As far as the monks are concerned, natural is better. They shun additives. Trappists at Spencer Abbey in Massachusetts produce more than two dozen exotic creations that include Kadota Fig preserves, a unique ginger marmalade, as well as a line of jellies with as many variations in taste as a well-stocked wine cellar.

When sales representatives relayed the existence of a market for a low-calorie version of the marmalade to the monks, they were immediately turned down. The same resistance met the suggestion of a pineapple-mint jelly, which the representatives calculated as a surefire success. According to monastery sources, the mint would have needed green artificial coloring and the low-calorie marmalade would have required sugar substitutes. Although the monks have nothing against dieting, they simply refuse to use artificial additives in their products.

The monks may be partial to food production, but they do involve themselves in other ventures. Spencer Abbey has long been known for the beauty and high quality of the vestments it makes, and one of their monks was attempting to develop a market for handcrafted sandals as this book went to press. The Abbey of Our Lady of Guadalupe in Lafayette, Oregon originally made furniture and ran a book bindery. They closed the furniture operation and now make date-nut bread and fruitcake, which they sell by mail order. Their fellow monks at Mepkin Abbey in South Carolina devoted their energies to the sale of eggs and were considering the possibility of producing T-shirts with inspirational sayings. "If you'll excuse the pun," said one Mepkin monk, "we see the wisdom of not putting all our eggs in one basket."

Beekeeping monks in Huntsville, Utah, sell sixteen flavors of honey by mail order. Their brothers in Snowmass, Colorado, look to the day when their cookies will sell well enough to allow Brother Arthur to avoid dealing with runaway llamas.

While some monasteries continue with an original income-producing industry, all devote time and thought to others that can be developed and which do not require as many man-hours to succeed, given the decline in that essential component. Gethsemani was originally involved in baking bread for commercial sale and developed its highly regarded Trappist cheese during that same period. It was test-marketing bourbon-flavored fudge at the close of 1989.

Fruitcake has been a major success for many abbeys, from the time of its introduction at Gethsemani. It can be made in advance, stores well, and despite the knocking it gets from comedians at Christmastime, enjoys a sizable market.

When I asked Dom Stephen how the abbey first began making fruitcake, he smiled and suggested I talk to Brother Saul. It seems Trappist fruitcake, for all its success, was born entirely of serendipity, with just the slightest touch of venial sin for good measure.

THE crowded basement storeroom appeared equal parts mess and mystery to Brother Saul. As he stood surveying the jumble of crates and cartons, he felt certain that only the good Lord himself knew their contents. The boxes might just hold junk that should have been discarded and then again, they might contain just the item someone needed desperately, if only someone else had bothered to make note of where it had been stored.

No matter. Necessity had forced the issue. The bumper crop of softball-size sweet potatoes that Brother Saul had raised in the monastery's garden took priority. Given the effort he had invested in planting and cultivating the vegetables, he was not about to see them ignored. The basement was perfectly suited to storing the potatoes for a year if need be. Whether junk or gems, everything else would have to be moved.

It turned out that the bulk of the boxes contained institutional-size cans, virtually all of which lacked labels. Some time ago, Saul recalled, the manager of a Louisville hotel had made a retreat to the monastery. Apparently, the experience had roused his spirit to the point where he sent the "poor monks" a truckload of marginally useful items that had accumulated over time in the hotel's own basement storeroom. Certainly, he wrote in a covering note, the monks, inventive souls that they were, would be able to redeem the value that lay hidden inside the unmarked cans.

Redemption had proven as elusive for the monastery's cooks as it had for their confreres in the hotel's kitchen. Although everyone agreed that the contents of the cans were eminently edible, there was some question as to whether Gethsemani's cooks could incorporate them into a menu that had been planned with a view toward gustatory balance. After a few surprises, the cooks had quietly set aside the gifts for some distant future when their courage and the community's sense of adventure might coincide.

Whether or not that fortuitous time had arrived, however, was not

Saul's concern. His potatoes needed space. By late morning, he and one of the cooks, Brother Robert, had worked their way to the storeroom's distant and dark corners, where they came upon a wooden barrel. While they had to estimate its capacity at about fifty gallons, its contents were clearly stenciled on its cover: mincemeat.

"Pie?" Saul asked, smacking his lips in anticipation.

Robert shook his head. Only recently Robert had run afoul of the "Saints" when they discovered that the superb taste of his corn bread was traceable to the use of lard. But their outrage would know no bounds if they believed the mischievous cook had tricked them into violating the rule of abstinence by baking pies with suet in them.

That jeopardy also shadowed any attempt they might make to see whether the mincemeat had survived its long storage, Robert added. It was their duty, Saul replied, and without waiting for argument, laid a chisel to the barrel's wooden cover. Several moments and hammer blows later, the cover was gone and the area where it had been was rich with a pungent, heady scent of alcohol and fruit.

"Booze?" Saul asked.

"The best," Robert answered.

"You go first."

"Could be contaminated."

Saul sniffed once more, looked at Robert, and made the sign of the cross over the barrel. Two hands dipped into it simultaneously and raised dripping tastes of the forbidden fruit to their mouths for testing.

Aside from everything else, it was too good to use for pie, Robert allowed. But fruitcake was a different story, and Robert had an old family recipe which produced a fruitcake that was highly regarded both within and outside the family, especially esteemed by those friends who were lucky enough to receive one at Christmas.

The monastery's version would of course bear with some experimenting, Robert said, since they would have to improvise, substituting materials the monastery might have on hand. Not as much cake flour, perhaps. And margarine instead of butter. But wouldn't such changes fail to do justice to so distinguished a principal component? Saul asked, still savoring (and sniffing) its spirited presence. Only if they proved disloyal to the call of monastic creativity, Robert reassured him. Only if they overlooked the providential existence of aged wine made from apples and raisins that had, upon tasting, proved unsuitably potent for use at mass.

One-pound circular tins were used to produce the fruitcakes because Robert only had one-pound circular tins. The cakes were then test-marketed by relatives of the monks, who saw that they were showcased at parish card parties and cake sales. More than thirty years later, a panel of gourmets assembled by the food editor and writers of *Newsday*, one of the nation's leading daily papers, would be no less intrigued when they removed the cover from one of that first fruitcake's descendants. The experts would sniff and taste and ultimately agree unanimously that the fruitcake born of a broken barrel of mincemeat, Trappist fruitcake, was not only tasty, but far tastier than any of its competitors.

"And I completely forgot to go to confession," said Saul.

24

After the Fire

"Men," she said angrily. There were men in the retreat house. She herself had seen them. Was this or wasn't this Ladies' Week at Gethsemani? she asked Mac, who listened quietly.

Exactly what had happened? he asked, trying to understand the nature of the complaint. He had offered to substitute for Brother Gio and was fielding calls on the switchboard, as well as in-person inquiries from retreatants. He told the woman that she was absolutely correct. This was the one week per month that the retreat facility was set aside exclusively for the use of women.

Not one, not just one, mind you, she emphasized, but two of them. Two men standing in the retreat-house kitchen, drinking coffee as though they owned the place. And as if that weren't enough, when she had asked them if they were aware that this was Ladies' Week, they had said yes—smiling all the time.

He was very sorry, Mac said. They were probably two of the long-term retreatants, since members of the monastic community were normally not allowed in the retreat house. She had not seen the two men during meals, had she? Mac asked. He doubted that, he quickly assured her, since everyone had been told to leave the retreat house for the women's use that week.

No, she said. She didn't think so. But she had not checked with all of the women—as she intended to do. By the way, she added, was Father

215

aware of the feminist cassette that had been played during meals? Really, it was terribly distorted—the type of exclusive propaganda that had plagued thinking women. Mac's brow knitted (it was a tape by Merton, on community) but he never got the chance to question her further.

And the liturgy, Father, she continued. Of all things, that mass. She had expected better of monks. Exclusive language. Gender tyranny. "God the Father indeed," she said.

She hoped things would change by the time she returned for her next visit. Perhaps in the meantime, she said, handing Mac a neatly typed list, the community might want to study the suggestions she and a few of the other women felt were important. But Father had to remember, she added, these were only the most critically important of the changes that were needed. There were many others, but those could wait for her next visit.

"Although, only God knows how these things can try one's patience," she said.

"How true," Mac agreed. "How very true."

HAVING finished my research, I was packing my truck to leave Gethsemani, the memory of my conflict with Father Bede still painfully vivid. I turned to pick up a carton and found it on his outstretched arms.

"Please don't leave without accepting my apology," he said. "God called you to this place and I was getting in the way. I'm sorry. Will you let me be your friend?"

I was quite overwhelmed, even more so when I reached out my hand and found Bede pulling me into a warm hug. "Come back soon," he whispered, and with one hearty squeeze, said goodbye.

A small package arrived from Gethsemani a week after I returned home. It had a wheel of Trappist cheese, a fruitcake, and a copy of the Gethsemani psalter.

"Dear Frank," an accompanying letter read, "I'm trying to get used to God coming into my life in very different and marvelous ways. It seems as though I've kept him at arm's length much as you say you had done. Now, he embarrasses me with his gifts. I wanted you to have these little tokens, a memento of the office you love so much as well as something both sweet and nourishing to help keep your Gethsemani brothers in mind."

Father Bede detailed some of the recent developments in his life and then added toward the close of his letter, "I make it a habit to pray the psalms privately every day as a personal devotion. I pray them five at a time, consecutively, and at the end I mention aloud the names of those close to me who have died. Praying those words that people have prayed for so many thousands of years reminds me of our oneness and its continuing presence before God. From time to time I add the names of people who come into my life in ways that are unmistakably instances of God's loving. (Especially now.)

"I wanted you to know that I have added the name of your son, Michael, to my daily remembrance. You should also know that you are in my prayers, in the same way that God has seen fit to make you part of my life. Come back to Gethsemani soon, to visit with your brother in Christ, Bede."

Bede and I exchanged letters after that and had one long conversation by phone in which he filled in his background for me. A long stretch followed with no communication between us, which heightened my anticipation of a reunion on my next visit to Gethsemani. I got there in time to join the community at compline, but when I looked for him, I noticed he was not among those in choir. When I asked Saul about him, he told me that, in a sense, Bede was no longer at the monastery.

For a time he had been given a leave of absence to be with his son Dick, to help nurse him back to health. On his return, he had been assigned the additional chore of abbey driver; he was responsible for picking up the mail and shopping for such items as were needed in town.

He was returning from the trip one day when one of the tires of the utility truck he was driving must have gone flat. The truck apparently went out of control and crashed into a telephone pole. Father Bede died from his injuries several hours later, without regaining consciousness.

The rows of white crosses stand in military order in Gethsemani's cemetery. Thomas Merton rests beneath one, as do all his brothers—those whose spirits Mac claims give special character and strength to the monastery. Grass had yet to grow on the rounded plot of earth in front of the cross at one end of the cemetery. The lettering noted simply that a monk named Bede was buried there in 1988.

I remember Saul hesitated, his eyes wet, several times during the days it took us to pray the psalter together by that mounded earth. We stood some of those times and at others we sat cross-legged, facing each other, in the warm sunlight. We mentioned Bede by name at the end of each psalm. He may be gone, but my brother Saul and I both know that like my son Michael, he will never vanish.

Bibliography

Benedict, Saint. *Saint Benedict's Rule for Monasteries.* Collegeville, Minnesota: Liturgical Press, 1948.

Braunfels, Wolfgang. *Monasteries of Western Europe.* Princeton: Princeton University Press, 1972.

Brown, Peter. *The Body and Society.* New York: Columbia University Press, 1988.

Capps, Walter. *The Monastic Impulse.* Crossroads, New York 1983.

de Waal, Esther. *Seeking God: The Way of Saint Benedict.* Collegeville, Minnesota: Liturgical Press, 1984.

Furlong, Monica. *Merton: A Biography.* New York: Harper and Row, 1985.

Griffin, John Howard. *Follow the Ecstasy.* Mansfield, Texas: Latitudes Press, 1983.

Hart, Patrick, ed. *Thomas Merton, Monk.* New York: Sheed and Ward, 1974.

Kardong, Terrence, *The Benedictines.* Wilmington, Delaware: Michael Glazier, Inc, 1988.

Kelty, Matthew. *Flute Solo.* Kansas City, Missouri: Andrews and McMeel, 1979.

Kelty, Matthew. *Sermons in a Monastery.* Cistercian Publications, 1983.

Lekai, L.J. *The Cistercians.* Kent, Ohio: Kent State University Press, 1977.

Levi, Peter. *The Frontiers of Paradise.* New York: Weidenfeld and Nicolson, 1987.

Lockhart, Robin Bruce. *Halfway to Heaven.* London: Thames Methuen, 1985.

Merton, Thomas. *Contemplation in a World of Action.* Garden City, New York: Image Books, 1973.

Merton, Thomas. *The Hidden Ground of Love.* [Merton's Letters.] Edited by William H. Shannon. New York: Farrar, Straus, and Giroux, 1985.

————. *The Monastic Journey.* Garden City, NY: Image Books, 1977.

————. *New Seeds of Contemplation.* New York: New Directions, 1961.

————. *The Seven Storey Mountain.* New York: Harcourt Brace Jovanovich, 1948.

————. *The Sign of Jonas.* New York: Harcourt Brace Jovanovich, 1953.

————. *The Silent Life.* New York: Farrar, Straus and Giroux, 1957.

Nouwen, Henri J.M. *The Genesee Diary.* Garden City, NY: Image Books, 1981.

Paulsell, William. *Letters from a Hermit.* Springfield, Illinois: Templegate Publishers, 1978.

Raymond, M. *The Family That Overtook Christ.* Boston: Daughters of St. Paul, 1986.

Raymond, M. *The Man Who Got Even with God.* New York: Guild Press, 1961.

Southern, R.W. *Western Society and the Church in the Middle Ages.* New York: Penguin Books, 1970.

Storr, Anthony. *Solitude.* New York: Free Press, 1988.

Ward, Benedicta. *The Wisdom of the Desert Fathers.* Oxford: SLG Press, 1986.

Wilkes, Paul, ed. *Merton, By Those Who Knew Him Best.* New York: Harper and Row, 1984.

Zarnecki, George. *The Monastic Achievement.* New York: McGraw-Hill, 1972.